A
Thing
Apart

Critical Issues in ———————

PSYCHOANALYSIS

cIp₂

A THING APART

Love and Reality in the Therapeutic Partnership

IRVING STEINGART

JASON ARONSON INC.
Northvale, New Jersey
London

This book was set in 11 point Palacio by TechType of Upper Saddle River, New Jersey, and printed and bound by Haddon Craftsmen of Scranton, Pennsylvania.

Library of Congress Cataloging-in-Publication Data

Steingart, Irving.
   A thing apart : love and reality in the therapeutic relationship /
by Irving Steingart.
      p. cm.
   Includes bibliographical references and index.
   ISBN 1-56821-304-2
   1. Transference (Psychology) 2. Countertransference (Psychology)
3. Psychoanalysis—Philosophy. I. Title.
RC489.T73S744 1995
154.2′4—dc20   94-41351

Manufactured in the United States of America. Jason Aronson Inc. offers books and cassettes. For information and catalog write to Jason Aronson Inc., 230 Livingston Street, Northvale, New Jersey 07647.

For my mother and father

together with

the children and adults with whom I do my work

Now it appears to me that almost any Man may like the spider spin from his own innards his own airy Citadel — the points of leaves and twigs on which the spider begins her work are few, and she fills the air with a beautiful circuiting. Man should be content with a few points to tip with the fine web of his Soul, and weave a tapestry empyrean full of symbols for his spiritual eye, of softness for his spiritual touch, of space for his wandering, of distinctness for his luxury. But the Minds of Mortals are so different and bent on such diverse journeys that it may at first appear impossible for any common taste and fellowship to exist between two or three under these suppositions. It is however quite the contrary. Minds would leave each other in contrary directions, traverse each other in numberless points, and at last greet each other at the journey's end. An old Man and a child would talk together and the old Man be led on his path and the child left thinking. Man should not dispute or assert but whisper results to his neighbor and thus by every germ or spirit sucking the sap from mould ethereal every human might become great, and Humanity instead of being a wide heath of Furze and Briars with here and there a remote Oak or Pine, would become a grand democracy of Forest Trees!

John Keats,
from a letter to John Reynolds
February 19, 1818 (Forman 1948)

CONTENTS

Foreword   xi

Preface   xv

Acknowledgments   xxv

1. Reality and Truth in the Analytic Relationship   1

    Real and Unreal Transference Experience
    Reconstruction in Psychoanalysis

2. Toward a Comparative Therapeutics   35

    Transference, Countertransference, and
        Analyst Work Style
    The Truthfulness of Interpretation as Object
        Relations Experience

3. Love in the Analytic Relationship   103

    The Analyst's Real and Extraordinary Love
        for the Analysand
    Transference at Termination

4. The Psychic Reality of Enacted Symbols   133

    Transference as Pathological Play

Language Concretization as Enacted Symbol
Acting Out as Enacted Symbol

5. Etiology of Pathological Play as Transference   199

Mind Emergence
Comparative Psychopathology
Projective Identification

6. A Clinical Episode   223

7. On the Comprehension of Psychic Reality   229

References   259

Credits   279

Index   281

FOREWORD

Irving Steingart's fascinating book uses psychoanalytic experience to give a rich, multilayered, wonderfully textured view of the nature of reality in the analytic situation.

In *A Thing Apart*, Steingart tackles the most complex philosophic issues that face psychoanalysis and indeed all of psychology today. He raises serious questions about the current emphasis on a narrativist, deconstructionist foundation for the treatment relationship. He asks: How can post-modernism support the *rationality* of a treatment relationship in which transference–countertransference experiences are *narratively coherent*, but in which the therapist typically does not verbally express his or her countertransference? He argues that this treatment situation only makes sense if it is based on the assumption of the patient's psychic reality existing independent of an intersubjective construction. Steingart applies this realism—which is not the naïve, empirical realism of logical positivism—to remembering and reconstructing in the clinical process as well as to experience in the immediate, treatment relationship. He shows how Freud was a realist in his construction of psychoanalysis, and how a realist-correspondence view can enhance rather than detract from the symbolism and sibylline meanings often encountered in the analytic situation.

In offering a new definition of the realist position, Steingart helps seemingly tired and worn ideas come alive with renewed conceptual and clinical vigor. For example, he offers a new framework in which to conceptualize treatment as a continuous intersubjective experience. This framework involves distinguishing among ways in which therapist subjectivity can influence the clinical relationship. First, Steingart contrasts the inevitable, ongoing impact of the therapist's personality or *work style* with the possible impact of the therapist's countertransference. Second, he contrasts the impact of the therapist's work style alone with the possible impact of an interrelationship between work style and countertransference.

He also faces factors rarely talked about, such as the analyst's love for his/her patient as a real and not-real part of every complete analysis. This *love for the patient's mind* is as real as any love, but a love absolutely unique to the treatment relationship. Steingart argues that the question of what is therapeutic—insight or the object relationship between therapist and patient—is, and always has been, a spuriously simplistic dichotomy. As part of his discussion, Steingart surveys some of our current major conceptions of clinical process, comparing and contrasting therapists who practice within a Freudian orientation with others who do not. This produces a comparative therapeutics that involves assessments of Beres and Arlow, Gill, Hoffman, Levenson, Schafer, and others.

Steingart also generates an innovative, developmental framework that relates enactment to the mentality of the young oedipal and preoedipal child *at play*. This basic structure allows the author to explain why it is that patients who tend to enact are also individuals who tend to possess and produce experiences of projective identification. Steingart then describes an approach for a classically productive handling of enactment. This approach applies especially to borderline and narcissistic individuals, who seem to need something more than language if transference and real aspects of the treatment relationship are to be felt as meaningful. With this innovative framework, Steingart demonstrates a generally underappreciated significance of the anal-rapprochement period: the emergence of one's sense that one has *a mind of one's own,* and that all others (mothers) also have their own minds.

Before I discuss my final point, I must confess to a distrust of the use of data from other fields to bolster claims about the analytic situation. Most often these attempts offer analogical results, which rarely clarify the topic they are intended to illuminate. These analogies too frequently cause clinicians to debate issues that they know little about and that have a questionable relationship to psychoanalytic theory or practice. Steingart has made me rethink my prejudice, for he weaves into an original, clinical tapestry data and concepts from a wide array of research, philosophic, and literary sources. Perhaps most interestingly he is able to use and give meaning to multiple psychoanalytic orientations and at the same time show what is unique about a contemporary Freudian perspective.

Regardless of one's theoretical or clinical orientation, any psychotherapist who is interested in a comprehensive and comparative view of therapeutic techniques will find reading this book an engrossing experience.

Steven J. Ellman
May 1995

PREFACE

In the preface to the first edition of *Childhood and Society*, Erikson (1950) remarks, tongue in cheek, that in writing a preface an author has a chance to express ideas overlooked in writing the book itself. My concern is not so much hitherto overlooked ideas but rather that I had, throughout the writing, a vague sense that I was not sufficiently aware *why* I was writing this book. Indeed, I resisted allowing myself to know something about my motivation to write it. On further (self) analysis, it now seems clear that I was concerned that if I were to let myself know this something else, it would mar my quite conscious and clear desire to write: the book represents my best effort to state what a psychoanalytic relationship is, and what it is not, to describe rationally what it is I have been doing for some 25 years, and why it is I *love* so much to do psychoanalysis. What I did not want to realize was that I also wished to justify that my love affair with psychoanalysis is *moral*. As a psychoanalyst I realize, of course, that one's motivation to do anything is many-sided. But it is clear to me now that I did not want to recognize that in writing this book my desire was not only to present a rational explication of a psychoanalytic relationship but also to justify the morality—in this sense the *goodness*—of this absolutely unique human relationship. Also, now I am able to realize clearly the psychic, emotional intimacy that always exists, for everyone, between *morality* and *morale*. That is, if one is doing something morally fulfilling in a clinically healthy way, then one will be suffused with morale—with spiritedness—in such doing. I am convinced that a psychoanalysis is distinctly—uniquely—therapeutic. The analysand becomes able to intentionally create more of the kind of a human life he or she wants, which is the reason for seeking psychoanalysis in the first place. This unique therapeutics is the result of a special kind of freeing-up of an analysand's use of his or her mind, enabled by experiences we call insight.

Psychoanalytic insight as self-contemplation is unique for three reasons: First, it enables an analysand to acquire dynamically unconscious, deeply felt understanding about him- or herself, which, by definition, he or she has never before experienced. Second, there is no constraint or boundary to the contents of these experiences. Third, what an analysand does or does not do with the insight is left entirely in the hands of the analysand.

A productive psychoanalysis can be likened to a physical event that produces awesome energic potential—such as that which occurs in the interior of our sun. But with the sun, the outcome of the awesome potential is known. In a psychoanalysis, outcomes are not at all known to the psychoanalyst, and indeed, a psychoanalyst should not invest in such questions. We realize, at this point, an irony and tribute to Freud's special genius, which is that through self-analysis he achieved significant insight about himself. But Freud's exclusive reliance on self-analysis could not, in principle, allow him the fuller opportunities for insightful experiences potentiated by the very special psychoanalytic *relationship* he himself had invented!

I have just said that Freud "invented" the psychoanalytic relationship, and in a definite sense he did. But how Freud came to create this relationship, centered as it is on the freest possible expression of analysand associations, is itself remarkable and revealing. This has to do with how Freud worked his way through—from hypnosis, to the cathartic method of placing his hand(s) on the analysand's (fore)head with an injunction to say what came to mind, to a (pun intended) "hands-off" relatedness wherein he simply listened and eventually came to appreciate the equal significance of resistances against free associations. A first point is that Freud (Breuer and Freud 1895) came to invent this relationship in *collaboration* with the early analysands who constituted the *Studies in Hysteria* and especially with Frau Cäcilie M. (Anna von Lieben), whom Freud called his "teacher" (Gay 1988, esp. pp. 67–74). A century later it is perhaps not possible to fully appreciate this point. Here is Freud, trained as a physician to conduct a systematic medical interview and to systematically examine a patient's physical symptomatology; in addition, here is Freud, trained in the classical research methods of experimental manipulation of variables. Now Freud is creating with his analysand a treatment relationship in which he spends much time simply listening, and listening with a state of mind very unlike anything emphasized in his formal, professional training. How did he do it?

I will suggest at least one important part of the answer. Breuer (Breuer and Freud 1895) obviously could not tolerate the emotionally charged, especially sexual, transference experiences that emanated from his patients. Freud not only tolerated but also responded deeply to such experience. Why? Because what Freud was discovering about how a *human mind can create* transferences (and dreams, symptoms, and so forth) became an object of his rapt emotional investment. Breuer could not make this emotional transformation and became increasingly anxious; Freud became increasingly committed.

Any *principled* departure from the three cardinal characteristics of psychoanalytically achieved insight moves us from a psychoanalysis toward a psychotherapy of one sort or another. It is not my purpose here to consider different types of psychotherapy, or the difference between any sort of psychotherapy and a psychoanalysis. At the same time, some qualifications need to be stated, and these qualifications exist to some degree in every psychoanalysis. I have used the language "distinctly therapeutic" and "create more of the kind of a human life." I believe the psychoanalytic relationship I describe in this book is real enough. But I say "enough" because the relationship involves an ideal; namely, it is completely, perfectly, and exclusively put in the service of enabling the acquisition of insight such as I have just described. Although the reality of this ideal permeates the relationship, the ideal itself involves perfection, and nothing is truly perfect, including an idealized psychoanalytic relationship. In other words, probably every psychoanalysis includes times when the relationship is used to promote not just insight but *selected* change in self-awareness and/or action, moments when the relationship is psychotherapeutic rather than psychoanalytic. But in keeping with the ideal of a psychoanalytic relationship, the analyst will attempt to make him- or herself aware of such a circumstance and attempt to understand with the analysand how this has happened *in terms of analysand dynamics*. This may or may not involve, or require, interpretation, depending on where the psychoanalysis "is" at such a point. However, I believe that for the psychoanalyst this kind of circumstance involves a countertransference experience of one sort or another. In this book I distinguish between countertransference experience and an analyst's individual work style, which is another thing entirely. However, I also argue that a psychoanalytic relationship, exactly when it is most productive, involves a paradox with respect to cure. This has to do with what I take to be a special sort of love that animates the relationship: although it can produce curative insight, which makes for psychic development, it is also provocative for the maintenance of a childlike transference love. In my view, a productive, reasonably successful psychoanalysis leaves an analysand with not just a tolerance but an appreciation for the childlike in him- or herself.

There are, of course, other limits to how much an analysand can effect desired change in him- or herself, dependent on the course of the analysand's life after achieving psychoanalytic insight. But again, the ideal of a psychoanalytic relationship centers on the acquisition of insight — analysand mind expansion — the content of which, in principle, has no bounds.

At this point it is pertinent to ask why psychoanalysts of all theoretical persuasions are called, jocularly, "shrinks," a word connoting just the opposite of mind expansion without constraint. Psychoanalysts of every theoretical persuasion maintain, at the least, an anonymity about their personal lives outside the psychoanalytic relationship. At the same time, the analysand is expected to do exactly the opposite. Even more, a Freudian psychoanalyst maintains a normative nonrevelation of countertransference experience. I believe it is this highly unusual relationship that produces, more so in some analysands and less so in others, concerns about possible *mind control* effected by the analyst on the analysand. Consequently, we have the appellation *shrink*. If mind control were the case, a psychoanalysis would be morally outrageous: the special therapeutics of a psychoanalysis would be not just a sham but immoral — nothing more than mind as product, a "stamped" and "approved" mind made in the analyst's office. I do not believe this to be true, and I take up this issue later in the book. And as a Freudian psychoanalyst, I especially want to examine the rational coherence for a type of practice in which nonrevelation of countertransference is normative.

For me, all of this leads to a conclusion that Freudian practice must be grounded in a philosophy of some type of realism. Thus grounded, a Freudian psychoanalytic relationship can then be understood to be highly moral. It is a good human relationship. Its abiding function and ideal is to promote analysand mind expansion through the acquisition of insightful experiences that can be acquired only by a normative nonrevelation of countertransference.

Such insightful experiences are not, in their essentials, imposed by the analyst. Although the influence of theoretical orientation is inescapable, one's theoretical orientation, while providing an overall interpretive framework, does not control the *particulars* of what will become insightful experiences for a *particular* analysand, the essentials of which already exist before analysand and analyst ever meet and discover them. But inasmuch as they exist outside the analysand's self-awareness, they are not available for self-contemplation. The simple but profound ethic of a psychoanalytic relationship of any theoretical persuasion is that such enhanced self-contemplation is a virtue, an idea hardly novel in either Western or Eastern civilization.

Finally, I stress that in a genuinely productive psychoanalysis, enhanced self-understanding is embedded deeply in one's ongoing life experience. If insight as self-contemplation is not felt to be deeply ingrained in one's love and work experience, an arid intellectualism is what is occurring, certainly not a psychoanalysis.

A few words on the overall organization of this book: three issues are currently receiving attention in our literature, and I have chosen to organize the discussion around them.

First, there is the question of how to view the place of a psychoanalysis among the variety of our knowledge-seeking, scientific, and literary pursuits. A usual way to state this question is to ask whether the practice of psychoanalysis is a hermeneutic (that is, an interpretative, narrative-creating) endeavor or a scientific activity. But the status of a practice, or method, is organic with the status of whatever content it produces. So a question congruent with the first is whether the body of psychoanalytic knowledge is a special kind of narration or whether it is scientific theory. But there is a

further, deeper question now being addressed in the psychoanalytic literature about this issue. Many psychoanalysts,
including Freudian analysts, now align themselves with a
philosophic position that the very distinction between a
narrative creation and a scientific theory is illusionary. Along
with this philosophic position, any sort of ontology of
realism, or correspondence notion of truth, is no longer seen
as tenable. As my earlier comments suggest, I do not
subscribe to this philosophic position, either in general, or
specifically for psychoanalysis. Chapter 1 takes up selected
aspects of this question.

A second, very lively theme in our current literature
involves questions about the more immediate clinical nature
of the psychoanalytic relationship. Two aspects are being
argued. One has to do with how to understand analyst
countertransference, and the question is how constant countertransference is, and how essential to empathic comprehension of analysand transference. My earlier comments
that a Freudian psychoanalyst does not, at least verbally,
typically (normatively) reveal countertransference perhaps
already suggests my belief that countertransference is neither constant nor necessary as a source for empathic comprehension. At the same time I cannot conceive (nor is it in
keeping with my own experience) that a psychoanalysis can
be without some circumstances of analyst countertransference. This has to do with the analyst's personality as
distinguished from any idea of countertransference. Another
controversial aspect of the psychoanalytic relationship has to
do with how to understand what it is that may bring about
analysand personality change. Is this process our original
and traditional (classically conceived) concept of analysand
insight? Or is it some more contemporary accounting having
to do with interactive qualities of the psychoanalytic relationship? I argue vigorously that this is, and always has been, a
false choice. I propose a synthesis that I believe always has

been latent in Freud's (e.g., 1912b, 1913) original ideas about what constitutes productive analyst involvement. These matters are taken up in Chapters 2 and 3.

Chapters 4 and 5 deal with enacted symbols. At the beginning of this Preface, I stated that a psychoanalytic relationship is a virtuous relationship, in which from beginning to end one individual, the analyst, devotes him- or herself only to understanding the mind of the analysand. Consequently, the analyst is offered the fullest possible expression and expansion of mind. One way to describe a natural and appropriate ending of a psychoanalysis is when both analysand and analyst now devote themselves to this same purpose and both find deep and sufficient fulfillment in the endeavor. The received wisdom, our traditional view of this exercise, has been that it occurs solely through language. By "language" I mean a condition of mind organization of the analysand, that is, that language-mediated experience is felt to be a sufficient realization for all manner of analysand experience, transferential as well as the reality of the psychoanalytic relationship. Yet, especially in the treatment of borderline and narcissistic individuals, this condition of language sufficiency is less likely to occur, at least for some critical circumstances in a psychoanalysis. Instead, what I have come to call urgencies for enacted symbols occur. I relate such enacted symbol urgencies to a play mentality and contrast this with a fantasy mentality, which is embedded in our more classical view of a transference neurosis. Such pathologically playful, enacted symbols can involve language itself and (at least) a great deal of what we have come to call analysand acting out. This section of the book argues a case for a conception of such enacted symbols to be just that—symbols; in other words, still, essentially, mental representation. I also propose at least a general clinical approach for meeting analysand transferences that feature, in some critical circumstances, such enacted symbols. I believe this extends the psychoanalytic virtue of the analyst's seeking only to understand the analysand's mind and how his or her mind expresses itself and militates against what I take to be a psychoanalytically naive and simple-minded prohibition against analysand acting out. Chapters 4 and 5 contain the most clinical material. I use examples from my own practice, and vignettes reported in our literature, as I seek to illustrate what I mean by analysand-enacted symbols as well as how best to treat them clinically.

In Chapter 6 I present a clinical episode that involves all the major topics taken up in this book: reality and truth, contrasted to not-real experience, in the psychoanalytic relationship; transference and countertransference; enacted symbolic transference organization expressed, here, via language concretization; and the issue of the real love the psychoanalyst possesses to understand the psychic reality of his or her analysand. It is my hope that at the conclusion what I have written will enable the reader to understand where I am coming from in my work as psychoanalyst and what I understand a Freudian psychoanalysis to be—clinically, theoretically, and philosophically.

ACKNOWLEDGMENTS

The preparation of this book involved an armada of high tech amanuenses! Seriously, and gratefully, I want to thank individuals who prepared text on computer screens other than my own and without whose assistance the typing of this manuscript would have been interminable. Such help extended into two states of our immediate tri-state area. These individuals who provided typing assistance in New York are Maria Bertucci together with Lawrence Schwartz and Tamara Richards; in New Jersey, these people are Laurie Knowles and Kathleen Tamalonis.

Also, I want to thank Sharone Bergner for her help in obtaining permission to use extended citations and help in checking the galleys.

There are a number of friends-colleagues who, in particular, provided useful criticism and/or emotional support. These people are Delia Battin, M.S.W., Lillian Gordon, Joan Schwartz, M.S.W., Lawrence Schwartz, M.S.W., as well as Drs. Phyllis Beren, Carolyn Ellman, Stanley Grand, Eugene Mahon, Arlene Kramer Richards, Arnold Richards, and Arietta Slade.

As always, the members of my study group gave me their critical counsel, together with their encouragement, and this involved their wholehearted willingness to examine carefully two separate drafts of this manuscript. Not simply intellectually, but emotionally, my experiences and relationships with these study group members have provided me with a kind of fulfillment over the course of my life that is like nothing else; this is because of its duration and the loving consideration we give each other with respect to not just our ideas but our lives. These individuals are Drs. Sheldon Bach, Mark Grunes, Martin Nass, and Norbert Freedman.

Another colleague and friend from whom I received incisive intellectual as well as generous emotional support is Dr. Steven Ellman, a co-editor of this series, who encouraged me to consider this book to be part of this collection. Also, I want to thank two individuals at Jason Aronson who facilitated the realization of this book from manuscript to hard cover: Dr. Michael Moskowitz, acquisitions editor, and Ruth Brody, production editor.

Giselle Weiss worked as the copy editor for this manuscript and I am fortunate to have had the benefit of her extraordinary skill. Each page—literally—of this book has benefited from her work.

Finally, I want to express my gratitude to my wife, Dr. Joyce Steingart. I thank her for her critical assistance, but even more, her forbearance with a spouse so invested in a labor that had the result of time together lost to us.

1

Reality and Truth in the Analytic Relationship

In what follows I will be talking a great deal about experience I characterize as real, and transference as not-real experience. I want, with the term *real*, to commit myself to a type of philosophical realism, or realist ontology: that a world exists as it is, both material and mental, both observable and nonobservable, and the essential nature of this world exists independently of our attempts to understand it. A correspondence concept of truth goes along with this philosophy of realism. That is, the truth of our beliefs about reality consists not in the way the beliefs fit together but in their corresponding to an actual, independent state of affairs.

A part of this world, which exists as it does, comprises beliefs about the world that are erroneous. In other words, false (*not-real*, or *unreal*) beliefs also exist, and the essential nature of these false beliefs exists independently of our efforts to understand them.

This realist posture puts me at odds with a noticeable, and notable, segment of opinion in our contemporary psychoanalytic literature (e.g., Gill 1985, Schafer 1983, Wallerstein 1973, 1985) who believe that only an antiobjectivist philosophy can be "coherent" (Schafer 1983) with psychoanalytic inquiry and its related subject matter. At the same time, an argument is raised against any consideration of the ultimate question of what is real for psychoanalysis, positing that it mixes levels of discourse that are better kept separate. But it is no solution, for example, simply to define psychoanalysis to be a science (e.g., Brenner 1955) with respect to method and subject matter; the very relationship between what is called science and the idea of reality is now a matter of intense debate among philosophers of science (e.g., Salmon 1984 or Smart 1963 vs. Feyeraband 1965 or Kuhn 1970). Obviously, this same point applies to any declaration that psychoanalysis is a hermeneutic discipline (e.g., Schafer 1983), in other words, essentially and only a retelling of what the analysand manifestly has said without resort to any philosophy of realism, or some mixture of hermeneutics and science (Ricoeur 1970).

It will be easy enough for me to document in this book that Freud himself was a realist and that he considered psycho-analysis to be a species of scientific activity devoted to discovering that reality. However, there are two related but separate features of the psychoanalytic situation where these issues particularly apply. The first has to do with the ongoing and present transference (or possible countertrans-ference) experiences that occur in every psychoanalysis. And with regard to this, Freud (1895) understood present trans-ference to be a "false [i.e., not-real] connection" (p. 302), something "not accounted for by the actual [i.e., real] situation" (Freud 1925, p. 42) with the psychoanalyst. The second feature is what Spence (1982) refers to as "historical truth" versus "narrative truth," clinically, the question of constructions about the analysand's significant past as nar-ratively assembled in a psychoanalysis. By the end of his writing Freud had, I believe, achieved a coherent if complex viewpoint on the issue of (re)construction, and this will be the subject of the last part of this chapter.

At least for psychoanalysts for whom it matters that psychoanalysis be intellectually coherent, the effort to work through to some appropriate ontology and epistemology is its own justification. But there is more to it. The very practice of psychoanalysis, I am persuaded, best rests on a realist philosophy and a correspondence concept of truth.

REAL AND UNREAL TRANSFERENCE EXPERIENCE

What I have in mind now when I use the terms *real* and *unreal* is how in the everyday psychoanalytic relationship we come to settle on and use ideas of real and unreal experience. To my mind, there are several ways to resolve this question. In the first situation, the question of whether an analysand's experience is to be considered real can be regarded as conclusively settled by recourse to some immediate observation—"immediate observation" being understood here to mean what we ordinarily call a fact.[1] For example, if an analysand reports a belief that I am masturbating while I sit behind the couch, and this is a so-called research analysis that is being videotaped, then a replay of the tape would show that I am, say, sitting and smoking a pipe and consequently that the analysand's experience is unreal. If the analysand, in such a circumstance, insists that his or her observation of the videotape is real, we would conclude that the analysand is hallucinating; and we would infer (theoretically conceptualize) that the analysand is treating his or her feeling and belief that I am masturbating as a perception.

A second type of circumstance involves analysand experience that stands in a different relationship to any immediate observations—facts—because here the analysand's experience is about the analyst's experience, and not anything obvious about the analyst's overt behavior. This can involve analysand experience that the analyst-as-a-person has certain attributes, interests, beliefs, likes or dislikes, ideas, fantasies, needs, and so forth. So, for example, an analysand can have the experience that the analyst has a very morally critical attitude toward the analysand. In such a circumstance, two things occur in a productive psychoanalytic relationship. First, implicitly or explicitly both analysand and analyst concur that, in principle, no immediate observation about their relationship, in itself, can either validate or disprove the analysand's experience about the experience of the analyst-as-a-person; in other words, no immediately observable fact can itself settle whether the analysand's experience is to be considered real or unreal.

This concurrence between the analyst and analysand I will call a *principle of equivocality*. Here I am using an idea already used by Gill (1984a):

> The analyst tries to avoid *behaving* in such a way that will be construed correctly and clearly as *obviously* reflecting some erotic or hostile intent but even so he can never take for granted that a particular behavior on his part has a particular meaning for the patient, both because he cannot have *unequivocal knowledge of his intentions and because of transference*. [p. 168, italics mine]

I believe this spells out what can be the only productive working attitude for both analyst and analysand in an analysis, ordinarily conceived. Further,

> a major role in the *resolution of transference* is played by the patient's coming to see that this plausible meaning of the situation is indeed no more than only plausible and not unequivocal, that is, that his experience of the situation is based to a greater or lesser degree on determinants within himself. [p. 165, italics mine]

Notice that with words like *obviously* and *greater or lesser* Gill commits himself to some kind of idea of a validatable reality (Schwaber 1992). How can we even conceive, let alone assess, whether transference or countertransference is gross or subtle unless we use some kind of a framework of realism? So, for Gill here also to say that the analysand must, presumably always, believe his or her transference only to be "plausible" confuses and conflates the use of this idea of equivocality. (This has consequence for Gill's more recent conception of clinical process, which I will take up in the next chapter.) Yet Gill does still make a clear, functional, and useful distinction. The analyst's observable and obvious behavior and (at least) conscious experience toward the analysand are contrasted with the analyst's (possible) dynamically unconscious intentions, about which no analyst can believe he or she has absolutely certain knowledge or control. I would stress that the analysand's willingness to adopt, with the analyst, this equivocal attitude is, at first, needed for the increasingly unreal elaboration of transference and later for its resolution. All of this I would understand to be part of Schafer's (1983) idea of "analytic attitude," which would apply to both analyst and analysand.[2]

But I think in other comments Gill muddies the water. He attacks what he calls the "myth" of an "uncontaminated transference," though this idea has a clear and useful meaning in terms of his own comment: the analyst does not consciously experience, behave, or speak in such a way that the analysand can observe "correctly and clearly . . . some erotic or hostile intent" (p. 168). To put this another way, of course things the "analyst has done as well as what he has not done" (p. 164) can have equally plausible meanings for the analysand. But the psychic reality with which the analysand interprets what the analyst has not observably done has a vastly different significance for the unfolding of the psychoanalytic process than a response to something observably done by the analyst. Put still another way, the analysand "behaves in such a way designed to get the therapist to justify . . . preconceptions which in turn lends further plausibility to them" (p. 165). Here Gill makes use of Sandler's (1976) idea of an analyst's "role-responsiveness." And Gill adds, "the patient stimulates counter-transference" (p. 165). But what matters here is what is to be considered *clinically normative* (see, e.g., Jacobs 1991), that is, what we believe usually to be an analyst's experience with respect to analysand transference pressures to relate to, and feel about, an analysand in a certain way. And my reading of Sandler's material is that he does not consider *readily observable* role-responsiveness on the analyst's part to be clinically normative or desirable, although, of course, it can occur. In any case, I do not, and I examine this later in more detail.

I have used expressions like *behavior, conscious experience, observe* to describe a context for assessing possible analyst countertransference. Such language is congruent with Gill's (1984a) depiction of analyst countertransference, with some qualifications. First, there can be circumstances in any psychoanalysis when it is not easy to decide whether countertransference on the analyst's part has become observably role-responsive. But such circumstances should not obscure what is clinically normative: that analyst behavior does not ordinarily correctly and clearly indicate some sort of interfering erotic or hostile intentions, and that, ordinarily, analyst (at least) conscious experience is not congruent with any such possible interfering countertransference. Because every 24 hours there are two ambiguous periods of light and darkness does not mean that in the rest of the 24-hour cycle we cannot usefully distinguish night and day, and such designations perform a useful orientation for us for the conduct of our lives. It is the same, I believe, with how we are to use this construct of countertransference to provide a useful organization of the experience of a psychoanalytic relationship for both the analysand and analyst.

A second complication is that clinically, we understand that countertransference occurs that is not readily observable. For example, Dahl and colleagues (1978) present data that suggest that not-conscious, hostile countertransference may be expressed in an analyst's syntax. Equally interesting, subtle, fleeting, not ordinarily detectable changes in an analyst's facial expressions (Haggard and Isaacs 1966) may also turn out to express countertransference. A body of data shows that certain varieties of hand movements as well as language constructions are related to types of clinical states and character styles (e.g., Steingart 1977, Steingart and Freedman 1975, Steingart et al. 1975), and it might be that such responsiveness can serve as a measure for counter-transference as well.

All of this—syntax, hand movements, facial changes that are not readily observable—is like the difference between ordinary looking and looking with an electron microscope. But there are no currently available, more finely tuned experimental data, or clinical observations, that prove the case for countertransference to be considered clinically normative; and any general significance of the effects on clinical process of such marginal or subliminal determinants is far from clear. Even if future research were to demonstrate such a regular, ongoing, finely tuned analyst responsiveness to analysand transference, at least some of this responsiveness might express an analyst's *empathy with transference*, which can be shown to be connected to facilitation of the treatment process.

Something else that is implicitly or explicitly agreed to by both analysand and analyst is that only further exploration about other analysand experience—particularly, of course, dynamically unconscious experience—will be used to settle the question whether the presently held analysand experience about the analyst's experience is to be considered real or transference. There is, then, agreement about the suspension of belief or disbelief, pending further exploration of the analysand's experience. For example, a later revelation that the analysand feels guilty about a hostile intention toward the analyst *may* then be understood as a reason (but also can be construed to operate as a cause) for the occurrence (Davidson 1980, Holt 1981, Holzman 1983) of the analysand's experience that the analyst harbors criticism toward the analysand; and therefore the analysand's experience about the analyst's experience as a person *may* now be understood to be unreal and the result of the analysand's own guilt and expectation of punishment. Another kind of possibility is that the analysand remembers a childhood memory that *may* now be understood to be experienced in the transference, that is, in an unreal manner.

Here I want to stress that in this book I do not concern myself with the issue of accuracy of any such childhood memory, the question of narrative versus historical truth. This issue obviously is important with respect to (re)constructional interpretation made by an analyst, which I discuss in detail later in this chapter. What I do maintain is that this issue can be validly separated from the matter of whether a childhood memory (however accurate) in the present is being reexperienced in an unreal, transferential way with the person who is the analyst. For this reason, when I talk about a childhood memory, I will use the term *reminiscence*—a childhood reminiscence.

The principle of equivocality can be stated another way, namely, that in place of an ontologically grounded idea of reality, it is the analysand's psychic reality that is "decisive" (Freud 1916–1917) in a psychoanalysis, and that it is the emerging complexities in this psychic reality that ultimately will settle whether experience is assigned a real or unreal transference status. An idea of an objective reality is treated, one might say, with a kind of benign neglect.

No contemporary psychoanalyst has devoted more serious and sensitive attention to this topic than has Schwaber, as some recent clinical material (Schwaber 1992) will illustrate:

> Two sessions before the summer break, Ms. T. [given to recurrent periods of silence] was quiet much of the time. She began the next hour, again, silently. When she spoke, she said she worried that something might happen to me and that I would not return, and she stopped. Then she said, "You're always more quiet before you go away. I want you to talk to me and you don't and I get angry. Before you go away I want to establish a stronger connection and I feel you want to establish more distance." [p. 1048]

Schwaber then describes her own effort, successfully and productively, not simply to write off the analysand's psychic reality as "distorted" (p. 1049). Instead, Schwaber considered how, from the point of view of the analysand's psychic reality, her (Schwaber's) own continued silence could be experienced as emotional distance making. Schwaber said to her analysand:

"It seems you're wanting me to reach *more* actively to you [than I am]."

"Yes," she said, unhesitatingly, her tone seeming now to sound more relaxed.

"Why then do you become [what appears] more quiet at this time," I asked. "Do you feel that, too?"

"Yes."

"Why do you think that is?" I asked. "As you say, it's not to establish more distance."

"Maybe it's just if I talk," she reflected, "then I wouldn't know if you really mean it when you respond."

"Oh, so you look for something *more* from me," I now could see, "especially at this time before we separate, for me to show my continued involvement."

"Yes," she said, as she spontaneously began to note parallel experiences that she had not quite seen in this light before; "I feel the same way about George [a friend], before he goes away. It's also hard for me to reach out; I only do that in desperation really." [p. 1050]

Schwaber then describes

a new direction [that] opened as [the analysand] recounted her feeling of not existing in the other's absence and her sense of increased risk before a separation; in later hours, she elaborated resonant memories from the recent and more distant past. As she felt her perceptions and her experience of them recognized she came to distinguish and acknowledge on her own additional nuances in the meaning of her defensive stance—her uses of quiet and retreat, and their interdigitation with her conflictual issues.

It is of course quite possible that in my taking the approach I did she may have felt me as reaching more to her, the very thing she had sought in the first place. But it was yet uncertain whether it was the

quantity of my words or the position from which they were
spoken—that is, the active search for her perspective, that had a
decided impact on what ensued. Whichever it may have been, or
both, was still to be learned. We could, in either case, observe that
there was clearly at the time *some relation between my response—silent
or verbal—and her ensuing one*, the meaning of which warranted
further elucidation. [pp. 1050–1051, italics mine]

I could not imagine a more sensitive, productive clinical
process.

But if I understand her correctly, the philosophical-
ontological conclusion for psychoanalysis that obtains for
Schwaber from such a process is something with which I
completely disagree. Earlier in this same paper, Schwaber
imagines a hypothetical analysand who is experiencing a
conflict-engendered hallucination. She says:

It should be noted that there is no suggestion of the absence of a
measurable or otherwise *validatable reality*. We utilize information
about life events and chronology, and surely employ our own
sensory apparatus in our clinical investigations. If, for example, a
patient (with no organic visual abnormality) sees a red dress where
the analyst is wearing beige, we may assess the inaccuracy in the
specification of the color. But this is a matter different from a
judgement about the correctness in the *experienced* reality—in this
case, the *experience* of perceived redness. Thus the analyst need not
surrender her or his own view of reality in order to locate that of the
patient, but may draw on the *discrepancy* between them as an
indication of something in the patient's perspective, which may be
conveyed metaphorically, bearing a truth still to be learned. [p. 1042,
first and last italics mine]

Notice that in this hypothetical example of an analysand
hallucination, Schwaber uses the word *discrepancy*, whereas
in the earlier cited clinical incidence she talks about "some
relation between my [Schwaber's] response and her [the
analysand's] ensuing one" (p. 1051). My intuition is that,
for Schwaber, *discrepancy* is, at the least, closer to *gross*
or *extreme*, whereas *some relation* connotes less deviancy.

But less deviancy from what, if not the reality of Schwaber's beige dress? And here I mean a philosophical-ontological realism, which is something Schwaber herself seems at least to lean toward with terminology like "validatable reality" (p. 1042).

I can maintain a philosophical realism and, at the same time, have absolutely no doubt that the hypothetical analysand hallucination—that Schwaber's dress is red—is true because it *must* have something to do with the objective reality of the patient's relationship with Schwaber. For example, it is plausible that the analysand is, dynamically and unconsciously, via primary-process thinking, equating the color red with menstruation, and it is true that Schwaber really is a woman. If it is not this it must be something else that is responsive to the objective reality of the psychoanalytic relationship with Schwaber. At one point Gill (Rapaport and Gill 1959) would agree (and see Hartmann 1939). Freud (1937b) had exactly the same belief: "The essence of it is that there is not only *method* in madness, as the poet has always perceived, but also a fragment of *historical truth*" (p. 267, italics mine). Later in the chapter I will discuss, at much greater length, Freud's idea of historical truth. But for now Freud had something else important to say about hallucination or delusion: "Under the conditions of a psychosis, [patients] can do no more than replace the *fragment of reality* that is being disavowed *in the present*" (p. 268, italics mine). In other words, for any analysand, psychic reality is in some way related to what can be (ultimately, ontologically) granted to be real about the present psychoanalytic relationship. Even individuals in a seemingly totally withdrawn catatonic stupor have been shown to express a responsiveness to what is real in their immediate life circumstances (Adams 1967). This is why Freud (1937b) could say:

> The *vain effort* would [really should] be abandoned of convincing the patient of the error of his delusion [hallucination, etc.] and of its

> contradictions of reality; and on the contrary, the recognition of its
> kernel of truth would afford common ground upon which the
> therapeutic work could develop. [pp. 267–268, italics mine]

Niederland (e.g., 1968) and, more recently, Lothane (1992) have demonstrated the relevance of this viewpoint for Freud's (1911b) work on Schreber's delusions.

What I mean, then, by psychic reality is something like the following: "The totality of a person's representation . . . thoughts, feelings, dreams and fantasies, memories and perceptions—whether or not they accurately reflect or correspond to objective reality" (Moore and Fine 1968, p. 83). Schafer (e.g., 1983) at this point would object that "objective reality" is never "recognized innocently" (p. 234); and I believe he is correct in his argument that a philosophy of "innocent" (or naive) realism cannot be appropriate to psychoanalysis. But I would respond that the way that Schafer uses the term *innocent* conflates a question of epistemology (truth value) that we place on any sort of belief (perception, interpretation, etc.) about what is real with what *is* real. However, the moment I so criticize Schafer's position with the term *conflate*, I have committed myself to *some* philosophy of realism (just as Schafer has committed himself to an antiobjectivist philosophy). Certainly, a term like *reflect* flies in the face of the constructional process involved in any conception of the real (e.g., Piaget 1937). But a philosophy of realism can be developed and maintained with due recognition of how "theory-laden and risky" (Devitt 1984, p. 133) are any of our beliefs about reality, and this is true whether our beliefs are related to immediate observations or theoretic unobservables. So I maintain that it is the business of a psychoanalysis to identify both real and unreal transference aspects of an analysand's psychic reality. Psychic reality is not, in this perspective, naively opposed to any "reflected," objective reality; rather, any feature of the psychic reality of an individual will *always* implicate the originating influences of *both* what is real and unreal (Freud, e.g., 1911b). But isn't a progressive enlargement of a patient's psychic reality in a psychoanalysis something that is *interpretively* articulated? Well, yes and no. When we use the idea of free association we mean not only a type of language but also a special (one could even say peculiar) state of consciousness such that mental contents not ordinarily available to an individual now become conscious. There is a congruent state of consciousness in the analyst (e.g., Beres and Arlow 1974, Freud 1912b). What the analysand's manifest, free-associational language accomplishes is that special mental contents are now made out-of-the-ordinary "facts" of immediate observation, and consequently there can occur interpretation that seeks to enlarge the analysand's psychic reality still further from such kinds of immediate observation. And, as I have said, this enlarged psychic reality may eventually settle adequately the question whether experience held by the analysand about the analyst's experience will be regarded as real or unreal transference.

The principle of equivocality, however, also applies to such interpretive revelation. Of course, I do not deny that an analyst's interpretations are shaped by a theoretical framework that implicitly or explicitly carries with it presumptions about the analysand's experience—it is impossible to conceive of any human being, processing experience of any sort, for any purpose, who is not using some such schematic orientation, and the analyst who interprets from manifest free association is no exception. But this need not violate the essence of what I mean by the principle of equivocality, and for these reasons. First, as Gill (1984a) has indicated, an analyst cannot ever be absolutely certain of possessing perfect understanding or control with respect to his or her dynamic unconscious. Second, our current limited knowledge about personality, treatment process, and certainly about their intersection also requires equivocality with respect to any interpretation based on immediate, free-associational language.

To put this another way, and using a term emphasized by Reik (1949), the possibility of *surprise* is to be regarded as a natural element in an analyst's attitude. The presence of such a readiness for surprise is a marker for a proper and productive analytic attitude (Schafer 1983). Thus it matters much whether interpretations are presented to the analysand with an attitude that here is something to consider (because of the principle of equivocality), or delivered with the air of a pronouncement. I believe that the analyst's attitude that presents interpretation as a *consideration* is an important aspect of what is meant by the idea of a therapeutic alliance (see, e.g., Greenson 1967). Such an alliance is not a relationship conceived somehow to be tacked onto the transference experience; it occurs at the very heart of analytic work, which is in the making, consideration, and effects of interpretation (Hanly 1994). I believe that Freud (1937b) also would use the term *conjecture* for this analyst's attitude. Interpretation delivered with an attitude of pronouncement must hopelessly confuse transference forces, making for suggestion (which is inevitable [Freud, e.g., 1916–1917]) with an actual attitude on the analyst's part that supports such suggestion. When I use such language as a readiness for "surprise," or interpretation given as a "consideration," I describe an analyst's attitude that is necessary for a *real*, collaborative clinical praxis. But this must also describe a context for the possible *refutation* of the hypothesis embedded in any clinical interpretation made by the analyst. And at least for analysts for whom such a thing matters, without an attitudinal context that generally includes the possibility of such refutation, a psychoanalysis cannot even aspire to be regarded as a natural-science activity (Popper 1959; and see Wisdom, esp. 1967). But I do not confuse, as important as this is, the difference between such an attitudinal context in an ongoing clinical process and controlled research that makes use of clinical process (e.g., Weiss and Sampson 1986).

There is a third type of circumstance with respect to settling whether an analysand's experience is to be considered real or unreal, and this involves still another relationship between an analysand's experience and immediate observation. Here the analysand uses, and is convinced that something from immediate observation serves to objectify, some aspect of his or her psychic reality about the analyst's experience as a person; and nothing from immediate observation can invalidate such a conviction. The purest example of this is a delusional system of some sort; to the extent that this enters into the psychoanalytic relationship, a progressive enlargement of the analysand's psychic reality cannot occur, and the analysand's language in such a circumstance becomes litigious. With an orientation provided by Mahoney (1979), one can say that such a paranoid, litigious use of language represents a type of rhetoric that (only) constantly aims to convince and persuade another; it is thus completely antithetical to a free-associational, psychoanalytic process and a collegial psychoanalytic relationship.

All of what I have said thus far might be considered only another way to describe an all-too-familiar contrast between schizophrenic and neurotic reality testing as this applies to the possibility of conducting a psychoanalysis, classically conceived. However, I believe this way of putting things is useful because it makes plain some important things that are perhaps so obvious they escape notice. In addition, it leads to the recognition of still another kind of question about what is to be designated real or unreal (transference) experience, one that I think is not so obvious.

What is obvious is that the psychoanalytic relationship, classically conceived, presupposes two kinds of agreement between analyst and analysand: mutual agreement about what constitutes (so-called) immediate observations, and agreement about the continuous, equivocal nature of the relationship between these immediate observations and whether analysand experience about the analyst's experience as a person is to be considered real or unreal. What I believe is not an obvious outcome of this approach is that a progressive enlargement of the analysand's psychic reality can occur, and language becomes, increasingly, personally expressive. However, while the relationship between immediate observations and the reality or unreality of analysand experience is acknowledged to be in question, this is not treated as equivocal, in the sense that I have used the term. Instead, what can arise is an acknowledged, intense, and persistent disagreement about whether some agreed-on immediate observation about the psychoanalytic relationship will be considered to confer a real or unreal (transference) status to some analysand experience about the analyst-as-a-person. When such a circumstance arises in any psychoanalysis, we have, in traditional terminology, concretization and a likely occurrence of acting out (see esp. Boesky 1982). Analysand acting out always gives rise to a greater likelihood of analyst "counter" acting out, and an unproductive psychoanalytic relationship may then prevail. More than this, what we are wont to call acting out can become essential to the transference and *real* psychoanalytic relationship of narcissistic and borderline individuals. This circumstance, which I term a psychoanalytic relationship of *enacted symbols*, or transference as *pathological play*, will be taken up later in this book.

When Freud (1906) early on devised the term *psychic reality*, he was not just constructing a conceptual tool for understanding and practice with respect to hysterical reminiscences of sexual seduction. His interest also was to use this notion of psychic reality to better comprehend the nature of what is real. Even in what we would conceive to be a most extreme, unreal construction of what is real—a schizophrenic delusion—Freud's (1911b) interest was to relate such unreal experience to an ontological issue of what is real: "[A] . . . paranoid *perceives the external world and takes into account any alteration that may happen in it*, and the effect it makes upon him stimulates him to invent explanatory theories" (p. 75, italics mine).

It is fair, however, to ask: Why must this be so? Why must all analysand psychic reality be related somehow to that which is (ultimately, ontologically) grounded in some idea of objective reality? The best answer, I maintain, for a Freudian theory of mind is that this is how a human mind *is made*. Certainly, at least since Hartmann (1939), it has become part of a Freudian theory of mind that we possess an initial and developing array of autonomous (i.e., conflict-free) capabilities to adapt to reality. Obviously, this is a reality bounded by these same autonomous capabilities, as would be true for any organism, but it is our autonomous inclination for adaptation to this reality that is the important point. Even more, Hartmann argued that if one considers this issue within a broader perspective, it is a reality principle inherent in evolution that would give rise to a pleasure principle in human mentality. This is not at all mysterious or difficult to understand. Surely it is in the survival interest of our species that it is pleasurable to reproduce, to eat, and so forth. But such a primacy for a reality principle in human mentality already is evident in Freud's writing. When Freud (1911a) formulated his two principles of mental functioning, he conceived that the human (infant) mind *first* makes a differentiation between "inner" (drive activation) versus "outer" (perceptual) sources of stimulation on the objective basis of whether or not such stimulation can be avoided by the infant's own physical movement. Hanly (1990), recently and incisively, has summarized Freud's argument to position psychoanalysis within a philosophy of realism and a correspondence doctrine of truth: (1) Mental capabilities have developed in order to adapt to a world, and it is likely that they have developed a structure to facilitate that adaptation. (2) Such mental capabilities themselves are part of the world and thus can be investigated as to their effectiveness, as can the question of what improves or retards such effectiveness. (3) Scientific knowledge, because of its methods, is determined primarily by the objects observed and not by our own mental structures and processes.

I want to return to Schwaber's (1992) sensitive clinical work with her patient. It was Schwaber's ability to put aside any "vain effort" (Freud 1937b) to convince the patient that the patient was distorting reality, and her ability to situate herself in the patient's psychic reality, that ultimately led to a spontaneous and genuinely felt realization by the patient herself that her psychic reality included a fantasy elaboration of the real situation obtaining between them. However, Schwaber also talks about her analysand's "*experienced* reality*" (p. 1042), which for Schwaber evidently has truth value in itself; and this analysand-experienced truth is to be contrasted with truth values to be obtained from our "validatable" [presumably objective] reality" (p. 1042).

I mentioned, in citing Schwaber, how her analysand spontaneously began to elaborate resonant "memories" in connection with her transference experience, and I have said that I think it more useful to use the term *reminiscences* than *memories*. It is this issue of analysand reminiscences, together with the matter of reconstruction in a psychoanalysis, that I would like, now, to consider.

RECONSTRUCTION IN PSYCHOANALYSIS

In an early paper, "Screen Memories," Freud (1899) brought his comments to a close with the following: "It indeed may be questioned whether we have any memories at all *from* childhood: memories *relating to* childhood may be all that we possess" (p. 322). Notice that Freud, here, refers to all memories, both within and outside a context of conflict. Earlier in this same paper, Freud comments that such a constructionist emphasis about memory—that is, memory that is not a simple copy of a taken-to-be-factual description of a childhood experience—is "something invariably happening in hysterical patients" (p. 317).

This is striking, because "Screen Memories" was published only some 4 years after Breuer and Freud's (1895) *Studies in Hysteria*, in which they describe memory after memory—all then considered to be veridical recollections of disturbing childhood occurrences. They contended that conflict was produced in a simple, direct way by these traumatic memories, which, in turn, produced hysterical symptomatology. From Freud's (1887–1902) correspondence with Fliess, we know that as early as 1897 Freud no longer believed in such a straightforward trauma, veridical memory theory of hysteria. With fantasy formation in childhood now seen as critical, a constructionist or "psychical reality" (Freud 1939) view of memory came to the fore. Nevertheless, a considerable time after this Freud added a footnote in 1924 to a paper that included comments on the etiology of hysteria (1896): "[actual] seduction retains a certain etiological significance" (p. 168) with regard to hysteria. It is important to be clear that what Freud meant by etiological significance at this later point in his theory was that an actual sexual molestation of some form or another will be a significant contributor to the formation of a hysteric's psychical reality (e.g., Freud 1939). But this psychical reality is not a simple copy of some sort of molestation. It is a construction that has another source: what the child makes out of this traumatic factual occurrence with respect to his or her psychosexual, and/or aggressive, fantasy formations.

A next step in this brief history would be Freud's (1915d) paper "Repression," one of his so-called metapsychology papers. A constructionist emphasis for remembering both within and outside of a context of conflict is at least implicated when Freud states: "[The] instinctual representative [representation] *develops* . . . in the dark, as it were, and this takes on extreme forms of expression" (p. 149, italics mine).

But in another of the metapsychology papers, "The Unconscious," Freud (1915e) plainly raises questions: "The system
Ucs. contains the thing-cathexis of objects, the *first and true*
object-cathexis; the system *Pcs.* comes about by this thing-
presentation being hypercathected through being linked
with the word presentation corresponding to it" (p. 201,
italics mine). And, "A presentation which is not put into
words, or a psychical act which is not hypercathected,
remains therefore in the *Uncs.* in a state of repression" (p.
202).

Notice Freud's (1915e) use of the word *first* and the
epistemic term *true* in connection with what he calls a thing
cathexis. At first reading, this is a more static conception of
dynamically unconscious representation; it would implicate
a fixed-copy view of memorial processes. Schimek (1975) has
understood this paper in just this way. And yet, just before
these comments Freud says something quite different about
this concept of a thing cathexis: "The [thing cathexis] consists in the cathexis, if *not* of the direct memory-images of the
thing, at least of remoter memory-traces *derived* from these"
(p. 201, italics mine). So here again Freud is employing a
constructionist emphasis formally similar to his statement in
"Screen Memories" (Freud 1899): "memories *relating to* childhood may be all we possess" (p. 322). Of Freud's use of the
term *true*, I believe this idea is what he (e.g., 1937b, 1939)
elaborated into his concept of historical truth, which I will
get to later.

But what are we to do with the terms *thing cathexis* and
word cathexis with respect to cognition in general, and
remembering in particular? And in this context, Freud also
introduces another term—*primary process*—which again
raises questions. Freud states the following about a con-
necting of the thing cathexis with a word cathexis: "[It]
brings about a *higher psychical organization* and makes it
possible for the primary process to be succeeded by the

secondary process which is dominant in the *Pcs.*" (p. 202, italics mine).

In *The Interpretation of Dreams* (1900), Freud said about primary process—which, by definition, is constructionist thinking—the following: "When I described one of the *psychical* processes as the 'primary' . . . I had in mind . . . a name which would give an indication of its *chronological* priority" (p. 603, italics mine). However, in the same book Freud is quite clear that it is only the dreams of 4- or 5-year-old children that demonstrate imagery requiring the concept of primary process. Before this age, the dreams are "quite uninteresting" and "raise no problem for solution" (p. 122). So if language encoding of experience starts before age 4 or 5, which it certainly does, but primary-process-produced dreams occur only at a later age, primary-process thinking cannot, chronologically, be first.

Here we are in a conceptual thicket and will remain so unless we make use of contemporary research into cognition (e.g., Kosslyn and Pomeranz 1981, Paivio 1986). Let us say that thing cathexis means not a fixed-copy view of representation but instead nonlinguistic procedures for imagistic encoding and storage of experience, as well as retrieval of memories, that develop throughout our lifetimes. Word cathexis, of course, will mean language system procedures for encoding, storage, and remembering that also develop. Bucci (e.g., 1994), in particular, has emphasized the usefulness for psychoanalysis of a multiple-code model for cognition, rather than Freud's perspective, which she correctly characterizes as a "mixed form of a verbal-dominance model." Our fundamental psychoanalytic construct of psychic reality requires us to consider that analogically encoded, prototypic imagistic experiences of intense emotionality are also subject to constructionist influence during development. But the important point is that a system of imagistic encoded experience exists that produces meanings, especially connected to emotionality, that are outside of language. Both verbal and nonverbal symbolic encoding systems operate for each of us, although the systematic, generative rules for nonverbal imagistic symbols (concrete form and function) obviously differ from those of the verbal system (grammatical rules).

Further, Bucci (1994) emphasizes how contemporary cognitive research points to a subsymbolic, or presymbolic, encoding of experiences that also operates for each of us; hence the designation *multiple encoding*. This parallel, multiple, subsymbolic processing and retrieval of experiences especially relates to our varied senses and is not at all difficult to understand. Imagine watching a newborn baby learning to nurse for the first time. If I say "learning"—and I believe I must—then in this very first nursing experience the baby is acquiring information. How? Simultaneously via its systems for perception, smell, registration of pleasurable affect with mouth muscle movements, digestive sensations, and so forth. We use these subsymbolic processes throughout our lives, for example, in the complex, multichanneled coordination involved in hitting a tennis ball or playing a musical instrument. Also, I believe it is *one* of the ways in which an analyst's dynamic unconscious continuously is influenced by the dynamic unconscious of the analysand, that is, outside of symbolic operations altogether (and vice versa [Freud 1915e]). Freedman and his colleagues (e.g., Freedman 1994) make the case that different patterns of hand and foot movements occurring between the two individuals in the clinical relationship ought to be understood as subsymbolic processes that may facilitate or interfere with symbolic operations (verbal and/or nonverbal). The basic idea of subsymbolic processing is what Werner and Kaplan (1963) some 30 years ago subsumed under the term *physiognomic apprehension* of experience; and it calls to mind Freud's (1923) statement that the ego is "first and foremost a body ego" (p. 27).

Psychoanalysis has much to gain, and nothing to lose, by adopting this multiple viewpoint about how life experience is encoded to build up psychic reality. Clinically, for example, it makes more natural, and therefore comprehensible, what we mean by insight achieved with language in a psychoanalysis, classically conceived. What analyst and analysand devote themselves to find with their language are the *right* words, which are *felt* to be meaningfully *connected*, especially to this nonverbal, emotionally encoded body of experience. Bucci (e.g., 1989, 1994) refers to this as "referential links" (p. 258). One could say that Freud's (e.g., 1915e) conceptual eye was too much in a verbal upward direction—"higher psychical organization" (p. 202)—and not enough in a sideways direction. Obviously, these two symbolic encoding systems for producing meaning for our experiences may interact with one another, whatever the context; and within a context of conflict there arises the possibility of psychoanalytic symbol formation. Evidently, our psychoanalytic experience with dreams (1900) and, one could add, symptom formation (Freud 1909) requires us to conceive that a certain measure of development of our verbal encoding system is necessary for primary-process-mediated symbol formation. But the symbols will always include elements of psychic reality from this nonverbal, analogically organized system of emotional, nonverbal, imagistic symbols "built on" subsymbolic, visceral, taste, and so on encoding of experience.

The critical simile used by Freud (1937b) likened interpretative reconstruction by a psychoanalyst to the work of an archeologist in the field. The following comments about transference are pertinent: "Our experience has shown that the relation of transference which becomes established toward the analyst is particularly calculated to favor the return of these emotional connections" (p. 258). And also, "What we are in search of is a picture of the patient's forgotten years that shall be alike, trustworthy and in all essential respects complete" (p. 258). And finally:

Indeed it may as we know be doubted whether any psychical structure can really be the victim of total destruction. . . . there are only two other facts which weight against the extraordinary advantage which is thus enjoyed by the work of the analyst. . . . psychical objects are incomparably more complicated than the excavator's material ones and . . . we have insufficient knowledge of what we may expect to find, since their finer structure contains so much that is still mysterious. [p. 260]

Has Freud, here, come "full circle" and returned as Spence (1982) claims to a correspondence, a copy theory of memorial processes, in doubting that any psychical structure can really be the victim of total destruction (p. 260)? I do not think so. Notice, especially, his distinction between the recovery of psychical objects and the archeologist's recovery of material objects.

This distinction was already in Freud's mind prior to his paper on constructions. It occurred in the first draft (1934) of *Moses and Monotheism*, especially in the third section (see Editor's Notes, pp. 3–5 [Freud 1939]). I emphasize this because in *Moses and Monotheism* Freud makes a careful distinction between historical truth (p. 129) and what he calls material truth (p. 129). Material truth for Freud corresponds to what we ordinarily mean by the term *real* applied to objects and events, past, present, and anticipated. Historical truth (1937b, p. 261) corresponds to psychical objects (p. 260), which are the stuff of what Freud (e.g., 1939) calls an individual's psychical reality (p. 76). Applied to the past, these psychical objects are the analysand's *reminiscences* of his or her interactions with significant others in childhood. Some of these reminiscences are available at the commencement of a psychoanalysis; other reminiscences first occur during a psychoanalysis and typically arise with some sort of transference experience with the analyst. In addition, and this certainly varies a good deal from one analysis to another, there can be constructions. Freud's (1937b) word for this was *conjecture* (p. 265), which is never remembered but "feels right" to the analysand. But whether we are considering reminiscences or constructions, the same applies. What will animate a Freudian analysis is how the analysand-as-child came to build up a psychic reality, which then is continuously elaborated; it is a meaningfully felt verbal connection to this psychic reality that can be therapeutic. A Freudian psychoanalyst, and psychoanalysis, assumes that at least some initial critical core of these reminiscences has been created jointly by childhood fantasies intersecting with factual occurrences in the analysand's childhood life with significant others.

It is, of course, such object relations fantasies that can infuse transference or (possible) countertransference experience. And I believe it is these dynamically unconscious, object relations fantasies that Freud had in mind when he spoke about how psychical objects have a "finer structure" (p. 261). In other words, the way in which reminiscences animated by sadistic fantasies may implicate the eventual experience of reminiscences animated by masochistic fantasies; memories informed by exhibitionistic fantasies may eventually instigate memories informed by voyeuristic fantasies; a feeling state of aggression may be sequestered from consciousness, and instead one may experience depression; and so forth.

What, for Freud, was the epistemic ground for this idea of truth within his concept of historical truth applied to an individual's past? The answer is complex, because Freud had now come to a more complex theory of remembering. Neither the factual occurrences of the child's past, nor the child's psychosexual and aggressive schemas for fantasy production, are totally created by the other; each have, in a significant sense, independent origins. But the particular elaboration of a psychic reality for a particular child is brought about by a mutual engendering. The idea of truth, for Freud, could be applied to the psychic reality of the reminiscences and possible constructions of the adult analysand, that is, historical truth, because Freud believed such reminiscences always, in their engendering, had to do with what he described as a "kernel of truth" (p. 268), for example, "Something [in the past] which was at that time terrifying . . . [and] . . . did really happen" (p. 268). What did really happen (material truth), and the possible fantasy elaboration about how it came to be so terrifying (historical truth), is the task of a psychoanalysis, and might be called the whole truth. We do the best we can, but every psychoanalysis remains vulnerable on this issue.

I believe Spence (1982) misuses Freud's concept of historical truth to mean material truth, for which Spence has no reference. He writes: "Historical truth is time bound and is dedicated to the strict observance . . . [or] . . . as close as possible to what 'really' happened" (p. 33). And he goes on:

> If we follow what Freud says in his writings we would find ourselves looking for historical truth. This emphasis comes out most clearly in his many references to archeology as the guiding metaphor, and in his persistent belief in the curative effects of the "kernel of truth"— historical truth being clearly intended. [p. 33]

But what did Freud (1937b) actually say about this kernel of truth and its relevance to the possible therapeutic effect of a psychoanalysis? "That [psychoanalytic] work would consist in liberating the fragment of historical truth from its distortions" (p. 268). And again, it is perfectly clear from the immediate context why Freud, here, uses the simple condensed term *distortions* (p. 268) to refer to psychic reality. Something did really happen and got to be terrifying as a consequence of an interplay with psychosexual and/or aggressive fantasy formation. What may be therapeutic is no longer an abreaction (Breuer and Freud 1895) of some taken-to-be-factual traumatic occurrence but an understanding of the psychic reality an individual-as-child has produced partly as consequence of that occurrence. Two other points need to be added. First, we certainly understand that this psychic reality need not only be terrifying; it can include all sorts of feelings that are gratifying, and this is illustrated in the clinical material I am about to present. Second, I referred to terror, that is, a feeling that, you may recall, I urge psychoanalysis to conceive of as experience that is not encoded linguistically. An individual's psychic reality is continuously elaborated linguistically, but it is not elaborated haphazardly. What are critical feeling states for a particular person will persist in his or her developing, conscious psychic reality, or the person protects him- or herself against some feeling, or more likely some combination of the two. This will also be illustrated in the following clinical material.

A Clinical Vignette

An analysand with whom I worked suffered a particular kind of malevolent object relations disturbance—she was sexually molested as a 4- or 5-year-old girl by her grandfather, someone for whom she had great affection and who had great affection for her. The best recollection she had about the sexual abuse was that he exposed and held his penis while she watched. It seemed to us likely that his penis was erect and he was masturbating, but the analysand had no such memory. She did remember that she felt an excitement in the pit of her stomach, which nevertheless also felt odd: at the same time she felt the excitement, it did not feel as if it was she who was having the excitement. The excitement seemed to be a (nonverbalizable) kind of "thing" (Freud 1915e) in itself, not easily represented out of subsymbolic experiences (Bucci 1994) and not connected to her self-representation. She also remembered thinking, incessantly, that her mother would disapprove of what was happening. There is no question in my mind that this sexual molestation occurred. The grandfather acknowledged it when the little girl told her mother about it. It ruined the intergenerational family. It was never talked out with her. The paternal grandfather was never again permitted any contact with any member of the family.

This relationship with the grandfather—prior to the sexual abuse—was remembered by the analysand as one of mutual, wonderful affection. The grandfather doted on her. They played together, he would give her sweets, and so forth. The little girl would demonstrate to her grandfather things she had just learned to do, and, at her home, show off her new clothes with a charming exhibitionism. It was, in a definite sense, the most fulfilling relationship the analysand remembered with respect to her childhood. The father and mother seemed to be drawn tightly together into a relationship of endless, mutual, acrimonious complaint about each other. There were some times of pleasure the analysand recollected with her father. These involved a certain music-playing talent they both possessed.

A dream, later on in treatment, was important in our further understanding. In this dream, a white horse is running around and around in a circle on the surface of a body of water. So long as the horse keeps running fast, it escapes drowning; the moment the horse falters, or even slows down, it will drown. To this powerful horse, she associated her grandfather's large penis she was forced to see. I conjectured that the whiteness of the horse could symbolize the grandfather's white pubic hair, but she could not remember seeing his pubic hair. But the analysand associated herself to this horse, especially her feverish work style, difficulty with relaxation, and the acute, really catastrophic, anxiety she could suffer if she believed something to be wrong with her job performance. It is important to understand that the horse in this dream was not at all like some winged Pegasus gliding effortlessly above the water. Quite the opposite; this white horse was agitated, intense, and endlessly concerned about its capacity to perform, to avoid sinking below the water. I conjectured with her that something of a past, actual agitated state of the grandfather—as he touched his penis and/or masturbated in front of her—was being represented in the manifest content of a horse with nostrils flared, sweating, exerting great effort to prevent death by drowning. This conjecture, like that of the white pubic hair, "felt right" (Freud 1937b) to the analysand, although again she could not remember. If so, the woman's vulnerability to develop extreme agitation over her work performance would be connected to an analogically encoded emotional state first experienced with her grandfather, who was agitated and struggling with his sexuality. But it would be a little girl who also suffered agitation about her own sexual excitement watching all of this. Reed (1993) has commented about the value that can accrue from such efforts at explicit reconstruction in a psychoanalysis. Spoken in plain, vivid language, it can enhance for an analysand the meaningfulness of the psychic reality he or she has created. The psychic reality expressed in this dream by my analysand obviously was no simple copy of what actually occurred during the sexual molestation. The great white horse, while no Pegasus, nevertheless was still an amazing animal, managing to stay on top of the water by dint of great effort.

But why did this particular little girl, suffering such sexual molestation, create the white horse fantasy *about herself*? It was her associations to the water that produced further, new, unexpected, important reminiscences, especially having to do with the nature of her early pre-oedipal experience with her mother. Initially, with a feeling of pride, she remembered reports by family members about how at the beach her mother would not "worry" about her as other mothers did with their children. What she remembered being told was that she could, even as a 2- or 3-year-old child, play at the water's edge, even dart into the surf, unmonitored by her mother. What further analysis developed was that this extreme self-sufficiency was not just allowed but required by her mother, who was prone to a chronic, depressive mood. As our work continued, it seemed to us that as a little girl my analysand developed grandiose, compensatory fantasies to cope with insufficient pleasure and security in her early attachment experience with her mother. And she continued to elicit and produce object relations experience congruent with such early grandiose self-sufficiency.

As a schoolchild, she could not remember a single morning when she ate breakfast with her father or mother. This was readily confirmed by her parents. Her father waited in the living room for his wife to arise at the latest possible moment, and they would then go to work together. The girl never complained or consciously felt complaint; she did remember having all kinds of pleasant daydreams at breakfast. Already as an 8-, 9-, 10-year-old, this girl routinely would cook dinner for her family. At age 17, she left her fairly small midwestern town to attend business school in a large eastern seaboard city, where she knew absolutely nobody. No regrets or sadness were felt or expressed by anyone over the separation.

The most stable way she felt pleasure and security in love as an adult was not with people but with her love for nature, a cat she loved, and growing tomatoes. This growing tomatoes commenced during the latter part of the analysis. She felt, initially in the psychoanalysis, mistreatment if, say, a subway train failed her; and later in the psychoanalysis a hopeless rage would occur with such an experience, together with an intense anxiety over loss of support from inanimate objects.

Notwithstanding her inclination to retreat as an adult into a grandiose self-sufficiency for her pleasure, together with her love for nature and her cat, she was never content for long with these solutions. But her pleasure seeking with others would erupt uncontrollably. While married herself, she carried on a torrid love affair with a married man. She would become irrationally possessive and jealous of his attention to any other woman, including his wife. Her inability to control her feelings disturbed her very much. What was remarkable about the love affair was the analysand's conviction that she could get the man to be faithful to her, although she knew, and close friends told her, that he was a notorious womanizer. She thus juxtaposed (split and repeated) the tepid, insufficiently fulfilling oedipal relationship with her actual father with the overwhelming, exciting, anxious, and guilt-laden experience with her grandfather. She would report compulsive bouts of masturbation that left her feeling disturbed and out of control, that is, masturbation where she would seem to need to go on endlessly. She reported a lifelong belief that she really could get any man to desire her if only she put her mind to it. She described with pride that she had the kind of figure on which a dress would "hang right," without need for alteration; she said this to me as she stood up and was about to leave the office.

Her sense of helpless rage, and her despondency over loss of support and mistreatment, entered concretely into our treatment relationship. This occurred after the white horse dream and focused on the time and day of one of her analytic sessions. The hour had to that point been suitable. But as a result of a change in her work schedule, this particular time actually did become difficult for her to keep; maintaining it would have required her to leave and return to work on a day that made her work life more pressured and hectic. She complained continuously about this, acting as if I forced her to keep up a pace that was unreasonable, that I didn't care that she felt so overwhelmed, and so forth. She readily could feel that she was now experiencing anger and dissatisfaction she never let herself feel or express as a child, particularly in connection with her mother. I interpreted from her associations that she was anxious that I, like her mother, would depressingly (angrily) withdraw because of her angry wish to obtain some better support from me. I also could interpret from her associations that she wanted me, as her mother, to feel guilty about bad caretaking. Also, from her associations, I could interpret her wish for me, as a man, to rescue her, knowing I would not. All this kept her needing to maintain herself in a beleaguered, mistreated, and deprived position. Eventually, at her initiative, we arranged another, mutually convenient session time.

But why did this analysand need to create such an extended period of anger and painful experience with me? She once said to me, before the white horse dream, "I can imagine saying words, but they're so disconnected to feelings, I'm afraid you won't believe me." It would be a vast error to conceive of this as an example of isolation of affect. First of all, this woman could experience all kinds of feelings and, in fact, was crying miserably when she made these comments. We came to understand that she herself could not experience any meaningful connection between words and her feelings when she spoke to me. Put another way, with me, both as a mother who forced her to do too much, as well as a father not available sufficiently for an oedipal "rescue" from such mistreatment, words, in principle, were not enough. Put still another way, no language, at this time, could provide a "referential link" (Bucci 1989) for this woman that felt meaningful for her. For this reason the analysand needed to create this "hectic schedule" experience with me; and once it was created, language for me could become meaningful for her. We are wont to call this kind of behavior an acting out (Freud, e.g., 1905b), that is, something that works against verbal expression of past experience. But I am more inclined to see it as an acting out (Freud 1914c) in order to make what had been remembered meaningfully expressible for herself, to me, *with* language.

After the hectic schedule experience, and our understanding not only of its dynamic significance but also of its significance with respect to making her experience with language meaningful, the patient increasingly made use of treatment to improve her work and love life. The work progress involved continuous career development into greater authority, and she eventually ended up in charge of her own business. She divorced her husband, who was practically sexually impotent, dangerously close to becoming alcoholic, and whose work took him away from her for extended periods of time.

The patient remarried and began to want and prepare to have a baby. At this time she would recall, mournfully, an oft-stated comment made to her by her mother: "Nice girls don't have babies." Subsequent to the sexual molestation by the grandfather, the mother became irrationally obsessed with the possibility that the patient would become promiscuous. The mother was always checking up on her as an adolescent, would not allow her to "hang out" at the neighborhood drugstore as did her other teenage friends, and so forth.

After this woman's (mutually agreed-on) termination, and for several years after the termination, she sent me a Christmas card inscribed with a note about her life, which was essentially satisfying. Enclosed with her Christmas card would be a picture and comments about her child. I believe her regularity in sending me these Christmas cards portraying and/or describing her growing child indicates a not sufficiently analyzed, oedipal transference fantasy baby. The analysand remembered the sexual molestation to have taken place in a back room of her grandfather's retail store. In the latter part of the analysis, she certainly felt some such connection to me and my office as a back room. But I also appreciate that this woman wanted to share with me what she had accomplished with her analysis and where she was in her life.

I will now end. But I want to do so by leaving you with a query. Why did this woman start growing tomatoes in the latter part of her analysis? I have the advantage of her associations. But I believe you have heard sufficient clinical material to make a good guess. And this guess would involve us, again, in these matters of connections between feelings and language, historical truth contrasted with material truth, as well as remembering and reconstruction in a psychoanalysis. I will give you a hint. It has to do with what she remembered being told about herself at the beach when she was a very little girl.

NOTES

1. Wallace (1984) uses the term *perception* for what I call a "fact."

2. Actually, for the psychoanalytic process, it really makes little difference whether, or to what extent, such "facts" are used by an analysand to support transference experience. The extent to which this does occur has to do with the character style of the analysand and this, then, becomes an important aspect of the analysand's psychic reality (see esp. Shapiro 1965).

As far as I can see, Spence's (1982) advocacy for "unpacking" the narrative truth assembled in a psychoanalysis, together with his more recently drawn contrast (Spence, 1990), between a "rhetorical" and "evidential" voice, only makes sense within some sort of perspective of realism. Schafer (1991), for example, who does not want to position psychoanalysis within any such objectivist framework, certainly appreciates this difference between himself and Spence.

2

Toward a Comparative Therapeutics

Transference and countertransference are, of course, the traditional Freudian constructs used to conceive interactional effects on clinical process. I believe that, as low-level clinical constructs, transference and countertransference are not immediate observation statements (Laudan 1990) about which psychoanalysts of difference theoretical persuasions can have a dialogue (in disagreement with Wallerstein [1990]). Also, I believe that while in a customary Freudian practice we normally withhold from manifest expression our countertransference, this does not mean we naively believe that a Freudian analyst exerts no influence on clinical process. Here we come to the matter (conception) of an analyst's work style. I think it can accurately be said that Freud spoke very little about analyst work style, and it is possible to conclude that analyst influence on clinical process is always and only a matter of an unproductive countertransference (e.g., Freud 1910c). But certainly contemporary Freudian analysts, increasingly, do talk about (conceive) a matter of analyst work style in distinction from countertransference (see, e.g., Poland 1986).

With a more-or-less-usual Freudian practice, an analysand's psychic reality can "expand inward." By this I mean that it can "open" toward object relations experience that is more and more felt to be "outside" a frame of time and place

altogether. This I contrast with any other psychoanalytic
process that keeps in the forefront how dynamically unconscious experience in the analysand relates to, or affects, the
current analysand–analyst relationship occurring in the analyst's office. This would be the case with a selective interpretation made of analysand associations to be about the
current treatment relationship (Gill, e.g., 1982); and it would
also be the consequence of a continuous revelation by the
analyst of his or her current countertransference experience
(e.g., Levenson 1972). That transference experience can exist
without regard to time and place is an important structural
aspect of what in Freudian practice we mean by regression in
the psychoanalytic relationship and the (always relative)
development of a transference neurosis (Freud 1914c), and
some allied term for other-than-neurotic conditions. This
altered, structural state of analysand consciousness optimally goes together with increasingly expressive, childlike
psychosexual and aggressive experience.

It will help, I think, as I go along to establish similarities
and differences among three types of psychoanalytic practice: (1) a more-or-less-usual Freudian psychoanalytic practice that continuously and exclusively empathically centers
and interpretively verbalizes only within the analysand's
psychic reality, together with a normative nonrevelation of
analyst countertransference experience; (2) a type of psychoanalytic clinical practice that includes a normative nonrevelation of analyst countertransference experience but that
emphasizes the analysand's psychic reality with respect to
contemporary experience of the interaction between analysand and analyst (Gill, e.g., 1982); (3) a type of psychoanalytic clinical practice in which, in addition to an emphasis on
the analysand's contemporary experience in the psychoanalytic relationship, the analyst utilizes and expresses countertransference experience to further clarify the nature of the
current, ongoing object relations experience (Levenson
1972). Levenson would object to my use of the term *counter-*

transference, and I will consider this later. Describing types of clinical practice along these lines becomes a useful grid for any future investigation of a comparative therapeutics of a more detailed sort: for example, I say nothing here about modern, Kleinian practice (e.g., Joseph 1989), something recently examined by Schafer (1994); and I have given only brief attention to Kohutian (Goldberg 1978) praxis or Gedo's (1979) "management" techniques, and so forth.

But my first purpose in this chapter is how to rationalize what is, after all, a highly unusual, one might even say odd, human relationship—our traditional Freudian practice of withholding manifest expression of analyst countertransference. I will consider as well how we are able to establish empathic understanding of the analysand's psychic reality, differentiating among concepts of transference, countertransference, and analyst work style as these affect the treatment relationship.

TRANSFERENCE, COUNTERTRANSFERENCE, AND ANALYST WORK STYLE

We conceive of an analyst's empathy with transference experience to involve a "trial identification" (Beres and Arlow 1974, Fliess 1942). But in such a conceptualization, the term *identification* is as crucial as the term *trial*. Trial importantly connotes an analyst's capability for an *instrumental* use of identification for the purpose not simply of grasping some sensibility about the analysand's unreal, transference experience but also of imputing an interpretive, interpersonal *meaning* to the experience.[1] This imputing of meaning I will call an empathic realization. It typically occurs to the analyst as a free association (Beres and Arlow 1974), that is, a not-cogitated understanding of some sort about the analysand's experience. The term *identification*, as Compton (1985) makes clear, has had a complex evolution in Freud's work, as

well as in the subsequent literature. But in this context I want
to use the following meaning of the term from Freud's (1921)
writing: "The ego has *enriched itself* with properties of the
object" (p. 113, italics mine), and "In . . . identification . . .
the ego makes a *partial* alteration in itself after the model of
the lost object" (p. 114, italics mine). If an analyst's ego
naturally becomes enriched—but only by some partial alteration of itself—then we are not dealing with dedifferentiation, that is, an imitative and/or merging object relationship
wherein the analyst's ego is "surrendered" or "lost" in
interactive experience with an analysand (see esp. Schafer
1959). But if this is so, the interpretation that flows from an
experience of empathic realization must also express something of the analyst's ego.[2]

The idea that an analyst inevitably must "shape" empa-
thized analysand transference experience appears contrary
to Freud's (1912b) description of how the analyst must use
his or her dynamic unconsciousness like a "telephone receiv-
er" (p. 115), and appears to contradict as well his recommen-
dation that the analyst "should be opaque . . . like a
mirror . . . show nothing but what is shown to him" (p. 118).
But with regard to the latter, as Gill (1983) has pointed out,
Freud was writing within a context of the advisability of the
analyst's sharing intimacies with the analysand. And with
respect to the former, Freud was writing about a dynamic,
unconscious *source* for empathic realization, which I think
still holds true, not about the *verbalization* of such source
material. Verbalization is never just a matter of attachment of
words to experience; rather, it implicates a "higher psychical
organization" (Freud 1915e). As such, verbalization implicates ego organization and functions so that something of
the person the analyst is must be expressed, in *some* way, in
any empathic realization of transference experience. It is, of
course, all a matter of the degree to which significant
libidinal and aggressive dynamics of the analyst find fulfillment in ways useful for the work of a psychoanalysis. From

another, object relations point of view, an analyst, no less than the analysand, is engaged in forms of object "refinding" (Freud 1905a) in his or her work as a therapist. This portrayal of the analyst as a person, necessarily dynamically involved and present in the psychoanalytic relationship, is not at issue in our literature, and such agreement extends over other points of controversy. For example, Brenner (1985), who is well identified with an objectivist philosophy for psychoanalysis and the maintenance of (so-called) classical procedure (minimal or no analyst self-disclosure of countertransference, etc.), states the following:

> Becoming an analyst, practicing analysis, necessarily involves for each individual analyst derivatives of that analyst's childhood conflicts. . . . It is when pathological compromise formations appear in an analyst's professional activity that analytic work may be disturbed. Instances of countertransference which interfere with analysis are examples of pathological or neurotic compromise formation. [p. 156][3]

Other analysts, such as McLaughlin (1981) and Schwaber (1983), who are identified with an antiobjectivist framework for psychoanalysis, together with a concept that analyst countertransference of some type is clinically normative with transference experience, but who still retain traditional Freudian praxis with respect to minimal or no analyst self-disclosure of countertransference, obviously will support a portrayal of the analyst as a person who is dynamically invested and present in the psychoanalytic relationship. McLaughlin, for example, states: "The analyzed analyst functions with his or her conflicts now altered (more or less sufficiently) by his training analysis into new psychic structures established through transference processes" (p. 656). And it is still more obvious that a concept of clinical praxis that involves continuous analyst disclosure of countertransference, exemplified, for example, by Levenson (1972), is grounded in a similar portrayal of the analyst-as-a-person, significantly involved in the psychoanalytic relationship.

What *is* at issue in our literature is how to conceive analyst involvement in the psychoanalytic relationɔhip. And, specifically, how are we to conceive analyst determinants for transference formation? If my use of the term *determinants* smacks, for some, too much of an (intended) natural science framework, then the same question can be put within a hermeneutic (i.e., narrative-constructing) perspective. In fact, it is important to realize that a Freudian analyst's ultimate philosophical position for psychoanalysis does not answer this question decisively. Schafer (1983), for example, working within a hermeneutic framework, states:

> The analysis primarily becomes the contemplation of the fantasy or invented aspects of the analysand's relationship to the analyst. This is so even when the analysand has temporarily succeeded in forcing or seducing the analyst into actualizing some assigned countertransference role in the relationship. [p. 123]

Schafer does not describe further this act of contemplation, nor does he say how it relates to an experience of empathic understanding (realization) of the analysand. But in any case, Schafer cannot mean contemplation in the sense of contemplation about something that exists in its essential nature independent of any influence emanating from the analyst who so contemplates, because Schafer is committed to an antiobjectivist positioning for psychoanalysis. Also important, Schafer clearly does not here view countertransference as clinically normative; he speaks about countertransference as something that can be "temporarily" activated.

Gill, on the other hand, while also committed to an antiobjectivist stance, holds quite a different concept of clinical process. I have already cited Gill's (1984a) contention that "the patient stimulates countertransference" (p. 165). And now I can add the following by Gill (1985):

> Transference is a *joint product* of the patient's intrapsychically
> structured patterns of relationship and of the interaction with the
> analyst. The proportions of the contributions from these two sources
> vary widely from one patient–analyst pair to another, and from one
> situation to another in any analysis. [p. 100, italics mine]

Notice again that any ideas about "proportions [that] vary
widely" are coherent only within some sort of framework of
realism. Gill obviously construes clinical process to be such
that transference–countertransference activation is clinically
normative, that in fact one cannot have a clinical process in
which one can occur without the other. I (or Brenner [e.g.,
1955] and others who adopt a realist positioning for psychoanalysis) would construe such an idea of clinical process in
this way: analyst-source determinants interact with anal-
ysand-source factors to produce, simultaneously and continuously, transference and countertransference experience;
and both kinds of determinants, thus, would be conceived to
have real (independent of the observer) causal effects on the
interactive clinical process.

But we can conceive of analyst-source factors in another
way, say, simply each analyst's own real, continuous *style of
work*—what makes his or her work "different in quality from
that of any other analyst" (Winnicott 1949, p. 195). Another
configuration of these effects will produce countertransference experience or behavior. The "opaque" (Freud 1912b)
image of a Freudian analyst suggests the possibility that *any*
sort of analyst-source determinants of transference experience are episodic and, when operating, not in any sense
significant with respect to the essential determination (or
narrative creation) of transference experience. As I have
indicated already, I believe the former aspect of this "classical" Freudian conception of practice is incorrect; it contradicts psychoanalysis itself as a thoroughgoing, dynamic
psychology, and it contradicts our concept of empathic
realization to involve trial identification. But I believe the
latter aspect is true; in some definite sense, what is an

inevitable, ongoing, stylistic analyst influence on analysand transference experience is, nevertheless, not essentially determining of what arises as the content of that transference.

Arlow's comment (in Schwaber 1985) that transference experience is ubiquitous, occurring before the psychoanalytic relationship begins, is, of course, true. But this in itself fails to argue compellingly that transference is not in *some* way influenced by the other person, analyst or whomever, involved in an interpersonal relationship with the analysand when transference occurs. Arlow (1985) also makes the point that the extent of the analyst's influence on transference can be likened to the effect of "day residue" (Freud 1900) material on dream formation. As useful as this analogy is, however, I think it does not give sufficient status to the shaping of transference that occurs as a consequence of the influence of the analyst's personality style in the psychoanalytic relationship. Freud, after all, emphasized how, as often as not, day residue material is of marginal conscious interest to the analysand, and this is hardly the case with the analyst-as-a-person in the psychoanalytic relationship. The day residue-to-dream relationship is obviously different from the ongoing, significant relationship that is clinically normative for analyst and analysand, and usually in manifest dream content the day residue experience is not even evident. Further, while analogic (Bucci, e.g., 1989) displacement is conceived to occur in usual sorts of transference formation, with typical dream manifest content, other, quite fantastic primary-process construction is wrought on day residue material.[4]

What I am after is an idea of the stylistic influence of the analyst-as-a-person (determination, creation) on analysand transference experience that encompasses the following: First, the influence is, in a definite sense, significant in forming analysand transference. Second, the influence is continuous. Third, the influence, while different from is also pertinent to inevitable circumstances of countertransference.

And fourth, notwithstanding the foregoing, this idea of a continuous, stylistic analyst influence must be meaningfully distinguishable from any connotation that the content of analysand transference is "essentially" or even "mutually" the result of analyst influence.

For these purposes, I want to use, and extend, a simile more recently used by Loewald (1975) but originally also used by Freud (1937a). And this is that analyst-as-a-person stylistic influence on analysand transference can be likened to the effect of a given material or medium on a creative production. The shaping opportunities for representation will differ in important ways according to the material or medium used by a creative individual. We can contrast a composer working with sound to a poet working with language to a plastic artist working with stone, wood, or oil on canvas, and so forth. Further, the shaping influences of these various plastic arts obviously will all possess more similarities to each other than, say, to musical composition. *But it is possible for a creative individual to produce—and an audience to recognize—an essential, identical representation of experience, whatever the medium or material used.* The same is true for transference expression in a psychoanalytic relationship, whatever the particular personality of the analyst.[5]

Obviously, at the least, a significant portion of this shaping influence on analysand transference is accomplished by how the analyst uses language. Language, here, must be thought of both as a sheer acoustical stimulus (pitch, volume, rhythm, etc.), and as a procedure (system) for communication; and in this latter respect, we deal with the manifold continuous choices an analyst makes in use of semantics and syntax, whether, and the degree to which, he or she uses metaphor and simile, and so forth. We now know, unfortunately, little about how the analyst's language exerts its systematic influence; and undoubtedly not the least reason for this is the degree of detailed analyst self-revelation it would require in the literature. One important exception to this state of affairs is a systematic clinical attempt by Poland (1986) to examine and observe effects of his language on analysand transference (see also Edelson 1975 and Panel 1986).

This same simile can be carried over to the formation of countertransference. A remarkable but routine observation is that countertransference can always become informative about the transference experience of the analysand (see, e.g., Jacobs 1991, Winnicott 1949). This can extend, in complex ways, into situations where it is not even the working analyst who experiences the countertransference but a supervisor, or case seminar member, to whom some clinical process is being presented (Gediman and Wolkenfeld 1980).

As I have indicated, any particular material or medium for creative expression will possess real attributes that facilitate a certain shaping for creative content. But these same medium or material properties will make more difficult, we can say "resist," the shaping of other creative representations. Examples of this are commonplace but nonetheless significant and real, the way, for instance, the grain "runs" in wood will facilitate one sort of creative representation and resist others.

We have, in our language, the expression "He or she rubs me the wrong way," and this is the heart of the matter. Each analyst—by virtue of the person he or she really is—must present potentialities for certain shapes of transference representation that at the same time make for resistance to other forms of transference. When the latter occurs, the analyst is more likely to be affected, consciously or dynamically unconsciously, by countertransference of some sort. If an analyst can achieve conscious realization of the countertransference without "obviously reflecting . . . erotic or hostile intent" (Gill 1984a), then countertransference can function as an effective signal for transference interpretation (see esp. Racker 1957).

Now, countertransference is always felt by an analyst to be (ego) passively suffered—even if consciously gratifying—

whereas empathic realization of transference routinely is felt to be a result of analyst activity (the ego is "enriched," Freud [1921]).[6] But whether we do (e.g., Gill 1985) or do not (e.g., Schafer 1983) conceive analyst countertransference to be a normative clinical counterpart to analysand transference, all current conceptions of psychoanalytic process agree that countertransference can, indeed optimally must, acquire this signal, informative function to be useful in any psychoanalysis. In one definite sense, this requires a modification of Freud's (1910c) view of countertransference: "We have noticed that no psychoanalyst goes further than his own complexes and internal resistances permit" (p. 145). In the rest of this context, Freud (1910d) makes clear his belief that in such a circumstance the analyst must seek further analysis to work through the sources of countertransference. Of course, Freud is still correct if the countertransference is unmanageable and seriously interferes with the conduct of a psychoanalysis; this is most usefully conceived to be a kind of "negative" clinical interference produced by the very same sources within any analyst that make his or her empathic realization facilitate certain other shapes for transference representation in the clinical process. A propensity for certain kinds of countertransference thus becomes part of each analyst's particular "work ego" (Fliess 1942), or "second self" (Schafer 1983), part of each analyst's stock-in-trade and overall instrumentality for being in touch with what is needed by an analysand for transference. Put another way, and now using a concept provided by Hartmann (1939), I can suggest that such an instrumental use of countertransference represents a productive, (relatively) conflict-free use made by the analyst of his or her transference experience in the psychoanalytic relationship.[7]

This idea that every analyst will (must) have potentialities that resist being used for some shape of transference experience has been reported by Schwaber (1983). The clinical material involved a point in a psychoanalysis where the analysand had decided to apply for graduate study, and schooling (achievement) had always been a source of intense anxiety. What now also emerged in the clinical material was "confusion and ambiguity" (p. 387) about the analysand's sense of sexual identity. Schwaber noted this conjunction: "I [Schwaber] thought that perhaps his engagement in formal learning might help to clarify further the sexual difficulty as well. I said this to him" (p. 387). What followed this comment was a rapid return to "symptomatic behavior which had long since receded—drinking, smoking marijuana, and engaging in sexual perversions" (p. 388). As subsequent material developed, it became clear that the analysand had transferentially construed Schwaber's comment as a coercion and/or lack of empathic support for his own emotional turmoil. The analysand felt that Schwaber was more invested in progress for the psychoanalysis than for himself. It was about such a transference experience that Schwaber was aware of resistance within herself to be perceived as such a person: "I felt a particular resistance to being experienced this way by the analysand, as central to another person's experience while so different from how I felt myself to be" (p. 389). Schwaber reaches this conclusion:

> Each of these factors—the centrality of my even unwitting participation in another's experience, as well as the lack of concurrence with my own experience of myself—seemed to stir a resistance which may have more ubiquitous significance; resistance to the acknowledgement that the truth we believe about ourselves is no more (though no less) "real" than the patient's view of us—that all we can "know" of ourselves is our own psychic reality. [p. 389]

In this way Schwaber has sought to resolve (or at least one could say transfer) a matter of clinically felt resistance into a kind of ontological resistance, a not wanting to acknowledge a plurality or relativity about what is real and true.

Here, I would maintain that there is *one* true and real answer to the clinical question. The question is whether

Schwaber was or was not involved in a countertransference experience when she made her comment to the analysand. Schwaber seems to be conflating two issues: (1) possible countertransference experience, and (2) how language may enter into the expression of such experience. The point here would be that any sort of gross examination of the manifest content of analyst discourse—be it language expressing an interpretation, or a clarification, or a confrontation, whatever—will most likely reveal little about the presence or absence of countertransference. Any ordinary examination of the structured language of the analyst's manifest discourse is as irrelevant for understanding possible countertransference as it would be for understanding, at least in the initial phase of a psychoanalysis, the analysand's transference experience. In the ongoing clinical situation, it is only the analyst's own self-analysis of his or her experience that can, one hopes, determine whether a countertransference experience has occurred; that is, whether some experience was "forced" on the analyst, as Schafer (1983) would put it, or whether the experience was something (ego) passively suffered. And what I maintain is that such descriptions as "forced" or "suffered" allude to a real, constant feature of countertransference not usually evident in the ordinary manifest discourse characteristic of the analyst's language (or behavior).

I can extend my argument to an extreme, and the same position would apply. Schwaber could make a discursive comment, as she reports, to an analysand, and she could be the only psychoanalyst now practicing for whom the experience expressed by such a statement is (or is not) a countertransference. But all of this is still only an important matter of how the individuality of the analyst's experience is obfuscated by a *communal* (by definition) language for discourse (just as this would apply to the analysand). Of course, self-deception on the analyst's part when he or she attempts self-analysis to detect countertransference is always a possibility; indeed, from an objectivist perspective, this is also a feature of reality that one would expect an analyst especially to appreciate.

If we approach this phenomenon of countertransference with a philosophical realism, a correspondence doctrine of truth, and a natural science perspective, as I do, then, in principle, I believe that there do exist procedures for objectifying the analyst's countertransference. As I say, it is highly unlikely that such an objectivization of analyst countertransference, which could be usefully applied to different analysts, will come simply from what an analyst says to an analysand at a particular moment. Of course, I can imagine the rare instance where, for example, an analyst calls an analysand by the wrong name, or begins shouting at an analysand, and so forth. But much more likely, procedures useful in objectifying countertransference will come from something subtle and not in focal awareness: the syntax of the analyst's language (see, e.g., Dahl et al. 1978; see also Steingart 1977 and Steingart and Freedman 1975 for another possible approach toward syntax); or some acoustical feature of language (e.g., Fónagy 1971); or some other-than-linguistic expression that subtly accompanies language, such as a fleeting facial expression (e.g., Haggard and Isaacs 1966, and see esp. the work of Ekman, e.g., 1980); or some combination of these (see Horowitz 1988). Actually, here we face a vast research terrain, unfortunately, still barely scratched. In addition, Holt (1962) has pointed out that another reason this investigation is difficult is that "we do not have . . . well established, unitary dimensions as [do] the physical [sciences], and not as simple and unarguable operations for measuring them" (p. 393). Certainly, countertransference is not something conceived of in a one-dimensional way. There is, for example, Racker's (1957) important differentiation with respect to "concordant" versus "complementary" identifications as these may be involved in countertransference; there is the matter of the various contents involved, the degree of consciousness, and so forth. Nevertheless, in principle (Holt 1962), whether such a research task is *conceivable* is a question of the philosophic positioning with which one approaches psychoanalysis. I return to a consideration of analyst empathy versus analyst countertransference in the clinical process. Olineck and colleagues (1973) describe the work ego of the psychoanalyst as follows: "We view the analyst's reactions as on a continuum, from trial identification (empathy) at the one end through more regressed phenomena of counter-identification and over-identification. Differentiation is made on the basis of evaluation of the degree of ego discrimination and mastery" (p. 144). A revised and, I believe, more useful conception would be to say that at the one end of the continuum of analyst reactions are both empathic realization of analysand transference experience and instrumental, informative countertransference. Both of these "reactions" are to be distinguished from counteridentification and overidentification that would be expressed in manifest conduct by an analyst that seriously interferes with the course of a psychoanalysis. Incidentally, this term *counteridentification* fits well with my earlier description of how each analyst's individual work style will resist certain transference. Indeed, we know from our own self-analysis how often it is that counteridentification is the other side of the emotional coin of threatened overidentification with precisely that which we resist in the analysand. Any psychoanalytic relationship will inevitably involve its own particular mix of these two sorts of analyst responsiveness. Neither a direct, empathic realization on the analyst's part nor an instrumental countertransference should, in itself, be considered clinically normative with respect to a responsiveness to analysand transference. This first kind of thinking would basically leave us again with a blank screen (Freud 1912b) idea of an analyst, albeit a more subtle version of such a notion. The idea now would be to grant that the analyst-as-a-person must shape transference in his or her interpretative activity; but still it would be maintained that only an (ego) enriched empathic experience is clinically normative. This view assumes that who the analyst is as a person (major dynamic sources of anxiety, defensive style, character traits, values, etc.) will *always* facilitate empathy for the analyst-at-work. In the next chapter, I will describe certain real but out-of-the-ordinary features of the psychoanalytic relationship that can enable an analyst to possess a degree of sensitivity, tact, tolerance, and so forth not evident in that analyst's "ordinary" significant relationships, all that is meant by an analyst's second self or work ego. But it still contradicts psychoanalytic theory itself, as it applies to the dynamics of the work experience for any analyst, to expect that who the analyst-as-a-person is will always facilitate empathy for the analyst-at-work. An analyst's personality is just that—a (one type of) character organization. To conceive that for the analyst only empathic realization is clinically normative is to require of the analyst a kind of perfection that is not really human (organization or function). In fact, such an expectation is itself a countertransference. On the other hand, if we conceive instrumental countertransference to be clinically normative, then an analyst *must always* conclude that he or she is involved in a self-deception should a countertransference not be consciously available in any particular transference circumstance in the psychoanalytic situation; I do not believe this conceptualization satisfactory with respect to our actual clinical experience.

This of course is not to deny the keenly felt difference in an analyst's experience with respect to these two sorts of reactions (Olineck et al. 1973). Instances of empathic realization "made" by an analyst involve, as Winnicott (1949) put it, countertransference "unfelt as such" (p. 196). Borrowing from Freud's drive theory (e.g., 1905a), we might say it is an instance of sublimation with respect to a dynamically unconscious experience that also has a countertransference potential, functionally similar to some sort of sublimation of a drive potential. Indeed, empathic realization must include sublimation of all manner of drive potential. But an analyst's experience of countertransference, even if the countertransference essentially functions only as an informative signal, is, nevertheless, still felt as experience that is (ego) passively suffered. Before I leave this subject, I want to suggest that an important work-style difference among analysts may be precisely whether countertransference occurs characterologically in the work situation that is a psychoanalysis. Following on what I have just said, and keeping in mind my characterization of countertransference always to involve an experience that is (ego) passively suffered, I can suggest that such an analyst's work style represents a productive, (relatively) conflict-free (Hartmann 1939) use of masochism enabled by the special situation that is a psychoanalytic relationship. Conceiving of characterological fluctuations with respect to countertransference in this way might help explain why some analysts (e.g., Heimann 1950, Racker 1957) want to define countertransference to be *all* that an analyst feels about the analysand, whereas others (e.g., Brenner 1985, Reich 1960, Schafer 1983) myself included, do not.

It is these inevitable times of analyst countertransference reaction to transference—rather than an analyst's realization of empathic experience with transference—that one can use to argue a case for a realist positioning for psychoanalysis, for two reasons: One reason has to do with how it is that in a usual Freudian praxis an analyst can make rational to him-or herself minimal or no self-disclosure of countertransference. The second reason has to do with phenomenology, what an analyst's consciousness of countertransference is like, how countertransference is (I would say) *necessarily* experienced as something suffered by the analyst.

I want, once again, to cite some comments by Schafer (1983): "The analysis primarily becomes the contemplation of the fantasy or invented aspects of the analysand's relationship to the analyst. This is so even when the analysand has temporarily succeeded in forcing or seducing the analyst into actualizing some assigned countertransference role in the relationship" (p. 123). And now we can ask: How is it that analyst and analysand can ever come to even a provisional agreement that some experience of the analysand's is indeed fantasy and invented, that is, a transference construed as not real, unless there exists some mutually understood idea of what is real about their psychoanalytic relationship? Schafer (1984) understands that "we cannot do without a conception of reality" (p. 368), adding as a qualification in keeping with his antiobjectivist, hermeneutic positioning for psychoanalysis, "even though we can attend to reality only by means of one or more versions or visions of it" (p. 368). And Schafer (1985b) recently has elaborated his hermeneutic framework for what counts as real: "The analyst relies on versions of common human situations and cause-effect relations that are so highly conventionalized that they serve as standards of good reality testing" (pp. 544–545). And:

> A . . . justification . . . for taking this stand on the factuality of certain representations of others . . . is the analyst's judgment that these representations . . . meet the criteria of *narrative good fit* . . . criteria of good fit derived partly from conventional commonsense. . . . For our idea of what hangs together in a story is founded on more than psychoanalytic understanding. . . . it rests as well on conventions of understanding that are shared by analyst and analysand. [p. 545, italics mine][8]

Are these "highly conventionalized" versions of human relationships, this "conventional commonsense" only, then, standards for a conception of reality that amounts to nothing more than a particular, local cultural consensus for narrative construction (Putnam 1981)? Or do such "conventions of understanding" arise exactly because of the influence of a reality that exists independent of any human narrators (e.g.,

Devitt 1984)? I have examined this question earlier in this book, and now I want to show its pertinence to our usual Freudian practice.

Restricting ourselves to our contemporary American culture, it is reasonable to say that both analysand and analyst have developed and live in, more or less, the same culture. Suppose we apply a criterion of narrative good fit to some expression of a transference by an analysand and the *possibility* of a countertransference by the analyst. Let us also say that this analyst countertransference, while ego (passively) suffered, is not manifest in any sense of obvious (Gill 1984a) interference with the clinical process. The analyst suffers the countertransference in silence. What becomes clear is that the basis for any justification that the analysand experience is a not-real transference construal, that is, fantasy and invented, is vitally different between transference and countertransference experience.

We can conclude that analysand transference is invented because it is not narratively coherent: the analyst is not conducting him- or herself in any way to justify a conclusion that a transference construal of the psychoanalytic relationship is real. For example, the analysand feels criticized, but the analyst is not manifesting criticism in any conventional way; the analysand feels sexually excited, but the analyst is not manifesting sexual interest in any conventional manner; and so forth.

But it need not be a matter of narrative incoherence by which a Freudian analyst concludes whether his or her own experience is countertransference, that is, also an invented construal of the psychoanalytic relationship. Countertransference may be an experience that narratively fits together with what sometimes is manifest, expressed analysand transference. The analysand may be – manifestly – insulting, and the analyst, countertransferentially, consciously feels angry; the analysand is – manifestly – sexually aroused, and the analyst consciously feels excitedly seduced; and so forth.

For the analyst it is, of course, more useful to be aware that he or she is having a countertransference experience, even if it is not obviously expressed and thus known to the analysand. But the Freudian analyst—notwithstanding how countertransference can even show such a narrative good fit—will nevertheless withhold expression of his or her countertransference.

What justifies the practice? I argue that a reality about the psychoanalytic relationship exists such that both transference and countertransference are a "false [not-real] connection" (p. 302) and something not "accounted for" by the actual psychoanalytic relationship (Freud 1925). A clinical circumstance can arise, especially (but not only) with borderline patients, in which the form of expression of some kind of analysand transference, let us say hate, is gross enough, or primitive enough, or enacting enough, in some manner annihilating enough, that it seems only human for an analyst to respond with a complementary countertransference experience of hatred. In fact, in such a circumstance Winnicott (1949) argues that if an analyst does not feel hatred, he or she is not productively engaged in the analytic relationship. This, as I understand it, would be a clinical realization of Winnicott's paradoxical concept of "truly objective countertransference" (p. 195)—objective in the sense that some irrational transference expression by an analysand is of such a sort that a felt, equally irrational experience on the part of the analyst is to be expected. Again, let us say the analyst (ego) passively suffers such hate in silence, or, at least, it is not obvious (Gill 1984a). Even here, Winnicott (1949) spoke about how the analyst's verbal revelation to the patient is "fraught with danger . . . and needs the most careful timing" (p. 202). And by timing Winnicott meant a point later in a reasonably successful analysis, when an initially very disturbed analysand now could productively realize the utterly irrational relationship that had been lived through by both analyst and analysand. The entire context of Winnicott's discussion of truly objective countertransference thus makes clear that he regarded it both as not clinically normative and as irrational analyst experience within a realist ontology.[9]

This realist rationale for a Freudian practice fits well with the phenomenology of countertransference for any analyst, and would extend to analysts who work with a very different concept of clinical practice wherein countertransference is to be expressed (e.g., Levenson 1972). I have already stated that an awareness of countertransference is to be conceived as a circumstance of (ego) passivity and suffering. The clinical marker that justifies this concept of passivity is that awareness of countertransference—even that which is consciously pleasurable—is regularly felt by the analyst to be not only passive but *disturbing*. But why should even exciting countertransference be experienced in this way, as disturbing? It is because an analyst's countertransference functions like the eruption of an ego-alien symptom, a phobia, say, or a compulsive ritual; because what is known and felt to be real about one's analyst-existence-in-the-world is now being subjected to an unreal (inappropriate) response. With a symptom like agoraphobia, what is real about one's relationship to walking on a street has become subjected to the effects of a dynamically unconscious, unreal fantasy. In the case of a consciousness of countertransference, what is real about the analyst's relationship to the analysand—and this is what is importantly connoted by Fliess's idea of the analyst's work ego or Schafer's second self—is being affected by the analyst's not-real transference, that is, countertransference. Put another way, countertransference no less than transference is an encroachment of unreal experience into the reality of the psychoanalytic relationship.

The situation of the Freudian analyst and his or her awareness of countertransference is akin to what we do—or really do not do—with our experience with (especially) drama. However impelling or personally significant our experience with drama may become, we do not interact in any usual way with the dramatic figures because our experience with drama is structured basically to be not-real. Yet it is a poor metaphor to conceive of the situation for the Freudian analyst to be that of the audience. The more apt metaphor would be to describe the Freudian analyst's experiences, countertransference or otherwise, to be like those of the Greek chorus (e.g., Reonhold 1959): continuously affected, and affecting, either through empathic work style, or countertransference, and expressing his or her interpretative commentary about the unfolding clinical relationship. As is well known, a young child will interact in such a circumstance. And my argument is that the young child does so because the child is not yet cognitively and emotionally capable of conceiving a reality that exists independently of his or her egocentric interpretation (Piaget, e.g., 1937). Actually, young children, already at the point they enter school, are in possession of an important degree of skill with respect to role-taking behavior in their interpersonal relationships (Flavell 1968); it is this understanding about conventional social interaction that in fact constitutes the basis of their "participation" with observed play or film. Thus, my conclusion is the opposite of that of Schafer (1983), who states:

> The official psychoanalytic conception of reality has been . . . reality is "out there" or "in there" existing as a knowledgeable, certifiable essence. . . . but this . . . telling is incoherent with respect to psychoanalytic inquiry . . . that limits us to dealing only with variants of reality. [p. 234]

However, Schafer continues to use "official" clinical procedure with respect to Freudian praxis, that is, no or minimal disclosure of countertransference. To repeat, my argument is that such a clinical procedure for psychoanalytic inquiry is both rationally and experientially more coherently grounded in a philosophy of realism.

This same argument, obviously, will apply to any type of antiobjectivist positioning for psychoanalysis that is also coupled in some manner to a clinical proposition that countertransference is always clinically congruent with transference experience. Two points immediately arise in this connection. First, it is clear that one can hold to some version of an antiobjectivist ontology for psychoanalysis but *not* conceive a psychoanalysis to involve a simultaneous transference and countertransference clinical process (e.g., Schafer 1983). Second, and as I have stated, one must conceive that an analyst exerts a continuous shaping influence on the emergence of transference experience. But this shaping, stylistic influence may or may not involve an analyst in a countertransference, and in either case, this influence is not essentially determining (in hermeneutic terms, narratively creating) what will become the core content of analysand transference (and see Freeman 1985).

Another subtle but important difference between Gill's (and others') version of an antiobjectivist philosophy for psychoanalysis and that of Schafer has to do with what constitutes the working through of transference experience. Gill's (1985) version of ontology is that reality is relative and that a working through of transference involves an analysand's (presumably) unconflicted acceptance that there are "other possible interpretations" (p. 136, i.e., of reality). This is a kind of Rashomon ontology. Gill, I trust, would consider comments like the following, if stated to an analysand, to represent an accurate portrayal of his viewpoint. Of course, I do not mean that Gill, or any analyst, provides an analysand with a characterization of his or her ontological commitment at the beginning of a psychoanalysis. I am only trying to spell out what for Gill rationalizes his clinical praxis. Here would be the comment: "I [the analyst] have my way of interpreting what is real between us and you [the analysand] have your way of interpreting what is real. What is crucial for our relationship, and therapeutic, is for both of us, genuinely, to respect each other's viewpoint." Such a comment obviously is not realism. Equally important, it is not the same as what I have described to be the only productive working attitude sincerely to be held by analyst and analysand.[10] This is that the question of the reality of the psychoanalytic relationship be treated with a benign neglect. All that matters is the meaning about the relationship that issues from the analysand's use of his or her mind (psychic reality) and the effort to understand how this meaning came to be.

Gill's ontology sounds egalitarian and it is—but that alone does not make it the productive, usual Freudian clinical working attitude I have just described. This clinical attitude is not at all egalitarian—*it gives primacy to the analysand's psychic reality*. It is true that I, or any other Freudian analyst committed to a realist positioning for psychoanalysis, and a Freudian analyst (Freud 1937b, Hartmann 1939) who works with a premise that all manner of analysand psychic reality must in some way be connected to validatable reality will believe that vital links will eventually be realized *by the analysand* in a productive analysis, ordinarily conceived. There is no necessary (i.e., logically required) connection between Gill's antiobjectivist positioning for psychoanalysis, or his idea that countertransference is clinically normative with transference experience, and his (1982) clinical emphasis on here-and-now transference interpretation. Transference material can be interpretively focused either on reminiscences, contemporary, other-than-analyst transference figures in the analysand's life, or on the analyst in the immediate psychoanalytic relationship, and Gill (1985) expects that each analyst will have his or her own prejudice for some such area. Gill (1984b) cites, approvingly, Wallerstein's (1984) comment about the "emptiness" of an injunction simply to focus interpretively on what is "there" to be interpreted, and this, of course, is an allusion to another important aspect of the classic idea of analyst neutrality: an analyst maintains an evenhanded attitude no matter the focus of the transference interpretation. To view this aspect of analytic neutrality as "empty" is rather like saying that an individual committed to be without ethnic prejudice is someone whose behavior and feelings reflect only an absence of something. What is certainly more likely the case is that such an individual possesses a positive commitment to an idea of civil rights for all. Analytic neutrality in this sense is an expression of an analyst's commitment that all major areas of analysand experience have "equal rights" to appear. Also, such an idea of analyst neutrality includes a belief that the analyst is always processing experience according to a theoretical (for me, Freudian) framework, and indeed, this is an "inevitable bias" (Gill 1984a). But within this theoretical framework an interplay among all major areas of analysand transference experience must appear, and reappear, and it is interpretative work within as well as between these areas that enables insight that contributes to the possibility of intrapsychic change.

Even if Gill (1984b) is correct, that over and beyond the bias of a theoretical framework there must exist a personal analyst preference for an interpretation of transference in one or the other major areas of analysand experience, it still matters much whether this interpretive bias is to be regarded as clinically normative or something it is the analyst's responsibility to try to minimize, along with a bias for any other area of analysand experience (see esp. Richards's [1984] and Stone's [1981] depictions of transference in the clinical process). Further, it can happen often enough in a psychoanalysis, especially (relatively) early on in the psychoanalytic relationship, that an analysand will displace transference experience *from* a significant, contemporary figure in his or her life *to* the analyst, and Gill's emphasis on a transference interpretation that focuses on the immediate, psychoanalytic relationship can more readily miss this kind of event.

In connection with this last comment, Stone (1981) has made the point that transference experience with other-than-the-analyst, contemporary figures has a kind of cogency that does not exist in the psychoanalytic relationship. Simply put, if an analysand, has, say, frequent, unreasonable, transferential, angry outbursts with a boss or spouse, the analysand can be fired or divorced. These, and any other, transferential experiences will not produce such real consequences in the psychoanalytic relationship. None of this works against everything we mean by the concept of development of a transference neurosis (or some allied term for other sorts of transference organization)—quite the opposite. It is expected that the psychoanalytic relationship will become, increasingly, but always relatively, an emotional center for the analysand's transference experience. However, this can occur not only because of the opportunities it offers for libidinal and aggressive expression but also because the psychoanalytic relationship is in reality a safe situation in which to develop such expression (and see, e.g., Loewald 1962). Here one realizes how a psychoanalysis presupposes the continuous influence of a reality that "frames" all manner of transference-countertransference to be unreal for both analysand and analyst, and that thus makes the experience safe for still further expression and exploration.[11]

But I do not see why one has to agree that Gill necessarily is correct even within his own philosophical position. Why can't it be, among the numerous ontologically valid viewpoints posited to exist in such a relativistic reality, that the idea of analyst clinical neutrality with respect to area of transference interpretation itself is one such viable perspective? An even stronger position, for which Gill (1984a) feels he can find support in Freud (1900), is to state that this analyst–analysand transference–countertransference is continuously and significantly influencing what is being expressed in any and all analysand associations from moment to moment. But even if we were to grant this is the case, we still have the clinical situation (Richards 1984, Stone 1981) in which presumed transference–countertransference-instigated free associations may appear in thoughts and feelings about the immediate treatment relationship, or in reminiscences, or in associative material that manifestly has to do with other-than-treatment, contemporary experience. From this angle, we can argue that it is more in keeping with a relativistic orientation that each area of experience be entitled to equal attention.[12]

A clinically normative intentional revelation by an analyst of his or her conscious countertransference will instantly effect a change in the structure of experience to align both unreal transference and countertransference experiences now taken to be real in the immediate interpersonal transaction. Levenson (1972) would say this is exactly what should occur. Of course, Gill (1983) knows that there is a developed rationale and clinical procedure for such a psychoanalytic process explicated especially well by the work of Levenson (1972; and see also, e.g., Epstein and Feiner 1979). But Levenson would object to these very terms *transference* and *countertransference*. Here is a clinical example, provided by Levenson (1972), which explains this objection:

> One might say [to an analysand]: "I thought you wanted help. I offered it and you felt attacked, criticized. I then felt rebuffed and insulted. That is the sequence. Let us agree that we both saw it correctly and that we call that out in each other and that probably the same sequence occurred with your father." [p. 184]

"The therapist and analysand," Levenson states later, "[really] become each other's creation" (p. 185), though it is the analyst's responsibility, and task, to "resist the [real] transformation" (p. 185).[13]

Prior to making these remarks and presenting the clinical example, Levenson states:

It will not be *distortion* or transference but an actual isomorphic replay in which the therapist participates. The therapist cannot avoid it by being "well-analyzed" or perceptive. It is not the therapist's uncoding of the dynamics that makes the therapy, not his "interpretations" of meaning and purpose, but rather, his extended participation with the patient. It is not his ability to resist distortion by the patient (transference) or to resist his own temptation to interact irrationally with the patient (countertransference) but rather, his ability to be trapped, immersed, and participating in the system and then to work his way out. [p. 174]

For Levenson, our traditional use of concepts like transference, countertransference, and interpretation are embedded in a more general construct of an individual's psychic reality, and he is quite right about this. Such ideas about how an individual "carries" around with him or her psychic structures that construe reality in certain ways is, for Levenson, a "machine" view of mentality, identifiably Freudian. And clinically, according to Levenson, this perspective must produce for the analysand a real experience of disrespect. Another perspective, which Levenson calls structuralism, obviates this clinical damage:

The structural perspective does not impugn the reality of the patient. His perceptions are seen as *real*, as a *consequence of the pull of the patient's system interaction with the real personality and organization of the therapist*. Nothing is projected onto the therapist. It is not a misunderstanding, to be alleviated by scrupulous communication. Respect for perspectivistic reality implies the recognition that one *participates* in it. [p. 183, second italics mine]

The more-or-less-usual Freudian praxis denies such conclusions, both theoretically and clinically. The Freudian analyst maintains that it is not a self-deception to believe that an empathic centering on the psychic reality construal of the analysand must really engender disrespect for the analysand's experience. Such an empathic centering, if it is genuine, is a trial identification; it requires authentic respect for the analysand's subjectivity, and provides a platform for the analysand to experience a nonjudgmental sense of his or her own agency in a way not possible in any other relationship. The more "regression" enabled by the Freudian praxis, the more startling and profound, albeit at times disturbing, can become this sense of agency for the analysand.

But, now, where and how does Gill's relativistic framework, together with his maintenance of the concepts of transference and countertransference, plus his continued nonrevelation of countertransference, fit in with all of this? Gill (1983), at least at one point, was quite clear that he did not advocate that a practice of analyst self-disclosure be considered to be clinically normative and for these reasons:

> I believe they [countertransference disclosures] have a tendency to shut off further inquiry into the patient's experience, not least because such inquiry might lead to the exposure of something on the analyst's part which he would rather not know about. Furthermore, the analyst must recognize that his subjective experience may be as defensive on his own part as he believes the patient's conscious attitudes are. He cannot therefore assume that if he reports his own experience that is the end of the story. But the pursuit of the possible hidden implications of his experience would change the analysis of the patient *into a mutual analysis of patient and analyst*. Some therapists advocate just that. I assume it is clear that I do not. The position that the analyst makes a major contribution to the transaction does not necessarily mean that a mutual analysis is desirable or perhaps even possible. [pp. 228–229, italics mine]

Hoffman (1983), in a paper published the same year, expressed congruent comments. But Levenson, and others like him who consider analyst self-revelation to be intrinsic to clinical process (e.g., Chrzanowski 1980, Epstein and Feiner 1979), can with justification level a criticism against Gill and Hoffman something like the following:

> You are engaging in self-deception. And it seems clear that at least part of your self-deception involves your need to maintain some

omnipotent, parental stance with your analysands. Who are you *to decide for the analysand* that the analysand would "rather not know" something about the countertransference experience of the analyst? A mutual analysis of the interpersonal reality is not only desirable, and possible, but it is this exactly that is psychoanalysis. If the analyst, in self-disclosure, is being defensive, this simply is part of the ongoing work of a psychoanalysis. If such analyst self-disclosure affects the analysand so as to "shut off" further inquiry into analysand transference experience, then this occurrence also becomes part of the psychoanalysis.

You say you believe transference and countertransference constitute a transaction and that the analyst, thus, always makes some "contribution" (Gill 1985). And you say your philosophy is that reality is "relative," so that the analysand's interpretation of what is real about the psychoanalytic relationship is as valid as that of the analyst. But your practice does not follow coherently from your stated beliefs.

And so forth. But after this, Gill (and his colleague [e.g., Hoffman and Gill 1988]) have taken a further important step, which, indeed, makes their practice coherent with their philosophy, and not now (at least quite) so subject to criticism.

Hoffman and Gill are clear that their more current view is a departure from any sort of "mainstream" (i.e., classical) idea of transference and that it represents a "shift in our thinking" (p. 57), "that it may be *desirable and useful* for the process for the analyst to participate partially and in a transitory spontaneous way in various kinds of transference–countertransference enactments which have important meaning for the patient" (p. 57). Hoffman and Gill do not say so in so many words, but we are left with a definite impression that revelation of analyst countertransference already is, or will become, a normative feature of the treatment process, albeit complexly normative from one circumstance to another.

This is what has happened. Hoffman (e.g., 1992a) now describes how various kinds of "expressive participation" on the part of the analyst can contribute to the therapeutics of a psychoanalysis. Along with this is a subtle but important revision of the concept of clinical process as it applies to transference or countertransference experience. This in turn grows out of Hoffman's (1993) current adoption of a positioning for psychoanalysis that he terms a "critical constructivism, . . . which connotes an interaction between an independent reality and the activity of human subjects" (p. 17). Hoffman prefers this term *critical constructivism* to *perspectivism*, and *perspectivism*, I assume, is equivalent to Gill's (1985) idea that "reality . . . is relative" (p. 136). One should say utterly relative, because this is the difference with respect to relativism or perspectivism. Hoffman (1993) does speak here about "an independent reality," but then goes on about human experience, including, of course, analysand–analyst experience in a psychoanalytic relationship: "Experience, taken as a whole, is partially constructed by what we make of it, retrospectively in the context of interpretation, and prospectively, in the context of experience-shaping actions" (p. 18). I will address, later in this chapter, the issue of interpretation. Hoffman does not appear to appreciate an important differentiation to be made about immediate clinical interpretation. But now it is this idea of experience-shaping actions in the clinical relationship, within his position of critical constructivism, that enables him to say that analyst expressive participation contributes to the therapeutics of a psychoanalysis.

> What I think is called for is an attitude that highlights the dialectic between the literal aspects of the analytic experience and its figurative, or "as if" aspects. With regard to the analyst's involvement, the tension is between viewing it as creating *opportunities for understanding in other terms*, particularly in terms of the patient's externalization of internal conflict, and viewing it as *important and consequential in its own right*. [p. 18]

Where all of this leads is to the following: A differentiation between countertransference and a clinically useful expressive participation (Hoffman 1992a) becomes not so hard and fast. Analyst responsiveness can be construed to mean countertransference *and* expressive participation, which can be therapeutic. I do not mean by this that Hoffman would not be able to assess a gross countertransference—say, a sadistic joke aimed at the analysand. But even here, Hoffman might consider that such a joke, heard in an overall context of a psychoanalytic relationship wherein the analysand feels the analyst to be devoted to a productive therapeutic process, can still have a clinically useful meaning for analysand and analyst. For example, the joke could be construed to be an expression of the analyst's pleasure in his or her hatred of the analysand's suffering. But other expressions of such expressive participation are, perhaps, easier to fathom. For example, Hoffman comments how an analyst's compliments to a patient, over his or her physical appearance, can be countertransferentially construed to be sexual flirtatiousness (from a father, I suppose), but then again, the same analyst is "equally attentive to his or her other qualities, and invested in the patient's development" (p. 9). Hoffman emphasizes that expressive participation is not at all like the "planned actions of Alexander [1950]"; rather, it is "genuine, responsive, sometimes creative [expression] of certain inclinations that arise within the analyst . . . that otherwise might be inhibited" (p. 7). I am, to put it mildly, not so sure. Hoffman includes, for example, an analyst deciding, in advance, how to dress for a particular analysand.

But let us consider a more detailed illustration (Hoffman 1992a):

> In the historical background [of the analysand] there was the fact that the patient had grown up in the shadow of her older brother. He had been worshiped by her parents and by her. Indeed she had always felt vastly inferior to him and never felt that she could hold her own with him in an argument. So whatever else it may have meant, our discussion about politics, to the extent that I was

> identified with the brother, seemed to foster, on the one hand, a
> differentiation of him and me and, on the other hand, the differen-
> tiation of the patient's self-image as the intimidated kid sister, and
> herself as an intelligent adult who commanded respect. [pp. 12–13]

The discussion of politics to which Hoffman alludes is his
spontaneous decision to engage in a "brief debate" with the
analysand, knowing that he and this female analysand
would have different viewpoints. Subsequent clinical material made obvious the powerful effect of this experience on
the analysand. She reported in the next session a dream in
which she and Hoffman were lovers in bed together, but
lovemaking was not consummated. Interestingly, and I
believe significantly, the analysand did not herself spontaneously associate (Freud 1900) the (unconsummated) lovemaking to this brief debate; she did so only when questioned
by Hoffman about any further associations. If, as I believe,
this was resistance, what could it mean? Several months
after this, a mutually agreed-on termination occurred, with
the analysand being aware that having had what she experienced as an unexpected, unconventional, treatment brief
debate produced a different, more confident experience
about herself.

Hoffman stresses this expressive participation he initiated
with his analysand to be something he also terms an "experience-shaping" (Hoffman 1993, 1992b), action-producing,
presumably, insight for the analysand, but *without interpretation* by the analyst. I mean, it seems to have occurred at the
moment without interpretation at the time. Hoffman (1992a)
does say "whatever else it may have meant" (p. 12), and here
he seems to be alluding to the analysand's sexual dream
stimulated by the political debate, and how he and the
analysand came to agree on an interpretation that the debate
also had a dangerous sexual meaning. However, the analysand herself was conscious only of being pleased about this
sexual dream and felt it to be a step forward in her sexual
expressiveness. But I want to venture another interpretation

that is not considered, or, at least, not reported. Again, why then would Hoffman's analysand not herself spontaneously associate (connect) the brief debate experience to the expressive sexuality displayed in her dream (and see Luborsky 1973)? In addition, and also reported by Hoffman, the analysand momentarily forgot, during the day, with whom she had had this brief debate!

One way to put the issue is like this: Can one be sure that Hoffman's initiation of this debate with his analysand really supported insight for her, so as not to experience herself as the "intimidated kid sister" either with her brother or transferentially with Hoffman, both intellectually and sexually? Is not the *opposite* possibility to be conceived? That by initiating this interaction with the analysand (notwithstanding his sincere respect for her as an intelligent adult), Hoffman can now be a "magical" (Hoffman 1993) "big brother" who *authorizes* for the analysand a new image of herself both intellectually *and* sexually? Hoffman (1992a) might answer that, if so, this can also be analyzed, although nothing suggests this possibility was analyzed. But I believe it makes for a different kind of therapeutics. Hoffman (1993) also might answer another way: if, indeed, such a transference "big brother" authorization for the analysand to now feel greater intellectual and sexual respect for herself did occur, this is the "ritual" and "affirmation" of the "analyst . . . [as] . . . an authority" intrinsic to the therapeutics of the psychoanalysis. I hypothesize that here we have two very different therapeutic concepts and effects. One is to fully appreciate with an analysand, especially in the termination phase, the "interminable" (Freud 1937a) about a psychoanalysis; and also, that there is no human relationship, including psychoanalytic, that is ever fully rational for both individuals, and devoid of childhood wish or (counter)transference (Freud 1912b, 1937b). Another conception of psychoanalytic therapeutics (Hoffman 1993) is to "not try to analyze away" (p. 20) the "moral authority" (p. 19) of the analyst that emanates from such childlike experience. As I understand the concept of the therapeutics of the clinical process envisioned by Levenson (e.g., 1972), he also would object to Hoffman's view of the desirability of this power of the analyst "as a kind of moral authority" (p. 19).

I do not dispute that this kind of analysis, which is, to use Hoffman's (1993) terminology, both "figurative ['as if']" and "literal," can proceed. But I think it impossible that this "dialectic" between the figurative and literal can become the same experience as is possible through everything that is meant by the terms *regression* and *transference neurosis* in a more-or-less-usual Freudian analysis. This is not to say that child*like* structures and experiences, however fantastic, do not continue to be relevant to some literal or validatable reality about the psychoanalytic relationship. This is always the case (Freud 1937b, Hartmann 1939), and as I have said, the possibilities for a regressive transference experience are always shaped by the real personality of the particular analyst.

The logic of the clinical rationale now proposed by Hoffman and Gill proceeds as follows. (It is important to understand, in what follows, that when I use the term *countertransference*, Hoffman [1992a] will want us to understand something different from any traditional idea about countertransference *expression*. That is, and as I have just described, countertransference expression can be desirable because it may also be constructed as an expressive participation, which has a therapeutic experience-shaping consequence for the analysand.) (1) First, there is a massive recruitment of analysand free associations to the here and now, transference–countertransference relationship (Gill and Hoffman 1982, Steingart 1992), notwithstanding any disclaimer to such selective emphasis (Hoffman and Gill 1988). In a paper subsequent to the article written jointly with Gill, Hoffman (1993) acknowledges that "an *emphasis* upon free associations . . . [is now replaced by] . . . an *emphasis* on the emergence of transference–countertransference configurations" (p. 18, italics mine). (2) Transference is conceived to be simultaneously figurative and literal. That is, the analysand's transference is at the same time an "externalization of internal conflict" and currently interpersonal inasmuch as transference is believed always to instigate countertransference. (3) Consequently, what needs "emphasis . . . [is] the element of *plausibility* in the patient's transference-based perceptions and his conscious and unconscious interpretations of the analyst's behavior" (Hoffman and Gill 1988, italics mine). (4) Finally, interpretation now centers on the "patient's pressure to impose certain kinds of patterns on the [psychoanalytic] relationship" (p. 57). Note that even with such a clinical rationale, what we might call the *essential generation* of this simultaneously conceived interpersonal and intrapsychic transference–countertransference experience still assumes the *analysand as agent*. Wallerstein's (1984) view, that Gill is only advocating an emphasis for here-and-now transference interpretation, can now be seen not to appreciate the degree of revision in usual Freudian clinical praxis advocated by Gill (and Hoffman).

It is worthwhile to repeat Schafer's (1984) subtle and important distinction in this regard. Schafer is clear that at least a working conception of reality is continuously required for a more-or-less-usual Freudian psychoanalysis. Otherwise, how can one have and emphasize (unlike Hoffman [1993]) interpretation into aspects of psychic reality that are invented, that is, not-real transference (or possible countertransference construals) of the reality of the psychoanalytic relationship? There is another matter about a concept of clinical practice expressed by Hoffman (1983) that seems to me misleading, or at the least confusing. Hoffman states his belief that there exists a "kind of informal 'school' of thought which cuts across the standard lines of Freudian, Kleinian, and Sullivanian schools" (p. 407). What Hoffman means here is a common conception that the analysand–analyst transference-countertransference constitutes the normative "unit" of clinical process. In one sense he is right, but in another very important sense he is wrong. The sense in which Hoffman is correct is that in our collective psychoanalytic literature transference–countertransference experience has come to be conceived as normative (among Freudian analysts, see, e.g., Jacobs 1991, McLaughlin 1981, Renik 1993; among Sullivanian analysts, see, e.g., Levenson 1972 or Chrzanowski 1980, or Epstein and Feiner 1979). Freud (e.g., 1925) obviously did not consider transference–countertransference experience to be normative, nor did Sullivan (see Will's introduction to Sullivan [1954]), for whom the notion of participant observation is equivalent to what I have termed an individual analyst's work style. Where Hoffman (1983) is in error, and what still marks his and Gill's concept of clinical process as a significant departure from mainstream Freudian practice, is the belief that an analyst's *expression* of countertransference is not only "desirable" but "useful." The only way I now can read the term *useful* has to do with Hoffman's (1992a) more recent transformation of the original meaning of the term *countertransference* into a concept wherein potentialities exist for an analyst's expressive participation in the psychoanalytic relationship that have a *therapeutic* experience-shaping consequence for the analysand.

Hoffman and Gill (1988, Hoffman 1992a) continue to cite comments made by Racker (1957) to the effect that it is sometimes useful for an analyst to express countertransference experience to the analysand to support their current concept of clinical process. Racker speaks about this as follows: "What I am referring to is . . . a transitory *performance* of the role induced by the patient, followed by an analysis of what has happened and what has been enacted" (p. 69, italics mine). And also, "We can in this way show the patient, *more vividly*, the *role* he desires the analyst to play and why he desires it" (p. 69, italics mine). But the context of

Racker's comments hardly characterizes analyst expression
of countertransference as desirable, and certainly Racker
does not advocate a clinical process in which revelation of
countertransference is normative. Racker ₅oes on to state:

> I believe that such actions on the part of the analyst constitute a
> crutch until we are able to walk without it. But in the meantime it is
> better to walk with a crutch than not to walk at all. On the other
> hand, given the dangers arising from the temptations of the coun-
> tertransference, such experiments are only advisable, I believe, for
> the analyst who already has ample experience in dealing with
> transference and countertransference. [p. 69]

Racker's terminology reflects, I think, the intention of a
Freudian praxis that the psychoanalytic relationship take a
"direction" substantially different from that of emphasis on
a continuous clarification of the immediate, taken-to-be-real
interpersonal field. This other direction emphasizes not the
plausibility (Hoffman and Gill 1988) of an analysand's transference but rather the analysand's "invented" (Schafer 1984)
transference experience. Certainly, Hoffman and Gill understand that an analysand may not experience the analyst's
revelation of countertransference to mean that the analyst is
"strong . . . and also dedicated" (p. 59). An analysand may,
in a particular circumstance, transferentially believe something quite different: that the analyst is fragile as a person, or
that the analyst is attempting to make the analysand feel
guilty, or whatever. Yet Hoffman and Gill operate with the
belief that such analysand transference experience is plausible because of their premise that some (however subtle)
analyst countertransference always occurs that is congruent
with transference. So another round of clarification of the
immediate, taken-to-be-real interpersonal field may occur,
with, to be sure, possible interpretation of the analysand's
genetic-dynamic process for generating the (real) transaction. But the point is that such transference–countertransference explication about the here-and-now psychoanalytic

relationship apparently becomes the entirety of the psycho-analytic process. With a mainstream Freudian practice, transference, whatever its *inevitable* (Freud 1937b, Hartmann 1939, Rapaport and Gill 1959) element of (ego) plausible connection to reality, is always used as a "window" into still other dynamically unconscious experiences (especially fantasies), and this is analogous to what occurs in dream formation (Arlow 1985, Freud, e.g., 1914c).

At one point in their 1988 paper, Hoffman and Gill illustrate their transference coding scheme with the following example: The analyst announces he will miss an appointment, and the analysand subsequently speaks about being left by others. Without doubt, the analysand's expression can be understood to be plausibly related to the analyst's stated intention to miss a session; this would be an example of resisted transference, inasmuch as the analysand is only indirectly expressing a sense of abandonment by the analyst. If this material is repetitively indicated in the treatment process, one would assume that, at some point felt to be clinically judicious, the analyst would make a resistance interpretation. Assume the interpretation is effective. Now another clinical situation is present. The analysand meaningfully feels transference abandonment, based on plausible analyst conduct that is so acknowledged by the analyst, but the repetitive nature of the analysand experience of loss is the expression of the analysand's psychopathology. This can be put another way, and I go back to my allusion to dream formation: there is nothing in this entire scenario that would regard the analyst's intention to miss a session to function the way a day residue does in dream formation. The analyst's intention to miss a session is, then, "drawn" (Freud 1900) into dynamically unconscious, unreal fantasies and exposed to intrapsychic conflicts imbued with such fantasies. In this inner psychic direction, what might turn out to involve further, invented aspects of the transference are beliefs about total abandonment, perhaps analysand guilt-instigated beliefs of this sort because of the analysand's sadistic wishes to possess the analyst's life completely, or to emasculate the analyst, and so forth. It is Gill's (e.g., 1985) downplaying of this further "interior" view of transference experience that enables him to conceptualize psychotherapy and psychoanalysis as processes importantly and essentially similar to each other.

I want, now, to return to the conjectured criticism with which I preceded this description of Gill's most recent position of clinical practice. The gist of such criticism would be as follows: Gill's belief that transference and countertransference constitute an organic, clinical unit, supported, for Gill, by his philosophy that reality is relative, is not coherent with any practice that does not make analyst revelation of countertransference normative (e.g., Chrzanowski 1980, Epstein and Feiner 1979, Levenson 1972). It is clear, now, that Gill and Hoffman have effectively dealt with such criticism (i.e., accepting it), and they have changed their ideas about clinical practice accordingly. My belief is that such a substantive change in (conceptualization of) clinical practice must make for a substantive change in the use of Freudian theory to characterize transference and countertransference experiences. Even if Gill and Hoffman continue to use certain Freudian terminology—say, involving psychosexual drive object relations concepts—to characterize a here-and-now transference experience, that experience cannot progress into a realization of a more thoroughly childlike (fantastic) psychic reality (Arlow 1985). It cannot because a further "interior" view of transference is opposite to a therapeutic effort to clarify presumed valid but different realities, operative in the immediate interpersonal field, notwithstanding a recognition that an analysand's intrapsychic conflict has essentially generated the dynamics (Hoffman 1993). I am here only expressing agreement with an earlier comment made by Gill (1983) to the effect that analyst countertransference self-revelation will tend to shut off further expression of the analysand's experience. But what I emphasize to be so shut off is not analysand expression per se but rather a type of progression of analysand experience; this is all that is referred to, from the perspective of more-or-less-usual Freudian praxis, by the terms *regression* and *transference neurosis* (Freud, e.g., 1912b), and this is something other than only a sort of examination of recurrent here-and-now transference–countertransference experiences. I can realize that the shaping influence of a particular analyst's real personality may constrain, to the point of eliminating, possible regressive experiences for a particular analysand. In fact, this is an acknowledged clinical experience. But still, to the extent a psychoanalytic process is occurring, it will be understood that the analysand's transference-instigated regressive psychic reality is there to be discovered (Schwaber 1992). Or, to use Freeman's (1985) terminology, a particular analysand psychic reality interpretively accessed via transference experience will have reference to what is, in a definite sense, independent of the analyst as the real person he or she is, and the investigatory procedure that is the psychoanalytic relationship (and see Bucci 1985, 1989).

What a more-or-less-usual Freudian concept of clinical process does share with any version of a psychoanalysis that emphasizes the here-and-now transference–countertransference dynamics (Hoffman, e.g., 1993, Hoffman and Gill 1988, Levenson 1972) is the idea that transference and countertransference are to be understood as fixed, compulsive repetitions, so that such experiences are prescribed. In other words, what is occurring in a transference and countertransference is a "repeating" (Freud 1914c) and nothing like a relating in which the full and real potentialities of both individuals can be emotionally apprehended for a spontaneous (not ordained) interaction of one sort or another. What distinguishes a Freudian praxis is that change—from ordained interaction to authentic relating—is achieved through interpretation. Such interpretation excludes a normative revelation of countertransference experience (Levenson 1972) or an idea that an expressive participation (Hoffman 1992a) transformation of countertransference is a critical part of what is therapeutic.

THE TRUTHFULNESS OF INTERPRETATION AS OBJECT RELATIONS EXPERIENCE

The multiple encoding orientation I described in the first chapter of this book enables some sort of correspondence idea of truth to be applied to psychoanalytic interpretation. There has always been clinical support, and now increasing experimental evidence, that each of us gives meaning to our experiences in formats that are not only linguistic. Throughout each of our lives, we provide meaning for ourselves with vivid, imagistic schemas that can be saturated with emotion together with subsymbolic encoding of experiences. A productive, language-delivered interpretation can be said to be *well connected*, and even transforming of one's psychic reality, but still it has *reference* to experience that essentially is neither language mediated nor organized (see Bucci 1994). I want to pursue some other aspects of such an idea of truth for psychoanalytic interpretation of object relations experience.

It is clear that neither analysand transference nor a possible analyst countertransference represents an authentic relating between two individuals. I want, now, to consider the object relations significance of analyst interpretation of the analysand's psychic reality. Here I am entering an area that Loewald (1960) 35 years ago termed "the therapeutic action of psychoanalysis" (p. 221). In this seminal paper, Loewald erased once and for all the untenable notion that the therapeutics of a psychoanalysis consists only of the acquisition of interpretative insight (self-understanding). Loewald states:

The transference neurosis, in the sense of reactivation of the childhood neurosis, is set in motion not simply by the technical skill of the analyst, but by the fact that the analyst makes himself available for the development of a new "object relationship" between the patient and analyst. The patient tends to make this potentially new object-relationship into an old one. On the other hand, to the extent to which the patient develops a "positive transference" [not in the sense of transference as resistance, but in the sense "transference" carries the whole process of an analysis] it keeps this potentiality of the new object-relationship alive for all the various stages of resistance. The patient can dare to take the plunge into the regressive crisis of the transference neurosis which brings him face to face again with his childhood anxieties and conflicts, if he can hold onto the potentiality of a new object-relationship, represented by the analyst. [p. 224]

Put another way, the analyst, in his or her act of interpreting, in a more-or-less-usual Freudian analysis, already and always is *relating* to the analysand. And the analyst is "saying" three very different things in every interpretation: "You have a wish to completely possess me, or hurt me, and feel this way in control of me, or take away from me my wife (husband), make me feel impotent, and so forth" (or some allied resistance to experience any such childlike, wishful experience). Still another array of interpretations would have to do with what Winnicott (1956) meant by matters related to "ego relatedness." Here the analyst could be saying, "I'm wondering if you feel either you exist alone with your experience or I exist alone with mine, because there is not enough space for both of us; if we connect one of us must destroy the other"; or "Could it be when I just spoke you felt coerced to pay attention to me about something that didn't fit right and you lost your own experience?"; or "You are silent now because you just expressed something hateful to me, and you feel I am not here anymore; you destroyed me, so there is no one to whom to talk;" and so forth (or allied resistance to any such experience). And all of this is a *prescribed* relatedness of one sort or another fixed into a "compulsion to repeat" (Freud 1920b) because of psychopathology. At the same time (Loewald 1971b), any of these interpretations can be experienced by the analysand to be saying: "You can engage with me in another, new and real kind of relatedness (at least relatively) freed of such prescribed, conflict-driven roles." And still at the same time, the analyst is saying with each interpretation: "You can choose which kind of relatedness will occur." Every interpretation, therefore, potentiates for an analysand a possibility for psychic regressive experience, or a psychic progressive development, together with an opportunity to collegially observe with the analyst what actually occurs. We consider in a Freudian practice that a productive clinical process is some optimal mix of all three experiences. I am assuming here an analyst making an interpretation who is free of any serious, interfering countertransference.

This last "saying," potentiated in every interpretation— "You can choose . . ." —tallies with notions of a therapeutic alliance (Greenson 1965) or, I think better, what Stone (1961, 1967) calls a mature transference, and it is this Loewald (1960) means when he speaks about "transference [that] carries the whole process of an analysis" (p. 224). Such ideas about a type of treatment-facilitating, nonpathological transference experience are also congruent with comments by Freud about a type of transference experience to be distinguished from either positive or negative transference experience-as-resistance. Freud described this type of experience as having two aspects: the analysand's "intellectual interest and understanding" (Freud 1913, p. 143), which we can understand to be the analysand's desire and capacity for interpretive insight, and (1912a) the analysand's "friendly or affectionate feelings which are [presumably at the inception of an analysis] accessible to [the analysand's] consciousness" (p. 105). All of this we can take to be "unobjectionable" transference (Freud 1912a, p. 103). For sure, every clinician must agree with a caution urged by Stein (1981) and Brenner

(1979) that this unobjectionable transference can be used to defend against negative and/or erotic transference experience that involves prescribed (infantile prototype) roles engendered by psychic conflict. Indeed, Freud (1912a) himself at least implies such a caution when he carefully discriminates among three types of transference: a conscious, or repressed, negative or erotic transference experience, both contrasted with unobjectionable transference.

Freud created confusion about this last idea, declaring that it emotionally arranges the analysand for "influencing" by the psychoanalytic relationship, and especially, of course, for "influencing" by interpretation. That a psychoanalysis is a relationship that is influencing would be absurd to deny — what other purpose would it serve? But influencing can occur in all sorts of ways, and Freud (1912a) at least at one point seems to equate influencing with suggestion:

> To this extent we readily admit that the results of psychoanalysis rest upon suggestion; by suggestion, however, we must understand, as Ferenczi (1909) does, the influencing of a person by means of the transference phenomena which are possible in this case. We take care of the patient's final independence by employing suggestion in order to accomplish a piece of psychical work which has as its necessary result a permanent improvement in his psychical situation. [pp. 105–106]

However, if we understand Freud's unobjectionable transference to be the equivalent of Stone's mature transference, or Loewald's (1960) "transference which carries the . . . analysis" (p. 224), or Greenson's therapeutic alliance, then influence by suggestion is the antithesis of the possible unique, therapeutic influence of a psychoanalysis. Instead, any therapeutic influence of a psychoanalysis is to be engendered in a real, mutual, that is, collegial, investigation by two adults of the psychic reality of one of them, the analysand. Conceived this way, the Freudian analyst does indeed have something to contribute that the analysand, hopefully and increasingly, will contribute him- or herself. This is not an authoritarian "teaching" of what is real, but simply procedures for an ever-deepening understanding of the analysand's psychic reality: the significance of free associations, together with the significance of resistance to the expression of free associations, how dreams can be analyzed and understood, and all that we mean by the adoption of an analytic attitude. Henceforth I will only use Stone's term, mature transference, since I believe it to be the most clarifying with respect to Freud's concept of the unobjectionable transference.

Freud (1915a) at another point said something quite different about the therapeutics of a psychoanalysis and its connection to transference and love. "It is true that . . . love consists of new editions of old traits and that it repeats infantile reactions. But this is the essential character of every state of being in love" (p. 168). And:

> Transference-love [in a psychoanalysis] is characterized by certain features. . . . in the first place, it is provoked by the analytic situation; secondly, it is greatly intensified by . . . resistance; . . . *thirdly, it is lacking to a high degree in a regard for reality, is less sensible, less concerned about consequences and more blind in its valuation of the loved person than we are prepared to admit in the case of normal love.* [pp. 168–169, italics mine]

All love, Freud is now telling us, is some transformation of transference love. Put another way, transference exists along a continuum from the not-rational to the (relatively) rational and clinically healthy. Thus it cannot be the therapeutics of psychoanalysis to "do away" with transference love. This is not just inconceivable but really absurd, inasmuch as transformations in transference love amount to one important way to talk about transformations with respect to processes that eventuate in psychic development, something especially understood by Loewald (1960).

It is very much the therapeutics of a Freudian psychoanal

ysis to be a vehicle for the elaboration of childlike transference experiences that have now become prescribed, conflict-engendered role behavior, so as to transform and augment this sort of transference love into one that is (always relatively) "normal" (Freud 1915a, p. 169). This is understood to be achieved through interpretation. What is more, I say "augment" because in a psychoanalysis, classically conceived, some sufficient presence of a normal (transference) love is assumed to be a given, affecting the analysand's feelings for the analyst from the inception of the relationship. From this perspective, I understand Freud's (1912a) idea about the analysand's unobjectionable (affectionate) transference to be a synonym for normal (transference) love.

I want to relate what I have said so far to why Freud did not sufficiently appreciate the possibility of therapeutics with pre-oedipal, nonneurotic disturbance. Freud seemingly believed that the essentials of all human states of love—childlike and pathological or (relatively) mature—lay the lovers open to influence by suggestion. But I think it is a contradiction in terms to say that the mutual influences effected between two lovers in a state of normal (transference) love is achieved by suggestion. It is this kind of conceptual "collapsing" of these concepts—transference love, therapeutic influence, and suggestion—that led Freud to his conclusion about a limited scope for the utility of a psychoanalysis. In one commentary on this subject Freud (1912a) had in mind matters of transference in relationship to pre-oedipal disturbance:

> Ambivalence in the emotional trends of neurotics is the best explanation of their ability to enlist their transferences in the service of resistance. Where the capacity for transference has been essentially limited to a negative one, as is the case of paranoiacs, there ceases to be any possibility of influence or cure. [p. 107]

But Freud's (1911b) own brilliant analysis of Schreber's material revealed the existence of Schreber's dynamically unconscious, intense homosexual love for his father. I use Freud's reference to "paranoiacs" to mean not only, or literally, individuals who express schizophrenic delusions, such as Schreber, but to mean a paranoid sensibility about what Winnicott (1953) called experiences of "impingement" that belong to what he called in 1956 matters of ego related-ness. A concept of therapeutic influence, agglutinated to notions of love and suggestion, is, exactly, a kind of thera-peutic "poison" for any notion of a useful therapeutics in such cases. Paradoxically, but understandably, what must be emphasized in interpretation is the real, collegial nature of the psychoanalytic relationship. This, in turn, can support the acquisition of a (relatively) mature transference—but it also can require a long time to establish.

When I use the term *interpretation*, I mean, by classical definition, a verbal statement to the analysand about an experience of his or her psychic reality that is dynamically unconscious. I have, in this chapter, fully appreciated the inevitable influence of an analyst's work style on discovery of the analysand's psychic reality. But I have sought to distin-guish the effect of analyst work style—even if it be the case where that style seriously limits or outright eliminates a psychoanalytic process—from a "discovered" (Schwaber 1992) analysand psychic reality when a psychoanalytic pro-cess is present and productive.

I am going to approach this issue in two steps—not, I think, sufficiently differentiated or appreciated in our litera-ture. For the first step, I want to use material from an article by Beres and Arlow (1974). On his return from the long Thanksgiving holiday, a patient reported:

> I am not so sure that I am glad to be back in treatment even though I did not enjoy my visit with my mother and father in the Midwest. I feel I just have to be free. My visit home was depressing. My mother hasn't changed a bit. She is as bossy, manipulative and aggressive as always. My poor father. He says nothing. At least in the summer time he could retreat to the garden and work with

flowers. But my mother watches over him like a hawk—a vulture—she has such a sharp tongue and a cruel mouth. You know, each time I see my father now, he seems to be getting smaller and smaller. Pretty soon, he will disappear and there will be nothing left of him. She does that to people. I always felt that she was hovering over me, ready to swoop down on me. She has me intimidated, just like my wife. I don't feel like getting involved, but when you are married, there isn't much you can do about it.

I was furious this morning. When I came to get my car, I found that someone had parked in such a way that I was hemmed in. It took a long time and lots of work to get my car out. During the time I realized how anxious I was. The perspiration was pouring down the back of my neck.

I feel restrained by the city. I need the open, fresh air. I have to breathe. I have to stretch my legs. I am sorry I gave up that house in the country. Next week, I'm going up to Massachusetts to look around for property. I have to get away from this city. I really can't afford to buy another house now, but at least I'll feel better if I can look.

If only business were better, I could maneuver more easily. I hate this kind of feeling of being stuck in an office from nine until five. My friend Bob has the right idea. He has arranged for retirement and now he's free to come and go as he pleases. He travels; no offices, no board of directors to answer to. I love my work, but I can't stand the restrictions imposed upon me. But I am ambitious, so what can you do? [pp. 29–30]

At this point the analyst called the patient's attention to the recurrence in the material of the experience of being "trapped and confined" (p. 30). Bion (1967) would call this a *selected fact*. What has the analyst contributed by way of this interpretative elaboration of the analysand's psychic reality? The analyst has called the analysand's conscious attention to a recurrent, but dynamically unconscious experience, of being trapped and confined. This is one kind of bona fide interpretation: it is, as Fenichel (1941) would put it, an interpretation about analysand dynamically unconscious experience just below the "surface" (and see Freud [e.g., 1926b]). The analyst calling attention to such an experience is rather like suddenly fixing one's attention on a melody. A melodic structure is, in one definite sense, manifest; in another definite sense, a melody is not "there" but "hidden" behind each moment of sound that fills one's consciousness.

My point is that the status of this dynamically unconscious experience—however one wants to view it from the standpoint of ontology or epistemology—is no different than it would be for any (so-called) observation statement (e.g., Bechtel 1988b, Fodor 1987, Lauden 1990, Quine 1969) like "I see the barn is painted red." And as such it constitutes what I will call our psychoanalytic, dynamically unconscious, experiential database. I believe, in principle, there is no difference between such a database of human experience and a database of any other science. To be sure, one must understand that the acquisition of this particular database requires an empathic capability; but this is essentially no different from the case that obtaining a database in any science requires instrumental skills. Also, in addition to empathic capability, this database of human experience in psychoanalysis emerges in a methodological context of analysand free associations, and an analyst state of "evenly suspended attention" (Freud 1912b), and so forth; this methodology, itself, is already theory laden (Devitt 1984), or embedded in an "ideal coherence of . . . beliefs" (Putnam 1981), however one chooses to put it. But again, this is characteristic of a database for any science. What justifies this conclusion? Simply, that it is our lot as human beings to share, more or less, a common core of human experience, and further, that this core of human experience extends into a realm of immediately apprehended but dynamically unconscious experiences.

Now, I have used this analogy to a (so-called) observation statement—The barn is painted red—so that it is incumbent on me to comment further. In fact, I want to use what we know about color perception, cross-culturally, to support my argument that it is viable to believe that a psychoanalytic database of dynamically unconscious experience exists.

The Dani of New Zealand, and a few other cultures, possess only two categories of color experience: first (and best translated), a dark cool (which would include our Western culture colors such as black, green, blue), and second, a (best translated) light warm (which would include our Western culture colors white, red, yellow). However, the work of Rosch as well as Berlin and Kay (cited, e.g., in Brown 1991, Lakoff 1987) makes clear that any conclusion that color perception is therefore an utterly relativistic and arbitrary matter is not justified. If, for example, one were to have the Dani people learn a more variegated color scheme, it turns out that they would most easily learn our prevailing Western color codification (Rosch's work, cited in Lakoff 1987). Or if one examines diverse cultures that possess increasingly complex color codification, it turns out there is regularity across cultures as to how this complexity will proceed. If there is a third color category, it will be red. If there is a fourth color category, it will be green or yellow, and so forth (Berlin and Kay's work, cited in Brown 1991). Finally, if people from diverse cultures are asked to choose which color is the best example of a color category in their culture, they will all choose the same focal color. Thus, if diverse cultures all possess the color category "red," the individuals in all of those cultures will choose the same red to be the best example of the perception of red, or the same blue to be the best example of blue, and so forth. There is also an apprehension of manifest emotional experience—an "immediately" sensed empathic understanding by a human of one culture how a human in another culture feels. Ekman (e.g., Ekman 1980, Ekman et al. 1969) first demonstrated a pan-cultural recognition of facial expression of basic emotions in this regard, and, more recently, argues cogently for a "wired-in" basis for such universal expression of affect

(Ekman 1992, 1993). Osgood (see Rieber 1983) has pointed out that a universal similarity also exists for a human cognitive ordering of experience. What a Freudian psychoanalysis adds is not only the realization that one human can empathically apprehend such emotionality even if it is dynamically unconscious but also that this could be accomplished via verbal free associations wherein the analysand's face is not seen by the analyst. This is what is evident in the analyst's empathically apprehended understanding that the analysand was, dynamically unconsciously, feeling both trapped and confined.

I already have mentioned, at the beginning of this chapter, that Beres and Arlow conceive this interpretive empathic capability to involve a trial identification made by the analyst with the analysand. Of course, this capability is not simply existent at one's birth, and it is not uniformly present in all individuals. So we might ask, What enables this trial identification? And what we believe enables it is an "unconscious fantasy that is shared in common" (Beres and Arlow 1974, p. 45; and see Sachs 1942). Now, Beres and Arlow go on to say: "The universally shared early biological experiences of mankind form the basis of universal fantasies, facilitating empathic communication between person and person, and person and group" (p. 46). But "shared" and "biological experiences of mankind" need further qualification. Empathic capability is not telepathy (and I do not believe telepathy exists).

Beres and Arlow themselves clarify this further with another clinical example of a shared analysand–analyst fantasy. In order to do justice to their example, I must cite from the article at some length. The analysand is first described as follows:

> A middle-aged professional man, tormented by feelings of guilt and depression, demonstrated a rather typical masochistic character

formation. Much of his problem centered around an unresolved feminine attitude and erotic longing for an uncle who had served as a father surrogate during his early years. [p. 36]

The authors go on to describe the analysand to be the only boy and youngest of three children. When the analysand was 2 years old, his father left the family in Europe and came to the United States. The family was not reunited until the analysand was 10. With the analysand's father absent, it was his uncle (mother's brother) who, increasingly, became the repository of grandiosity displaced from the absent father. The uncle became an idol for the analysand as a little boy with whom he played and whose bed he shared. The analysand became depressed and did not want to leave the uncle when the time came for the family to be reunited in America. Once in the United States, the analysand longed for his uncle, and tried to have the uncle emigrate, but the uncle had no intention or desire to leave Europe, even with the impending threat of war and Nazism. This aggrandized image of the uncle was quite unrealistic, as the uncle appeared to be a ne'er-do-well who lived by his wits. But this information, obtained about the uncle by the analysand in later years, did not affect the analysand's idealized image. When war broke out in Europe, and the Nazis seized the analysand's hometown, the analysand was convinced the uncle would survive. More than this, the analysand was convinced the uncle would display bravery and resourcefulness in the face of Nazi oppression. Later, during the analysis, the analysand learned that his uncle had suffered quite a different fate. The uncle had been shot the first day the Germans occupied the village because of some foolhardy, defiant gesture.

The analysand began a session with a dream:

Last night I had the following dream. I saw myself in a house with some cousin of mine in the country. It was not yet dark, but it was no longer light, and I seemed to be all alone in the house. My cousin was elsewhere; I could not see him. I called out "Peter" and somebody, in a joking way, called back "Joey." [p. 37]

Beres and Arlow go on to say:

The therapist heard no more than this of the patient's material when he suddenly found himself having a vivid, visual fantasy. He saw himself at a European airport, standing in the terminal. It was the kind of airport typical of many European cities: the passengers debark from the plane at some distance from the terminal and are brought in by bus. As the therapist was standing and waiting, a bus approached the terminal. Among the passengers, he recognized his father who had been dead for a number of years. Many thoughts came into his mind about this fantasy. As a matter of fact, the last time he had seen his father alive had indeed been in an airport except that the circumstances had been reversed; his father was waiting for him at the airport in New York upon his return from a visit to Europe. The visit had included a sentimental journey. The therapist had made a trip to his father's native land, and had in fact, gone out of his way to visit the city where his father had spent his youth. It suddenly came to him that he was in a twilight zone between life and death, in that in-between land where it is possible for the living and the dead to be reunited.

The therapist's next thought was the patient's dream. The patient had been in a house in the country; it was not yet dark, but it was no longer light. The patient, too, was in the twilight zone and the therapist realized immediately that the names Peter and Joey, which occurred in the dream, were actually Anglicized forms of the names the patient and his uncle used to call each other. At this point, the therapist began to emerge from his intrusive visual fantasy and heard the patient speaking: "Last night I was watching television. The show was 'Twilight Zone.'" [pp. 37–38]

And, finally, these comments:

It was not hard to interpret the patient's dream. It expressed the wish to be reunited with his uncle. The dream was based upon the unconscious fantasy of reunion in the twilight area where the living and dead find each other once again. The patient and the therapist both had the same "dream" and, with no immediate associations to the manifest content, an unconscious fantasy of the therapist congruent with that of the patient's appeared in his mind. Without the benefit of associations to the dream, and before the process of intuition could become operative, the therapist had grasped the meaning of the patient's dream and responded with his own version of the identical unconscious fantasy. In truth, the therapist had created his own unconscious fantasy before he had any conscious awareness of the meaning of the patient's dream.

Clearly, this empathic process by which the patient's fantasy stimulated the therapist's own had taken place entirely at the unconscious level. An identification between the two of them had been effected through this shared unconscious wish that led in turn to an almost identical fantasy in both their minds. [pp. 38–39]

Clearly, what has occurred, and is appreciated by Beres and Arlow, is a fantasy that is shared but congruent between analysand and analyst. In other words, the analysand's dream has important meaning in terms of his own life development, and the analyst's fantasy has a similar but different important meaning in terms of the analyst's life development.

Should this kind of a consciousness of an analyst fantasy be construed as countertransference? Beres and Arlow do describe the analyst's fantasy as "intrusive"; in a quite obvious sense, it interferes with the analyst's "evenly suspended attention" (Freud 1912b, p. 111), which of course is always to be centered on the analysand's verbal free associations. I think to maintain clarity this sort of absorbing emergence into an analyst's consciousness—the very (usually) dynamic unconscious fantasy formation that enables identification—ought to be conceived as a species of countertransference. But, if so, it is at least clear that it is a kind of countertransference that, phenomenologically, is not (ego) passively suffered in a way typical of countertransference experience. In addition to the issue of the analyst's work style, it may be that such an occurrence is a kind of trade-off. Something in an analysand's free associations has provoked congruent analyst fantasy formation of great emotional significance for the analyst's life experience. Such a momentary intrusion of fantasy in the analyst's consciousness accomplishes an emotional catharsis (like a play experience perhaps); if this analyst's fantasy had remained repressed, what was only a momentary self-absorption might have had another sort of countertransference consequence even more disturbing to the clinical process: a faulty interpretation, some inappropriate confrontation, or the like. In any case, what we can take to be the regular activation of congruent— but not telepathically identical—dynamic unconscious fantasy formation between analysand and analyst is exquisitely shown in this illustration.

In my own clinical practice experience, I can cite a fantasy I developed, which was momentarily so absorbing that the analysand's free associations no longer had my (evenly suspended) attention. The fantasy was very simple, but very intense, and involved both visual and auditory experience: I could "see" and "hear" Frank Sinatra singing the song "My Boy Bill" from the Soliloquy of the musical *Carousel*. This was interesting and intriguing for a number of reasons, not the least of which was that I had this fantasy in response to the associative material expressed by a female analysand.

However, the congruence between my fantasy formation and this female analysand's experience was immediately evident. This woman was complaining, vividly complaining, as she had done many times before, about her father's male chauvinistic attitude toward his only daughter (herself) with respect to his expectations for her vocational identity. The father was a physician and easily as well as eagerly could express his expectation, at the birth of a son, that a son of his also could become a physician. In fact, one son, the youngest of the three children as I recall, did become a physician. But no such expectation was held out for his daughter, my analysand, at her birth. Obviously, this fantasy of mine was congruent with the experience being expressed by the analysand and had to do with my relationship with my own father. It was immediately evident to me that this Frank Sinatra-"My Boy Bill" fantasy had to do with my learning, as an adult, that my father had purchased for me a set of encyclopedias prior to my even beginning school and how moved I was by this experience. The point I want to make here is that this fantasy, while momentarily distracting, also, I believe, was very facilitating with regard to my making a transference interpretation to the analysand. This had not so much to do with the content of the transference toward me, which was fairly obvious, but the *form* in which I made the interpretation. As I say, this analysand had emphasized bitter comments about her father many times before. I had made numerous interpretations in a straightforward way about her transference wish for me to be a different kind of father for her. This time, the dramatic performance quality of my fantasy, I believe, in quite a definite sense, carried over to a different form for my interpretation, and this seems to have had a productive result in terms of a revelation of clinical material never expressed before by the analysand.

There is something else important to consider that may be related to the analyst's work style, and that is the extent to which dynamically unconscious fantasy formation, out of which the analyst is able to make empathic identification, emerging into the consciousness of the analyst may represent an important difference in work style among different analysts.

I want to return to the initial clinical material I cited from Beres and Arlow and cite the analysand's free associations immediately after the analyst interpreted the analysand's feeling of being trapped and confined (p. 40).

I do get *symptoms of claustrophobia* from time to time. They are mild, just a slight anxiety. I begin to feel that perspiring feeling at the back of my neck, and begin to have a sense of restlessness. It happens when the elevator stops between floors or when a train gets stuck between stations. I begin to worry how I'll get out. You know, I have the same feeling about starting an affair with Mrs. X. She wants the

affair and I guess I want it too. Getting involved is easy. It's getting
uninvolved that concerns me. How do you get out of an affair once
you're in it? [p. 30, italics mine]

Now, I certainly would maintain that this analysand's manifest free associations include experience that is theory laden
or part of an ideal coherence of beliefs, however one wants to
put it. Here, the analysand talks about "symptoms," specifically, the symptom of claustrophobia.

I am really chicken. It's a wonder I was ever able to have relations at
all and to get married. No wonder I didn't have any intercourse until
I was in my twenties. My mother was always after me. "Be careful
about getting involved with girls—they will get you into trouble.
They will be after you for your money. If you have sexual relations
you can pick up a disease. Be careful when you go into public toilets.
You can get an infection, etc., etc." She made it all sound dangerous.
You could get hurt from this, you could get hurt from that. It
reminds me of the time I saw two dogs having intercourse. They
were stuck together and couldn't separate. The male dog was
yelping and screaming in pain. I don't know how old I was then,
maybe five or six, perhaps seven, but I was definitely a child and I
was frightened. [p. 30]

And some final comments by Beres and Arlow about this
particular vignette:

At this point, [while] the existence of claustrophobia could be
deduced in a rational way from . . . the material, claustrophobia was a
new element in the treatment. . . . But there was another idea that
presented itself to the therapist's perception. *This was the idea that the
patient was under the influence of an unconscious fantasy in which his penis
would be trapped or injured if it entered the vagina, originally his mother's.*
A corollary of this notion was that the patient fantasized his whole
body as his penis and it, too, would be subject to the same danger
that threatened his penis in the preceding fantasy. Considering this
insight, there was much less evidence than for the conclusions
regarding claustrophobia. [p. 31, italics mine]

Beres and Arlow here do clearly recognize that both analysand and analyst now, decisively, have moved beyond what

I have called our psychoanalytic, immediately apprehended, dynamically unconscious database of human experience. As I have already said, the analysand's use of terms like *symptom* or *claustrophobia* implies a theory- or belief-laden coloration of experience; and certainly now the analyst's conjecture that the analysand possessed a dynamically unconscious vagina dentata fantasy is similarly affected by a theory or belief system. All of this demonstrates the seamless way in which our psychoanalytic database is taken up, organized, and elaborated according to one theoretical (or belief system) framework or another in an ongoing psychoanalysis (Grossman 1992). Thus, when Beres and Arlow talk about how "shared early biological experiences of mankind form . . . universal fantasies, facilitating empathic communication" (p. 46), we must understand a second important qualification. Not only are shared fantasies congruent (not telepathic), but what we take to be the nature of these shared early biological experiences differs according to our theory (or belief system). Beres and Arlow have in mind universal fantasies that emanate from Freudian psychosexual theory; a Kleinian analyst will have another version of what is so "universal"; an Adlerian analyst will have yet another version; and so forth. Someone like Levenson (e.g., 1972) will stress a universality of experience that does not use concepts of biological experiences that inform our experiences of social relatedness (Erikson 1950), but fundamental experiences of social relatedness that inform our biological experiences. This is why there can be no conception of a "common ground" (Wallerstein 1990) of transference and resistance among our various psychoanalytic orientations. At the same time, I hope to have demonstrated that this entire question about the theory-ladenness of observation is not like whether or not a woman is pregnant—it is not all or nothing. There is a real and significant difference between the ladenness of theory with respect to what I have called our "immediate" database, conscious or dynamically unconscious (Bion's [1967] selected

fact), versus a concept about the existence of a symptom and
the like (and see esp. Meehl 1969).

Finally, I can proceed directly to the question about
whether one must conceive psychoanalytic interpretation
only to be a narrative truth (Spence 1982), or a narrative
"retelling" (Schafer 1992), in other words, whether an analyst's work style puts a clinical gloss (Spence 1982) on
interpretation, and, further, whether an analyst's theory
amounts only to one sort of story line or another (Schafer,
e.g., 1983). We cannot dispute the theory-ladenness of
observation or the effect of work style. But notice that the
three versions of clinical process discussed in this chapter are
all in a certain basic agreement about how a psychoanalytic
relationship is *emotionally arranged*. I believe what makes for
this agreement is a matter of reality and not storytelling.
Perhaps this agreement can be usefully understood in terms
of a medical metaphor. For a more-or-less-usual Freudian
view of clinical process, and that of Levenson (1972), as well
as that of Hoffman and Gill (e.g., 1988), the analysand is like
a patient possessed of an infectious medical illness: the
analysand's dynamically unconscious experience "infects"
the analyst with the analysand's illness by producing within
the analyst (at the least) the potential for the same illness.
Kohut's (e.g., 1977) idea of narcissistic disturbance, or
Gedo's (1979) idea of mental psychopathology "beyond
interpretation," is not like a physical illness that is infectious
in this way. Rather, such mental psychopathology is like a
severe allergy, which does not infect another person but
creates out-of-the-ordinary demands for a very special kind
of environmental provision. It would be like having a guest
in one's house with an extreme allergy to dust and pollens
and attempting to provide for this guest an extraordinary
atmosphere that, inevitably, could not be perfect. In this
way, Kohut (e.g., 1977) advises that the analyst with the
narcissistically disturbed patient must acknowledge "empathic failures," but without guilt, owing to these extraordi-

nary demands for empathic provision in the psychoanalytic relationship. But this concept of a dynamics of provision is a very different idea than a concept of an infectious dynamic interplay between analyst and analysand in the clinical process.

Another illustration of this important difference is provided by Hanly (1982). Hanly has produced a theory, together with illustrative case material, to argue that one can conceive a narcissistic personality to be a "defense," though not in the ordinary sense of the term (A. Freud 1936, S. Freud 1926a). Still, Hanly uses the term *defense* because he conceives this ego "defect" (Pine 1990), that is, a narcissistic, nonautonomous self-esteem regulation, to exist within an overall drive (wish)-object relations conflict matrix.

Hanly states:

> The absence of a satisfactory maternal response causes injury not because it fails to confirm the child's narcissistic needs but because it repudiates the child's phase-appropriate demonstration of object love and exerts a pressure upon the child for a regression to narcissism. [p. 430]

"[It] . . . can serve," he continues, "both as a disguised gratification for unconscious anger and hostility [I would emphasize sadism] and as a means of maintaining them in an unconscious state" (p. 431). But Hanly works here with a concept of narcissism used by Freud (e.g., 1914a, 1915c) that I believe is confusing and problematic.

For example, in one paper Freud (1915c) describes narcissism as a psychic condition at "the very beginning of life . . . and . . . [a] way of obtaining satisfaction [that is] 'autoerotic' " (p. 134). Yet elsewhere (1914a) he states "there must be something added to auto-eroticism—a new psychical action—in order to bring about narcissism" (p. 77). He describes an early psychic organization for loving such that "an object . . . is loved . . . but it is also incorporated into the ego" (1915c, p. 136). But again, "a unity comparable to the ego cannot exist in the individual from the start; . . . [it] has to be developed" (Freud 1914a, p. 77). So where are we with all of this? To examine this thoroughly is not a purpose of this book (but see Loewald, e.g., 1971a). But here I will simply state that Kohut's (1977) idea of a narcissistic selfobject can be equated, theoretically, to what Freud (1915c) meant by how an object "is loved" and also "incorporated into the ego," and that this kind of love is an attribute of an overall anal-rapprochement psychic organization. Later in this book I will discuss mind emergence as a phenomenon of anal-rapprochement development, and how the toddler's sadomasochistic fantasy life relates to issues of mind control. Now I simply am saying that narcissism as a concept must adhere within a psychic organization of mind that enables a consciousness of one's self (or object) of some sort. In the myth, after all, Narcissus is not just looking at but *recognizing himself* in his reflection in the water. I believe Hanly presents clinical material illustrating this. A female analysand's longing for affirmation from the analyst is expressed with a fantasy about good care (providing firewood) to the analyst, who is an idealized selfobject (imagined as an old man). Hanly's initial *only extended enabling* of such experience is followed by quite sadistic fantasies toward this idealized, loved selfobject; and then, ultimately, oedipal dynamics become expressed and worked through with a now individuated love object.

It should be clear that such a difference in interpretative orientation—which I have analogized as an infectious dynamic interplay contrasted with an allergic dynamic press for some sort of extraordinary environmental provision—would apply to the entire variety of ego defects (Pine 1990) we consider with such terminology as a lack of inner-object continuity (e.g., Winnicott 1955), or the analysand's lack of an inner container (e.g., Bion 1962), or the analysand's inner lack of a holding environment (e.g., Modell 1976), and so forth.

At the same time, I believe that this infectious concept of clinical interaction need not at all produce a unitary kind of psychoanalytic experience for the analysand, and can even result in an important similarity with the notion of allergy with respect to clinical process. I suspect (hypothesize) that the concept of clinical process such as that used by Levenson (1972), as well as Hoffman and Gill (e.g., 1988), or Kohut (e.g., 1977), produces "transference scenarios" for Hoffman (1993) and Kohut, or real interpersonal paradigmatic replays for Levenson (1972), that emerge early and change little (if at all) compared with a usual Freudian practice (and see Richards 1991, Schafer 1985, Steingart 1990). I suspect (hypothesize) the same with respect to an analysand's descriptions of important contemporary figures in his or her life including the analyst (see Schafer 1985b). And I suspect (hypothesize) the same with respect to critical reminiscences (see Shapiro 1993).

So to whatever extent a productive psychoanalysis is occurring, analyst gloss shapes but does not eliminate the essential expression of aspects of the analysand's psychic reality there to be discovered by analyst interpretation. One human mind, that of the analyst, can understand something about the conscious and dynamically unconscious experience of another human mind, that of the analysand, which is true according to a correspondence doctrine of truth. But what about the inevitability that an analyst's interpretations will, seamlessly, be taken up and elaborated in one theoretical "persuasion" (Schafer 1983) or another? I want to inject, at this point, some beautiful and powerful language by Loewald (1970): "To discover the truth about the patient is always discovering it with him and for him as well as for ourselves and about ourselves. And it is discovering truth between each other, as the truth of human beings in their interrelatedness" (pp. 297–298). I believe Loewald's use of this idea of discovering—and this means discovering by interpretation—is the same idea expressed by Schwaber (1992) when she speaks about an analysand psychic reality to be discovered by interpretation. But Loewald, like Schwaber, is now not only talking about a truth having to do with what I have called our immediately apprehended but dynamically unconscious database of feeling states of one sort or another. What Loewald means by truth is how this psychoanalytic database is taken up and elaborated by him according to his version of Freudian theory.

But if this psychoanalytic database in fact exists as I describe it, then it constitutes an array of observation statements (e.g., Laudan 1990) like that possessed by any science. This, in turn, enables not just a comparison but a testing among different psychoanalytic theories in the arena of clinical process. An analyst who construes psychoanalytic interpretation to be always and only a narrative truth (Schafer 1983) cannot subscribe to what I have just said. Such an analyst believes either that the database does not exist or, if it does exist, is inconsequential in comparison with the overall theoretical framework that immediately takes up and elaborates this common lot of human experience in an ongoing psychoanalysis. Further, such an analyst may believe that our various psychoanalytic theories, in themselves, are only some ideal coherence of beliefs. This tells us nothing about either a mind-independent conceived psychic reality, or a validatable reality, or objectively conceived connections between them.

All the foregoing has to do with two components of what may be therapeutic about interpretation in a psychoanalytic relationship: what we customarily call the acquisition of insight and how providing that insight is a type of relating. But there is much more to it. What Freud (1912b) meant by analysand transference that is unobjectionable, that is, "friendly or affectionate feelings" (p. 105), and that I believe equates with Stone's (1961, 1967) idea of a mature (love) transference, is met by an extraordinary but real sort of love that emanates from the analyst in a psychoanalytic relationship, expressed in the analyst's every interpretation.

NOTES

1. To speak of an interpersonal meaning is descriptively accurate. But this, of course, hardly means that these attributions by the analysand have no relevance for the analysand's psychic structure (superego projections, etc.).

2. A good deal has been made that Freud's (1912b) "blank screen" depiction of the analyst was an inevitable consequence of his realist philosophy (e.g., McLaughlin 1981, Schwaber 1983), but I think this is greatly overdrawn. In any case, realism as an ontology can be maintained and separated from inescapable, inevitable epistemological hazard, including that of clinical, empathic realization made by an analyst. But more to the point, I believe Freud's idea of the analyst as a blank screen has more to do with sociology than philosophy. In this same paper, Freud uses the term *purification* to describe an analyst's need for periodic reanalysis. Why use such a moral sounding term? Freud was obviously advancing a theory and type of treatment radical in its emphasis on sexuality and the revealing of sexual intimacies to a professional "stranger." And for this, Freud was subjected to harsh social-professional criticism. This blank screen idea of the analyst, I submit, no less than the analyst's need for purification, was heavily influenced by Freud's understandable need to defend psychoanalysis against such criticism. It is interesting to realize that the title of the paper in which these ideas were presented included a reference to (fellow) physicians – "Recommendations to Physicians . . ."

Also, we tend to forget that when Freud in his "Recommendations" paper described his use of the couch to be personally better suited for himself, he alluded to a matter of work style he did *not* consider an issue of his countertransference. However discovered, the clinical, Freudian justification for the use of the couch is something else. Philosophers of science refer to this as the difference between the "context of discovery" and the "context of justification" (see, e.g., Kaplan 1964).

3. But if I understand Brenner correctly he would use this same term, *countertransference*, to include analyst experiences that interfere with as well as facilitate an analysis. This is why Brenner states: "There is truly

no need for a separate term [countertransference]. Countertransference is the transference of the analyst in an analytic situation" (p. 156). I do not think it useful to use the same term, *transference,* for such different effects of analyst experience on an analysis; and I will say more about another important difference shortly with respect to an analyst's transference experience in the psychoanalytic relationship.

4. Of course, the more an analysand approaches schizophrenia, the more these distinctions dissolve and we have delusional and/or hallucinatory transference experience.

5. A very tangible example of this, in the domain of music, would be Elgar's work *Enigma Variations,* which are musical "portraits" of individuals, including one of himself.

6. My use of the terms *passive* and *activity* in this context refer to conceptualizations of analyst ego functioning (see esp. Rapaport, e.g., 1958).

7. I stress "in the psychoanalytic relationship." How manageable (conflict-free) an analyst can be with his or her transference experiences in his or her other "ordinary" life situations is another matter, and certainly of no concern to the analysand. Further, special features about the psychoanalytic relationship that promote a signal function use (Beres and Arlow 1974) of the analyst's countertransference experience do not exist in the analyst's other "usual" life situations.

8. But Schafer elaborates another criterion for reality in the psychoanalytic situation when he speaks about assessing the analysand's "cognitive activities" (p. 544): "for when this estimate is relatively high, the analyst will be more likely to ascribe some truth value to reports of past and present actions performed by other people" (p. 544). I would immediately add that this assessment applies as well to self-reports of analysand performed actions and judgment about analyst action toward the analysand in the psychoanalytic situation. Wallerstein (Panel 1985), correctly, I believe, has argued that Schafer's commentary is inconsistent with his basic nonobjectivist positioning for psychoanalysis. Schafer's response (reported by Roughton in Panel [1985] is that on a "high theoretical plane" it is still possible for him to maintain a basic hermeneutic positioning for the psychoanalytic situation. Also, Geha (1984) may be correct that Schafer is holding on to some type of realism with his statement that "we cannot do without a conception of reality" (p. 368). But, if so, it is what Devitt (1984) terms a weak realism.

9. I will allude to Winnicott's realism later in this book when I cite certain of his comments about the relationship between fantasy (I would prefer to say play) and reality (I would prefer to say actuality) in the young child. Of course, a mutual, irrational, transference-distorted relationship may be expressed and be characteristic of a nonanalytic relationship. One

thinks, for example, of the marital relationship depicted in Edward Albee's (1962) play, *Who's Afraid of Virginia Woolf,* in which wife and husband constantly, sadistically attack each other, each locked into irrational transference experiences about the other.

10. Gill can object that he would not, in the first place, accept my depiction of transference-countertransference in the here and now to be unreal experience. But then, in my opinion, he would have to make more intellectually coherent than he has thus far (Gill 1983) his past maintenance of "classical" Freudian practice with respect to minimal or no revelation of countertransference experience. Gill is, of course, aware of another kind of analytic praxis (e.g., Levenson 1972), which treats and *expresses* countertransference as real experience. I will discuss this shortly. Gill (Hoffman and Gill 1988) more recently appears to be changing his idea of clinical practice toward the revelation of countertransference, and I will discuss this shortly as well.

11. Also, there is an important analyst counterpart experience of safety with regard to transference regression. This has to do with a vital, and real, difference in the analyst's experience of *responsibility* in the psychoanalytic relationship contrasted with the responsibility the analyst experiences in his or her "ordinary" significant relationships.

12. And, considered from this perspective, I believe the idea of analytic "neutrality" has much in common with the psychology of scholarship. I use this idea of scholarship in another context, as an important analogy for what transpires in the psychoanalytic relationship with respect to love.

13. At least to me, this conception of clinical process suggests that a kind of confrontational stance is clinically normative.

3

Love in the Analytic Relationship

At the end of the last chapter, I said that the mature, loving feeling state on the part of the analysand—the unobjectionable transference—is "met" by a love on the part of the analyst that is real. Now, to say that a state of love is real, even such a state of (always relative) mature love, is to state a paradox. Because even such a state of mature-equals-real love involves, as Freud (1915a) puts it, "departures from the norm that make up the essential elements in the condition of being in love" (p. 169). Elsewhere (Steingart 1983) I have described how these departures involve a simultaneous and natural psychic "elevation" of the experience of one's self, beloved other (or animal, inanimate object, etc.), and the quality of the pleasure experience itself. The result is that a simple, sexual pleasure now is exalted into romantic and/or passionate states of love, the loved other is idealized, and the lover experiences him- or herself to be suffused with narcissistic enhancement. At the same time, Freud differentiated between departures in a (relatively) mature love from departures in a childlike transference love, and essentially this differentiation focused on how a childlike transference love is "to a high degree lacking in regard for reality" (pp. 168–169). Of course, everything I have just said about childlike transference love on the side of the analysand applies as well to infantile countertransference love that may be engendered in the analyst.

Where I disagree with Freud has to do with his seeming contention that in all states of love the lovers influence each other by suggestion and compliance. This is exactly what is not true about a mature love; it *is* true about a childlike transference love. A lover in a mature love relationship with another person in a similar mature loving state will naturally become deeply concerned about the fulfillment of the needs of the loved other. But at the same time this lover will not feel any need for compliance, or influence by suggestion, to automatically fulfill the expressed needs of the loved other person. A lover in a mature love relationship is also deeply secure that the same fulfillment of his or her own needs is no more or less important than is the satisfaction of the loved other's needs (Sullivan, e.g., 1954). It is this deeply felt realization that realistically anchors the psychic departures from the norm in a mature love. In a mature love there is a reality of two individuals who are wanted by each other to live out their own separate existences within the intimacy of their love relationship. This certainly is true for the mature love that can exist in the psychoanalytic relationship for both analyst and analysand, in other words, the love that can exist outside childlike transference and (possible) countertransference experiences. Freud is most clear on this point when he attempts to apply his psychic energy constructs to the phenomenon of narcissism (self-love).

> We may even venture to touch on the question of what makes it necessary at all for our mental life to pass beyond the limits of narcissism and to attach the libido to objects. The answer which would follow from our line of thought would once more be that this necessity arises when the cathexis of the ego with libido exceeds a certain amount. A strong egoism is a protection against falling ill, but in the last resort we begin to love in order not to fall ill, and we are bound to fall ill if, in consequence of our frustration, we are unable to love. [Freud 1914a, p. 85]

And it is clear in this context that Freud is not speaking about narcissistic love objects (see also Kohut 1977, Reik 1944, Sullivan 1954).

There is an important irony and consequence of all of this for treatment, especially a psychoanalytic treatment relationship with other than neurotically disturbed analysands. A psychoanalysis, traditionally conceived, assumes a sufficient presence of what I take Freud to have meant by the unobjectionable transference; again, these are (relatively) mature friendly and affectionate feelings that are neither positive nor negative childlike transference love and hate. But it is not that "paranoids," to use Freud's (1911b) example, are possessed only of a negative childlike transference, and so make a psychoanalytic treatment unable to "cure." I have already referred to Freud's (1911b) own brilliant analysis of Schreber's delusions; this analysis revealed the dynamically unconscious presence of intense, childlike, positive homosexual love. It is the profound anxiety over influence, vulnerability to suggestion, compliance to the point of Schreber's expected surrendering of his own existence (sexual identity) that made him delusional. Put another way, Schreber, one assumes, did not possess sufficient development and presence of an unobjectionable, mature loving capability to enable a psychoanalysis. And this is the irony for the psychoanalytic relationship as treatment procedure. I assume that other-than-neurotic psychopathologies—what we refer to as borderline or narcissistic disturbances, or schizoid, or perverse, and so forth—all present the possible therapeutics of the psychoanalysis with a similar issue and problem. The irony is that, with more deeply disturbed individuals, a mature loving condition must be augmented along with interpretation of dynamically unconscious experience. Again, continued discussion of these considerations would involve me in a book about a theory of psychoanalytic technique, and this not my purpose. I do, at least, want to make the comment that an emphasis on what I have described to be the real, collegial nature of the psychoanalytic relationship is absolutely vital in connection with the treatment of other than neurotically disturbed individuals, whereas its experience is taken for granted in our treatment of neurotic psychopathology. However, use of this term *collegial*, with reference to nonneurotic analysands needs further explanation about what I believe actually occurs.

So I need to return to my contention that the nature of the psychoanalytic relationship is such that the analyst possesses a real love for the analysand. These considerations obviously apply to other-than-neurotic as well as neurotic sufferers. In fact, these considerations have a special pertinence for other than the neurotically disturbed. This analyst love is not only real but extraordinary. And what makes it extraordinary follows, directly and naturally, from the altogether extraordinary nature of the psychoanalytic relationship. This has to do with what Freud (1915a) meant when he said that the psychoanalytic relationship "is one for which there is no model in real life" (p. 166).

THE ANALYST'S REAL AND EXTRAORDINARY LOVE FOR THE ANALYSAND

Let us suppose an analyst becomes aware of angry, countertransference feelings that have arisen within him- or herself in the context of manifest analysand transference that is insulting or demanding, whatever. Are these feelings real, say, like the anger generated in the context of offensive behavior or attitudes expressed by a friend, spouse, or children? I say they are not, and to argue that they are is to engage in a kind of self-deception; because the analyst who is angry with a friend, spouse, or child will naturally express that anger and want *to change* in some way the offensive behavior or attitude experienced as a significant, real threat to his or her security. But for an analyst who is countertransferentially angry to want the analysand to change whatever it is that is manifestly offensive is inconceivable in a viable therapeutic relationship. To want the analysand to change —

rather than, or in addition to, only understanding what is happening—hopelessly confuses what is uniquely real about the analyst's needs in a psychoanalytic relationship with the analyst's desires in a real, significant, "usual" life relationship. The analyst's desire only to know the analysand's psychic life hardly means that this desire is unconnected, within the analyst, to diverse voyeuristic, sadistic, and so forth fantasies and feelings; quite the opposite: only if the analyst's desire to know does realize such deeper, personal desires can the analyst be present as a person in a psychoanalysis in a useful way (e.g., Brenner 1985, McLaughlin 1981). But inasmuch as the emotional position of the analyst is essentially only to know, the analyst's experience of responsibility for how the analysand conducts his or her life, inside or outside the psychoanalytic relationship, really is quite unlike that which obtains in an "ordinary" significant relationship. Paradoxically (but understandably), the opportunity for a uniquely psychoanalytic resolution of transference experience can only occur if the analyst's conduct toward analysand transference is mediated by these real but out-of-the-ordinary states of desire and responsibility.

And what I have just said about analysand transference extends as well to analyst countertransference. The psychoanalyst's desire and responsibility with respect to his or her countertransference is not to eradicate it but surely to know it; and the analyst's responsibility to change his or her countertransference extends only to the degree to which such countertransference moves beyond being essentially a source of important information for furthering the psychoanalytic process. We conceive countertransference, in Freudian or non-Freudian practice, to be generated by the analysand (Hoffman and Gill 1988, Levenson 1972), or forced (Schafer 1983) on the analyst by the analysand (Heinmann 1950), or passively suffered by the analyst; this is due either to a subtle influence (Freud 1912b) of the analysand's dynamic unconscious or to the analysand's manifest behav-

ior. The basic idea here is that the psychoanalytic relationship is emotionally arranged so that the analyst's experiences
are *counter*transference experiences. If we now consider the
entire course of a psychoanalysis, it is not simply that analyst
countertransference can occur but that certain fluctuations in
countertransference are expectable and always congruent
with variations in analysand transference. This variability is
not at all to be expected with respect to transference experience an analyst may have in his or her "ordinary" significant
relationships; to the extent that an analyst has transferences
in his or her ordinary life, these experiences will tend to be
stereotypic and repetitive, as is the case with anyone.[1]

It is these out-of-the-ordinary states of analyst desire and
responsibility—only to know—that enable the development
of what Fliess (1942) meant by the analyst's work ego, and
what Schafer (1983) more recently has described to be the
analyst's second self. That is, the analyst as analyst can
possess a degree of tact, sensitivity, tolerance, and so forth
not at all necessarily evident in that analyst's ordinary significant relationships. All that is really wanted and really
required in the psychoanalytic relationship is an understanding of what is happening between two individuals,
transferentially (or countertransferentially), as well as in experience that is validatable reality (Schafer 1985b, Schwaber
1992). "The feeling that is most dangerous to the analyst,"
wrote Freud (1912b), "is therapeutic ambition" (p. 115).

This concept of an out-of-the-ordinary relationship, mutually committed only to knowing, is both separate from and
related to the matter of the theoretical framework being used
for such knowing. It is separate in that the relationship is a
reality in and of itself; but it is related to the framework being
used (usual Freudian or other) because the commitment to
knowing must include understanding of the framework
itself. The crux of the matter is that Freud created not only a
new theory of human nature but, interrelated with that

theory, a new type of human relationship, whatever might be the theoretical orientation of the analyst.

I want to return to the simile of drama to examine further, and contrast, more-or-less-usual Freudian practice that involves minimal or no revelation of countertransference (e.g., Schafer 1983) with the idea of praxis in which the analyst is a "participant," always or sometimes (Hoffman, e.g., 1992a,b, Levenson 1972), in some transference-countertransference. This latter idea would correspond to the analyst as an actor or actress in a play; the former to the analyst as a member of the Greek chorus (Reonhold 1959), who, while emotionally affected by (e.g., Beres and Arlow 1974) and in turn affecting the actors, nevertheless does not interact or participate in any usual sense of the words *interact* and *participate*. Whichever concept of clinical process is employed, it is an established consensus that (at least some) countertransference is significant and inevitable in any psychoanalysis. But whether one expresses the countertransference (Hoffman and Gill 1988, Levenson 1972), or only uses it to inform prevailing transference (e.g., Schafer 1983), neither process extends to countertransference responsibility for change that could arise naturally for an analyst in any of his or her ordinary relationships.

An easy, but I think erroneous, implication that can be drawn from the concept of the therapist as "a total participant and observer" (Levenson 1972, p. 215) is to think that emotional involvement of the therapist in a psychoanalytic relationship applies only to the participation aspect of the entire complex experience. Actually, the term *observer* hardly does justice to the experience held by an analyst or an analysand when he or she is attempting to understand transference in a certain way. *Observer* (observation) does, indeed, connote emotional detachment, solely a registering of something perceived to occur. Schafer's (1983) term *contemplation* is both more apt and accurate, connoting an idea of invested, extended, and serious consideration of experience. And what is especially implicated is a sense of the personal importance, for both analyst and analysand, of understanding the experience, and this naturally makes the experience itself important. The outcome (purpose) of such contemplation is to objectify an important analysand dynamically unconscious experience, but this does not mean the psychoanalytic relationship itself has become impersonal in the sense of emotionally detached. An act of contemplation on the part of either analysand or analyst amounts to an offering of a kind of relationship, one to the other, an invitation to devoted study of an analysand experience. Earlier I described how important it is that analyst interpretation be delivered with a genuine attitude that an interpretation is being offered as a consideration, and not a pronouncement. Now it is clear, and I can add, that only with such an attitude is there a chance to develop a contemplative psychoanalytic relationship.

If I use more familiar language to describe what I have just been saying about the psychoanalytic relationship, it would be an argument for insight as the critical, potentially therapeutic feature. But what I conceive here is not insight simply as what comes to be known—that is, content as outcome; insight also is *how* something comes to be known, and both aspects are uniquely real about the psychoanalytic relationship. The usual Freudian version of a psychoanalytic relationship is one in which both individuals, analyst and analysand, are devoted to achieving insight to dynamically unconscious experience one person (the analysand) has with the other (the analyst). It is a false and simplistic notion somehow to separate this idea of insight as outcome from a conception of a vital, unique relationship that makes the insight possible. Loewald (1980) has put it this way:

> It seems to me that an interpretation is not so much the result of understanding as it is the means by which understanding pro-

ceeds. . . . It is a curious fact that unless the patient feels understood we feel we have not fully understood him. Understanding would seem to be an act that involves some sort of mutual engagement, a particular form of the meeting of the minds. [pp. 381-382]

Eagle and Wolitsky (1986) have made a similar point about how an idea of insight as content cannot, conceptually, be separated from the how or type of relationship that produces it. A related consideration applies to what I have now described to be three kinds of experiences that support knowing in a psychoanalysis and, collectively, subserve both the process and the outcome of the relationship:[2] contemplation, together with immediately felt transference or (possible) countertransference, or an experience of some sort of empathic realization.

But I have not yet fixed on the idea and experience of the analyst's real (noncountertransferential) love for the analysand. It is an extraordinary sort of love because it occurs in the context of this absolutely unique human relationship in which two people, analyst and analysand, devote themselves always and only to expressing their knowing about the psychic reality of the analysand. At least, such is the case with a more-or-less-usual Freudian clinical practice. The Freudian analyst in his or her every interpretation expresses this love of the analysand. But a love of what about the analysand?

I have in mind something more about the kind of knowing that is psychoanalytic interpretive insight. An analogy can be made to scholarship. What do we mean by and what is distinctive about a scholar's relationship to the ideas of his or her subject matter? A person's relationship to ideas—ideas now thought of as potential objects for love or hate—can be as varied, dynamically, as that person's relationship to another person or some inanimate object. Ideas as subject matter can become dynamically invested objects for unresolved, childlike (i.e., not sublimated) exhibitionistic gratification, or pleasures in sadistic control, or castration urges, and so forth. But when we say that a person is a scholar, what we have in mind is a kind of love: devotion to the ideas in themselves—a care about their use (rather than abuse)—and this is like the devotion a lover can have for the needs of the beloved in a (reasonably) mature love relationship. Further, just as is the case with a mature love for another person (Steingart 1983), scholarship is animated by its own kind of idealization of the subject matter from which springs the ideas the scholar contemplates. But the subject matter of psychoanalysis is about experience that emanates from the psychic reality of the analysand. In other words, there is a type of analyst love in knowing about the psychic reality of the analysand that properly and really exists in a psychoanalysis. Put still another way, Freud created not only a theory of personality and a therapeutic praxis, but a new type of love relationship that occurs uniquely in a psychoanalysis. For the (so-called) classical patient it is presupposed that this relationship is operative and sufficient at the inception of treatment. As I have said, for analysands who possess other-than-neurotic emotional disturbance, this unique love relationship is only potentiated by a psychoanalysis; its augmentation is organic with any possibility of a productive, interpretive revelation of the analysand's dynamic unconscious experience.

I believe my emphasis on this idea—that an analyst, naturally, loves what is to be learned about the analysand's psychic reality—also elaborates something stated by Freud (1913) about the clinical process.

> It remains the first aim of the treatment to attach . . . [the patient] to it and to the person of the doctor. To ensure this nothing need be done but to give him time. If one exhibits a *serious interest* in him, clears away the resistances that crop up at the beginning and avoids making certain mistakes, he will of himself form such an attachment and link the doctor up with one of the images of the people by whom he was accustomed to be treated with affection. It is certainly possible to forfeit this first success if from the start one takes up any

standpoint other than one of *sympathetic understanding* . . . such as a
moralizing one, or if one behaves like a representative or advocate of
some contending party – of the other member of a married couple for
instance. [pp. 139–140, italics mine]

It is, of course, "serious interest" and "sympathetic understanding" that I have in mind. Earlier in this book I spoke
about the nitty-gritty of the everyday psychoanalytic relationship: the – really – countless incidents of negative transference that, as Freud states, "crop up"; the continuous
underlying resistance contributed by the repetition compulsion as this applies to each analysand; the working through
of insightful experience; the eventual resistance supplied by
each analysand's positive transference with respect to the
resolution and termination of the psychoanalytic relationship; and so forth. I can see no other way to account for an
analyst's steadfast devotion only to understanding the analysand's psychic reality unless this psychic reality, in itself, is
loved by the analyst. This means that each analysand, in this
special way, is loved because his or her analyst loves
understanding even the repetitious minutia of the analysand's unique psychic reality, and not only that which is
new, interpretive revelation.

This unique kind of analyst love that produces insight is
also supported by a novel but real sort of mental state held
by the analyst, one that Freud (1912b) termed "evenly
suspended attention" (p. 111). To characterize the novelty of
this analyst mental state only in the negative – that is, an
absence of focused attention – is to miss entirely its contribution for the therapeutic action of a psychoanalysis. This kind
of mental state, by its very nature, cannot be a source of
"impingement" (Winnicott, e.g., 1953). Or, put another way,
we might say it "wraps" itself about the analysand's associations and thus provides a holding environment (e.g., Modell 1976) for the analysand's mind-produced experiences,
offering a "new beginning" (Balint 1968) for what Freud
(1915c) once called the analysand's "total ego." Again, the

significant irony here is that it is other than neurotically disturbed individuals, those most susceptible to experiences such as impingement and psychic annihilation, who need the steady maintenance of such a state of analyst suspended attention in the face of extreme transference provocations, which sometimes can be quite subtle (or, of course, gross). All of what I have been saying must be at least part of what Grunes (1984) means by a "therapeutic object relationship."

It is true that ordinary significant loving relationships (between friends, parents and children, lovers, etc.) will sometimes center on efforts at mutual understanding. But only a psychoanalytic relationship is—throughout and essentially—insight centered to the exclusion of all else. An analyst who desires, or believes, that he or she can live out a life of significant usual life relationships with significant others with an analytic attitude (Schafer 1983) is not really living, and not living sufficiently in the real, usual world. The psychoanalytic relationship was never conceived to be (Freud 1915a), and is not, a simple, straightforward model for mental health with respect to our familiar, real, important human love relationships. And, paradoxically, it is just because it is not a familiar, natural, human loving relationship that it is capable of empathically realizing and interpreting all manner of dynamically unconscious experiences. If an analyst does not sufficiently enjoy, or sense sufficient aggression, and consequently succumbs to an urge to make a psychoanalytic relationship actually and significantly more natural with regard to purpose(s), we know that the analysis must suffer. And if an analyst attempts to make out of any of his or her other familiar, important, human relationships an analytic relationship, we know that what emerges must be grotesque.

Talk about an analyst's love originated with Freud (e.g., 1937a): "The analytic relationship is based upon a *love* of *truth*—that is, on a recognition of reality—and . . . it precludes any kind of sham or deceit" (p. 248, italics mine).

Because we know that Freud was philosophically a realist, we can be sure that the "truth" he speaks of here is a correspondence type of truth, and that its application is twofold: (1) that an analysand's conscious and dynamically unconscious psychic reality exists as it is independent of the analyst's work style and the psychoanalytic relationship through which analyst and analysand attempt to understand it; and (2) this truth also applies to that aspect of the psychoanalytic relationship, as well as to the analysand's entire life experience, that is a validatable reality (Schwaber 1992) or "outside" psychic reality (Schafer 1985b).

And what about "love" of truth? It is Loewald (1970) who first took this positioning for psychoanalysis espoused by Freud (1937b), looked at the nature of the psychoanalytic relationship, and did not conceptually "blink":

> Scientific detachment in its genuine form, far from excluding love, is based on it. In our work it can truly be said that in our best moments of dispassionate and objective analysis, we love our object, the patient, more than at any other time and are compassionate with his whole being. In our field scientific spirit and care for the object flow from the same source. It is impossible to love the truth of psychic reality, to be moved by this truth as Freud was in his life work, and not to love and care for the object whose truth we want to discover. All great scientists are moved by this passion. [p. 297]

Loewald here uses a notion of truth—"truth of [the analysand's] psychic reality." Schafer (1992), because of his hermeneutic positioning for psychoanalysis, chooses to understand this idea of truth as a narrative truth; I conceive it to be a correspondence truth. However, with respect to the analyst being in a real but extraordinary state of love about the analysand's psychic reality, Schafer certainly concurs.

In elaborating his idea of an analyst's work ego, Fliess (1942) stated: "It is not the analyst as an individual who approaches that 'rare and exalted perfection,' but the temporarily built-up person who does so under the circumstances and for the period of his work" (p. 225). Put another way, this means simply that it is the psychoanalytic situation—so long and to the degree that an analytic process is occurring—that brings about the analysand's unreal, childlike idealizing transference for the analyst. However, Fliess's concept falls short on two counts. First, his portrayal of the analyst-at-work as a "temporary built-up person" seems to say, inconceivably, that an analyst's work ego is literally built anew with each treatment hour. Rather, I believe the analyst "as an individual" continuously must possess some attribute that promotes "clicking into" the psychoanalytic situation and relationship. One can think here of an idea like psychological mindedness, though it fails to convey fully how the analyst as an individual must be someone, characteristically, who loves what is to be learned about psychic reality. Second, the way Fliess emphasizes the "exalted perfection" of the analyst tallies with the analysand's childlike idealization of the analyst, which will, of necessity, include erotic wishes. But this transferential "exalted perfection" is not connected to what Stone (1961) means by a (relatively) mature, reality-based transformation of childlike transference love onto the actual personage of the analyst. And it is here that Schafer's (1983) contribution of the concept of an analyst's second self, in his or her work as an analyst, is such a useful advance beyond Fliess's idea of work ego. Schafer (1983) states:

> In our best work as analysts we are not quite the same as we are in our ordinary social lives or personal relations. In fact, we are often much better people in our work in the sense that we show a greater range of empathizing in an accepting, affirmative, and goal directed fashion. . . . On this basis, a special kind of empathic intimacy, strength, appreciation, *and love*, can develop in relation to the analysand which would be a mistake to identify with disruptive countertransference. [p. 291, italics mine]

Still more recently, Schafer (1992) has commented about how such an analyst's "love in work . . . [is] an essential component of the engaged analyst at his or her best" (p. 308). Schafer is, with such comments, describing not an analyst who is simply an (ego) passive receptacle for the analysand's childlike, erotic, and idealized positive transference but a (relatively) mature, (ego) active person in his or her work situation.

But this elaboration of a second self possessed by an analyst at work cannot escape ontological consideration; indeed, it calls out for it. Schafer is telling us that when a person works as an analyst, at least to the (never perfect) degree to which he or she is free of disruptive countertransference in such work, this analyst is now importantly different as a person compared with how he or she is in other life circumstances. Everything about Schafer's writing about the second self suggests that he considers this to be something real, that is, real and different personality features of the analyst that essentially exist apart from any conceptual effort to formulate them. In other words, it is an ontology of realism that, I believe, best supports the concept of the analyst's second self; in turn, the analysand's encounter with this real but highly unusual analyst second self provides a platform for all manner of not-real transference construals about the actuality of the psychoanalytic relationship.

Also, I would not, within this perspective of a second self, with which I agree, venture how an analyst's work "does call for a significant subordination of the analyst's personality to the analytic work" (Schafer 1983, p. 290). Phenomenologically, the analyst's personality is no more felt to be subordinated than a violin is subordinated to the use made of it by the violinist. At the same time, the particular make and composition of a violin will affect the music produced in some determinant manner. This maintains my idea that the analyst's actual personality exerts a mediumlike effect on a psychoanalysis, but this influence is on an analysand's psychic reality, which exists as it is in some essential manner. So I think it confusing to describe either the analyst's

loving contemplation or empathic realization of the analysand's psychic reality as "creative" (Hoffman 1992a) in the
customary sense of the idea of the work of a creative artist of
one sort or another; even more, this applies to analyst
experiences of countertransference even if such countertransference is not disruptive and can be used information-
ally. The point is that there is a certain natural way in which
the narcissism of the creative artist is "figural" in creative
work, whereas in analytic work this kind of narcissistic
organization of oneself is not natural for the analyst at work.
The analyst's narcissism, at work, is as I (and G. Steiner
1990) have said about the narcissism of the scholar with his
or her subject matter: "The scholar . . . melts the strength of
his own personality and technical virtuosity into the . . .
[subject matter] . . . he is analyzing. . . . that . . . [subject
matter] . . . will become his without ceasing to be itself" (p.
133). Finally, I am concerned that what I have described as
this special sort of scholarly analyst love for the subject
matter, the psychic reality of the analysand, may appear to
describe to the reader an intellectual experience. I want to
emphasize that what I intend involves a full loving sensibility, which certainly includes, but is not only the equivalent
of, a deep sense of intellectual comprehension.

I take it that Lear (1990) would agree with everything I
have said about this real analyst love for the analysand as a
way to understand why it is that the analytic interpretation
that offers concepts is, in its own way, a "loving response to
the experienced instinctual life" (pp. 179–180). But interpretation can only be a "loving response" within the matrix of an
overall analytic relationship that itself is lovingly and respon-
sibly devoted only to knowing the analysand's psychic
reality. I want to explicate my conception of this real analyst
love because it has a somewhat different accent compared
with the other versions just described (Lear 1990, Loewald
1970, Schafer 1983, 1992). The analyst possesses a real,
(relatively) mature love for the analysand's mind and all that

the analysand produces with his or her mind. It matters not whether what the analysand produces with his or her mind is expressive, resistant, creative, perverse, adaptive, maladjusted, loving, hateful, or whatever—all are equally loved by the analyst because they are ways in which the analysand produces his or her psychic reality with his or her mind.

It is my positioning for psychoanalysis that an analysand's psychic reality exists, in some essential manner, as it is, apart from the analyst's conceptual efforts to understand it, as well as the particular empathic realizations by which he or she proceeds to comprehend dynamically unconscious experience. This kind of realist positioning for the analysand's psychic reality (mind products) naturally would be conjoined with such a perspective for analyst interpretation. But if this is accepted, and what I have just been describing to be an extraordinary but natural kind of analyst loving of the analysand's psychic reality is also accepted, then effects can be produced that are as ironic as they are disturbing. Suppose an analyst makes an interpretation that is consensually assessed by others (say, in a research program) to be valid; valid in this context would mean "true" according to a correspondence doctrine of truth about the analysand's psychic reality. Now, suppose that it is also valid (true) that the analyst makes this interpretation with subtle but nevertheless obvious (Gill 1984a) sadistic countertransference. For example, the sadistic aspect of the interpretation could be "delivered" via the analyst's syntax (Dahl et al. 1978). This interpretation cannot remain a good interpretation. In fact, because the interpretation, in a narrow, "technical" sense can be assessed to be valid, the analysand will suffer more from the analyst's sadism than if the valid interpretation were not "technically" correct. This is because the technically correct interpretation, while it will make the analysand fully understood, and in this analytic sense loved, is disturbingly negated by the sadistic pleasure expressed by the analyst in making the interpretation. If the interpretation had been technically incorrect, the analyst's sadism actually would be less destructive. Suppose it is considered true (valid) that an analyst is in a good, empathic contact with an analysand, up to the point of making an interpretation. And let us say that this good, empathic connection involves 20 minutes of silence that began with the beginning of the session. Then the analysand says something, briefly, and the analyst immediately makes an interpretation. Now, let us say that the analyst's interpretation is assessed to be not valid (true) about what is pertinent about the analysand's psychic reality at the moment. Suppose further that it is concluded that the analyst's not-valid interpretation was due not to some interfering countertransference; rather, the analyst has not understood that the analysand would experience any verbal initiative by the analyst as an intrusion into his or her psychic reality (something one hopes is correctable with further experience). As I have made clear, I do not believe analyst countertransference is normative, so I believe the kind of clinical incident I have just described can happen. Here the point would be to realize that the analyst's good empathic contact during the silence, prior to making the not-valid interpretation, produces more disturbance than if this contact had not existed. A certain kind of very disturbed person will experience great, anxious confusion in such a circumstance (hopefully, in time, to be connected to enormous rage). Another kind of analysand will experience oppressive impingement (Winnicott, e.g., 1953), or another will experience what Kohut (1977) calls narcissistic rage, another deep depression, and so forth. Of course, I recognize that these same disturbing ironies could be understood as contradictions that produce disturbance in a cohesive narrative, or story line, and this would be the approach taken for someone who wants to position psychoanalysis as a hermeneutic enterprise. However, at the least, such examples, which are not esoteric, make clear that the notion of "good narration" has to be stretched beyond what we ordinarily take to mean by telling a good, compelling story.

An objection to what I have been describing to be a special state of analyst's love for the analysand's mind-produced psychic reality could derive from our psychoanalytic concepts of sublimation and idealization. Freud (1905a), early on, understood the process of sublimation to be the way in which our pregenital, libidinal drive aims are transformed into socially useful achievements of one sort or another. And in his paper on narcissism, Freud (1914a) carefully distinguished between sublimation, which has to do with drive aims, and idealization, which has to with an object's elevated love status. Why do I not simply define what I call this special analyst's love for the analysand's mind-produced psychic reality as sublimation? Because as sublimation this analytic attitude (Schafer 1983) is more in line with what Fliess (1942) meant by the analyst's work ego, a very special work to be sure, but not touching on any sort of special experience of analyst love for the analysand.

I do not think this is a viable understanding of the nature of the analyst's work, the peculiar and extraordinary thing about which, if one wants to call it work, is that it is not at all devoted to any sort of *adaptation* (Hartmann 1939). The analyst's work is devoted only to both feeling and understanding the structure and subject matter—the analysand's psychic reality, now lovingly elevated in importance—and the analyst's responsibility is only to desire such understanding. I can return again to the similarity between the analyst's loving devotion to the analysand's psychic reality and the same state of mind in a scholar with regard to some particular subject matter. Odd as it may seem, a scholar is not, in any way, fastened on any desire for adaptation in his or her study of subject matter. All that matters for the scholar is understanding. And I can draw another similarity: the analyst's loving interest in the analysand's mind-produced psychic reality is akin to how one experiences an emotionally moving work of art—all that matters is the experience itself. However, in another way, with the realist position I have maintained in this book, I would insist that the analyst's contemplation of the analysand's psychic reality is not at all like contemplating a work of art. A great work of art can be said to have universal *appeal*, but it is grounded in variable interpretation for the individual observer. It is my conviction that an analysand's psychic reality exists, in some essential manner, as it is, apart from the individual analyst's effort to understand it.

This leads to a still deeper question about the emotional possibilities of this extraordinary psychoanalytic relationship. In order to consider this question, I use a concept given us by Winnicott (1956), that of "primary maternal preoccupation" (p. 300), a real, expectable condition in the mother in which the mother's total psychic life, cognitive and emotional, is absorbed in a rapt, fascinated attention to her infant's thriving. Considered as an object relations experience, the real, special state of mind Freud (1912b) called an analyst's "evenly suspended attention" (p. 111) without "therapeutic ambition" (p. 115) is part and parcel of the loving idealization of the analysand's psychic reality. It is a not-focused-but-encompassing absorption with every detail of the analysand's psychic reality expressed via free associations, and as such it has an affinity with Winnicott's concept. It is easy enough to see how such a real organization of the analyst's subjectivity would facilitate, for the analysand, a deep and early transference experience in which the analyst becomes someone who is holding (Winnicott, e.g., 1960) or is someone who contains (Bion 1962) experiences for the analysand.

But I only use the term *affinity*. Should this kind of evenly suspended, all-absorbing attention, really possessed by the analyst for the analysand's free associations, be construed to be the result of a normative creation within the analyst, even a dynamically unconscious fantasy, that he or she is a mother? Not, I think, in an optimal psychoanalytic relationship. Such a fantasy is an illustration of therapeutic ambition and constitutes a potent source for a suggestive or coercive influence on the clinical process. For one thing, the adult analysand is not a child, but an adult, who certainly may have gifts and talents not possessed by the analyst—so to develop a dynamically unconscious fantasy of mothering is inappropriate. For another, a real mother with a real child takes a natural pleasure and responsibility in her child's *development*. The analyst as analyst only takes a natural pleasure in the analysand's mind production of his or her psychic reality, which, from another "external" perspective, may be assessed to be psychic development. I realize that these comments take exception to Stone's (1961) contention that the analyst is the "mother" of "intimate separation" (p. 86). I only say here, and repeat, Freud's (1915a) claim that the psychoanalytic relationship "is one for which there is no model in real life" (p. 166).

Now, Freud (1915b) called ambivalence a "law" of life, and this special sort of analyst's loving idealization of the analysand's mind can be no exception. But clearly the analyst's general (personality) style of work, what I have termed his or her being used as a medium, has nothing to do with ambivalence, so where does it come into play? According to Winnicott (1949), an ambivalence natural to the psychoanalytic, loving relationship is the analyst's maintenance of a definite period of time for each analytic session. Another example is the analyst's satisfaction in a vacation break away from the analysis. Any other sort of "ordinary" countertransference is a derailment of the psychoanalytic relationship, although such countertransference may still function essentially only as a valuable source of information about what is occurring in the transference experience of the analysand at the moment.

I have, up to this point, only described my belief in the

existence of a (relatively) mature love had by an analyst—as analyst—for his or her analysand's psychic reality in terms of a usual version of Freudian practice.

But how does this relate to the concept of clinical practice advocated by Levenson (1972, or Epstein and Feiner 1979)? As I understand Levenson, there is a fundamental agreement, notwithstanding a fundamental difference. Levenson speaks of the analyst's *"ability* to be trapped, immersed and participating in the system and then to work his way out" (p. 174, italics mine), but I think this must be supported by the kind of analyst love I have described. Levenson's desire and, I would say, loving responsibility is, with words, only to interpret to the analysand to understand what is now happening between them and to them.

But it is another matter with Hoffman and Gill (1988, and Hoffman, e.g., 1993). In the last chapter, I said that Hoffman (e.g., 1992a) ascribes an important therapeutics to circumstances of analyst "expressive participation." Neither I, nor Freudians who believe in a transference–countertransference "unit" of treatment experience, nor, I believe, Levenson, accept this possibility. The opposite view is that the act of interpretation potentiates the therapeutic action of a psychoanalysis (Loewald 1960), that is, makes possible a new object relations experience. But with respect to the "conditions for loving" (Schafer 1983) in a psychoanalytic relationship, Hoffman (1993) says even more:

> I think it undeniable that the boundary between the analyst and the patient defines a relationship that is, in part, hierarchically organized. The psychoanalytic situation can be viewed as a unique kind of contemporary social institution in which one of the two people involved [analyst] has a special kind of power to affect the other. [p. 20]

First, notice that for Hoffman to say that something about human experience is undeniable is an unusually powerful statement. This is because, as I have already described in the last chapter, Hoffman wants a critical constructivism to be the positioning of psychoanalysis.

And I will add the following by Hoffman (1993) about a psychoanalysis:

> Constructive activity goes on in relation to more or less ambiguous givens in the patient's and analyst's experience. In fact, some of these givens are virtually indisputable elements in the experiences of the individuals, and any plausible interpretation would have to take this into account—or at least not contradict them. [pp. 17–18]

So Hoffman has given up (I presume) his earlier agreement with Gill (1985) that "reality is [utterly] relative" (p. 136) and acknowledges an "independent reality" such that certain "givens" in the psychoanalytic relationship are "virtually indisputable." One of these givens is this hierarchically organized boundary between analyst and analysand. Now, he does go on to speak about a "delicate integration" between such a "ritualized asymmetry" and "the patient's perception of the analyst as a person like himself or herself" (p. 22). Nevertheless, when all is said and done, the therapeutics of a psychoanalysis emanates from an analyst's "affirming power," which in turn emanates from this ritualized asymmetry. Here is Hoffman's pertinent commentary:

> The source of that power is precisely in the ritualized asymmetry that promotes a view of the analyst as superior, in some sense, and as beyond the patient's reach. In that context the analyst's emotional and personal availability can become a kind of magical gift that is assimilated in a manner that has continuity with (although it is hardly equivalent to) the way that the love of parents is assimilated in childhood. *You might argue that there is something magical associated with one person winning the love of another no matter what the circumstances, and I would agree that what I am talking about is very closely related to the experience of love in other contexts.* However, I am arguing that the analyst's personal involvement in the analytic situation has, potentially, a particular kind of concentrated power because it is embedded in a ritual in which the analyst is set up to be a certain kind of authority. [p. 22, italics mine]

Hoffman believes he finds support for this conception of the
therapeutic notion of a psychoanalysis in Freud's (1926b)
description of the analyst as a "secular counselor." Even
more, Hoffman is correct that Freud (1915a), as I also
indicated in the last chapter, conceived every sort of love,
childlike or (relatively) mature, to bring about states of
compliance and/or effects through suggestion. Here,
Hoffman uses this comment by Freud (1916): "Love is the
great educator; and it is by love of those nearest him that the
incomplete human being is induced to respect the degrees of
necessity" (p. 312). But just as I have taken exception to
Freud, I do not agree with Hoffman that the affirming power
of a psychoanalysis, that is, its therapeutic action, is "lever-
aged" by such childlike inducement.

One is, however, never done with Freud. Freud (1912b)
also said about the therapeutic action of psychoanalysis in a
context of the analysis of transference that "psychoanalytic
treatment is founded upon truthfulness. In this fact lies
a great deal of its educative effect and its ethical value"
(p. 164). Here, once again, Freud is asserting his correspondence doctrine of truth and realism positioning for psychoanalysis. It is not that love is absent in the therapeutic action
of psychoanalysis. But it is a (relatively) mature love of both
individuals in the psychoanalytic relationship for each other
that animates and is conjoined with a search for a particular
truth. The analysand's mature (love) transference (Stone
1961, 1967) is for an analyst who, in reality, is as he or she
really is, and lovingly desires and takes on the responsibility
only to understand the analysand's (especially dynamically
unconscious) psychic reality. This is why I say that every act
of analyst interpretation is an expression of such a love, and
it is only interpretation in a psychoanalysis through which a
therapeutic action may occur. So there is nothing "magical"
about the analysand's "winning the love of another [the
analyst] no matter what the circumstances" (Hoffman 1993,
p. 22). The analyst's loving desire really is only to know

every nook and cranny of the analysand's psychic reality. This analysand psychic reality now is elevated, as is true for any loved object, and this ensures that an analysand has the analyst's love. The analyst's own self—as analyst—is narcissistically suffused and enhanced as is true for all love (Steingart 1983).

Levenson (1972), I suspect, would regard the idea of magic as something that contributes to "mystification." Working within a more-or-less-usual Freudian concept of clinical process, I would agree. But I understand the issue more in terms of Schafer's (1983) "conditions of loving" (p. 113), that is, a differentiation, and availability, of the analysand's childlike transference love contrasted with this same analysand's mature (love) transference. Both these sorts of love are continuously "met" by the analyst's (relatively) mature love for the analysand's mind-produced psychic reality. This psychic reality is to be interpretively understood by the minutia, the unexpected, the perverse, the beautiful, whatever, of the analysand's free associations, all now idealized as loved objects as is true for any love. If all that Hoffman wants to say is that such an analyst's love cannot be perfect, this, of course, is true. But it is part of a mature love to realize and accept that such maturity is imperfect, that no relationship is completely rational for both analyst and analysand.

But Hoffman also means something else: that the "analyst's involvement"—other than and in addition to interpretation—is "important and consequential in its own right" (p. 18) for the therapeutics of psychoanalysis. This analyst involvement, for Hoffman, is something other than the inevitable constraints and opportunities of the individual analyst's work style interacting with an individual analysand's potentialities for the fullest expression of his or her psychic reality. Hoffman (1992a) seems to mean, rather, that various sorts of analyst expressive participation are as necessary as interpretation in the expression of this love. Not to believe this, for Hoffman (1993), is "intrinsically irrational" and does "violence to human nature" (p. 22). Neither I, nor Loewald (1960), nor Schafer (e.g., 1983) agree. Nor do other Freudian analysts agree (e.g., Jacobs 1991, McLaughlin 1981, Renik 1993) who work with an idea of clinical process that conceives of transference and countertransference as a clinical "unit."

Hoffman's concept of clinical practice is, understandably, organic with his vision of what it is to have a human existence. It is a social-relational core vision of human existence. This is not the same as a vision of a human existence that is organic with a concept of a psychoanalytic relationship in which a possible therapeutics is enabled essentially by analyst interpretation and not by any other sort of expressive participation. This view is that a human existence has at its core a solitude—not to be confused with non- or asocial experience—but nevertheless a solitude. I want to cite Hanly (1990) in this regard: "In the end, each person has only his own life, however shared with others. At the core of the being of each person there is a solitude in which he is related to himself . . . the ground of genuine analytic work is his attitude of respect for this solitude" (p. 382). It is the Freudian analyst's mature love for this analysand solitude that naturally makes the analyst want to bound his or her possible real therapeutics within the expression of interpretation. Hoffman might say that what I have just said is, at best, an illusion, and, at worst, inhuman. I would answer that his belief that a ritualized asymmetry, something magical, is as critical for the therapeutics of a psychoanalysis as interpretation exactly takes away from a psychoanalysis the thing that makes it unique. But Freud himself did not sufficiently realize that in devising psychoanalysis he created conditions for an extraordinary, (relatively) mature love relationship that exactly exorcises magic because its ambition is only to know. That an analyst brings his individual work style, and theory, to this extraordinary loving relationship complicates but does not contradict the reality of this love.

TRANSFERENCE AT TERMINATION

Obviously, at the termination phase of a reasonably successful analysis, we can expect a significant degree of working through of the problems that brought the analysand for treatment. Also, we can expect that at termination the analysand can now do for him- or herself what analyst and analysand did together. Put another way, a psychoanalytic process is, now, a useful instrument for self-analysis for the analysand. This is the termination outcome of what Loewald (1960) means when he describes how, in a psychoanalysis, the analysand is increasingly "an associate, as it were, in the research work" (p. 227). But it will come as no surprise that I want to add something else: at termination the analysand will have obtained—really deeply identified with—a (relatively) mature love for the way he or she uses his or her mind to create a psychic reality. This analytic self-love at termination is the very opposite of a childish narcissism. It is a kind of narcissism; but it is a narcissism that involves a sober realization of how clinically unhealthy potentialities within can do damage not only to the analysand but to significant loved others. At the same time, this analytic narcissism excludes, or, at least, should significantly modify, both self-punishing and "interminable" (Freud 1937a) tendencies to repeat psychopathology (Freud, e.g., 1914c). This analytically obtained narcissism is, we might say, human sized. Also, the termination phase of a reasonably successful analysis should include the analysis of analysand transference experience about this real but extraordinary loving had by the analyst for the analysand's way of using his or her mind to create psychic reality. Obviously, it is a mistake to minimize the emotionality for the analyst involved in the need to terminate this loving attitude; giving it up amounts to losing a loved other.

Another question has to do with how to characterize the status of transference experience at termination. It cannot be the goal of the psychoanalysis to do away with the particular psychosexual and aggressive themes that have informed the variety of transference experiences lived through in a psychoanalysis. I make a distinction here between a psychodynamic theme and how such a theme may, or may not, be caught up in a conflict-driven repetition compulsion (Freud 1920b). For instance, a society will use humor to realize eternal love and hate themes about human existence and to apply such themes to whatever or whoever is significant and emergent in that society's development. We are not surprised to find jokes about the astronauts, the current president and his family, inflation and recession, whomever and whatever; we expect a society's humor to be au courant.

It is the same with the psychodynamic themes that have been interpretively revealed in the analysand's transference experiences and that analysand's future development after termination. What is a reasonable goal for a psychoanalysis is to significantly free up and transform transference themes from the repetition compulsion so that the analysand now can bring an enlivened but not pathological self-awareness to the realities of his or her existence. Each of us brings our own particular transference tragedies and farces to the realities of our lives, transference themes that are larger than actual life, but that can in a special, unreal way inform us about who we are, what we have been through, and to what we aspire. Transference themes can become a source of enrichment in the face of the realities of our lives because they provide a personal significance above and beyond such realities. This view is congruent with the more general perspective about unreal experience stated by Loewald (1975): "But fantasy is unreal only insofar as its communication with present actuality is inhibited or severed" (p. 362). And Loewald adds, specifically with respect to transference:

> The resolution of the transference neurosis surely does not consist of renewed repression or any ultimate relinquishment of recovered memories and fantasies, but of employing them, revived and made available for development and change in the transference play, in actual living. [pp. 367–368]

These last words by Loewald—"in actual living"—I believe to be identical with my idea that a reasonably successful transference resolution involves a useful integration of unreal personal significance into the realities of one's life. A statement by Winnicott (1971a) seems similar: "The work done by the therapist is directed toward bringing the patient from the state of not being able to play to a state of being able to play" (p. 38). Of course, what Winnicott and Loewald have in mind here is a state of healthy play or fantasy. Thus, not only is it impossible for a psychoanalysis to eliminate transference themes, even to conceive of such a possibility is inhuman, and this naturally applies as well to the analyst-at-work.

NOTES

1. This is why, unlike Brenner (1985), I believe it is necessary to retain the term *counter*transference. Such experience normatively is expected to vary in a psychoanalytic relationship.

2. There is, obviously, something to consider here about a difference between a psychoanalysis and either an expressive or supportive psychotherapy relationship; but to do this is not related to my present interest.

4

The Psychic Reality of Enacted Symbols

In psychoanalysis what we call acting out has always been tied to some idea of "discharge"—that is, a discharge of "energy" or "tension" that operates against any possibility of achieving insight (e.g., Freud 1905b, 1914c, 1915e). Our human (especially brain) neurophysiology simply and fundamentally does not function to discharge any such tension (e.g., Pribram 1989). But in "Beyond the Pleasure Principle," when Freud (1920b) transformed his concept of libido into a life instinct, he changed his prior thinking. Now, at least, one fundamental function of the human nervous system had to do with an individual's natural inclination to develop, that is, to achieve even more complex psychic structure and function (see esp. Loewald 1971a). But Freud also retained his original notion of discharge and brought it to a kind of sober, ultimate conclusion with his introduction of the concept of a death instinct.

Because acting out always has been so tied to this idea of discharge, it has not been conceived to be an expression of a possible, genuine, mental *symbolic* activity, in other words, not a legitimate or genuine mind product. Acting out thus does not appear to be "deserving" of that analyst love for the analysand's mind, and every manner of psychic reality the analysand produces with his or her mind, discussed in the last chapter. Acting out, classically, has not been

viewed— incorrectly I believe—to be a type of expression of
an analysand's psychic reality.

All of this produces an "analytic attitude" (Schafer 1983)
that must only consider acting out to work against a psychoanalysis. Consequently, acting out is prohibited, or, at least,
expressly discouraged, by the analyst. Put another way, an
analyst cannot feel free to empathically situate him- or
herself in the analysand's psychic reality in a circumstance of
acting out. The result is a treatment relationship that is
precisely what a psychoanalysis should not be: now the
analyst really is attempting to exercise mind control over the
analysand.

I conceive that what is happening in an analysand's
psychic reality in a circumstance of acting out essentially can
be appreciated as one would symbols expressed by verbal
free associations. And for this reason, I want to replace the
term *acting out* with the concept of *enacted symbol*. At the
same time, I want to express a certain constraint with respect
to the use of this concept. The term *enactment* enjoys an
ever-increasing popularity in our literature (e.g., Jacobs 1991,
McLaughlin 1981, Renik 1993), risking a kind of conceptual
promiscuity. It is not to be equated with some general notion
of wanting to influence the analyst—every sort of expression
by an analysand is a desire to influence the analyst in one
way or another; it is not to be equated with a specific notion
of "communication" such as can only be achieved through an
authentic use of language; it is not the same as various kinds
of characterological nonverbal expressiveness, for example,
an analysand who characteristically rubs his chin, which
have become functionally autonomous (Hartmann 1939)
from dynamically unconscious experience (fantasies); it is
not the same as analysand nonverbal expressiveness, which
still remains only a physiognomic apprehension of experience (Werner and Kaplan 1963), say, a typical constriction of
body movement on the couch, which has never achieved a
symbolic representation (Bucci 1994). I mean by enacted

symbol the expression, either consciously or dynamically unconsciously, of a symbolic vehicle that incorporates an urge for action of one sort or another in the psychoanalytic relationship. Language, every sort of language used in the psychoanalytic relationship, can also serve as enacted symbol. These distinctions I have just cited are not always easy to make in the clinical process. But they are real and important distinctions with respect to the organization of an analysand's psychic reality and require different kinds of clinical interpretation to promote, eventually, authentically verbal insight as "higher psychical organization" (Freud 1915e, p. 202). I already have argued for a differentiation between an analyst's work style versus an analyst's possible countertransference. Now I would add that I do not think it useful to conceive that all countertransference is enacted symbol. Countertransference, as well as transference, may or may not be enacted symbol.

I want to make what I have just said tangible, and to do this I want to make extended use of some rich, clinical material supplied by Jacobs (1991). Jacobs describes the first session with an analysand, Mr. V., as follows:

> A few seconds after the buzzer sounded announcing his arrival, I started for the waiting room to greet him. I did not get far. When I opened the door of my office, there he was, filling the entranceway, standing not more than a few inches in front of me. Nodding curtly, he swept into the room like a linebacker blitzing the quarterback, took off his jacket and stretched out on the couch. I was stunned. I felt as though I had opened the door to a tornado which, within seconds, had ripped through my office, leaving in its wake a disquieting and eerie calm. [p. 33]

Then Jacobs describes how, in this first analytic session, Mr. V. in a "modulated controlled voice" (p. 33) described a plan to get revenge on an employee Mr. V. felt was "infringing on his territory." Mr. V. went on to say how this employee would "forever be his enemy" and that Mr. V. "would go out

of his way to make his [the employee's] life miserable."
Jacobs then became aware of his own experience while
listening to this free association material expressed by Mr.
V., as follows:

> I found myself sitting forward in my chair, my musculature tense,
> my eyes fixed on the patient as he lay remarkably still on the couch.
> Watching him I was reminded of the famous painting by Rousseau
> which depicts a large tiger, eyes burning, lying among high grasses,
> waiting to spring. But who was that tiger? Viewing the immobile
> figure in front of me who, in muted tones, spoke of stark vengeance
> and observing myself, the concealed analyst, listening in a state of
> tension, poised to interpret my patient's covert aggression, I could
> not be sure. [p. 34]

"Clearly," Jacobs continues,

> *important transactions* were occurring between Mr. V. and myself.
> Swiftly, aggressively, he had moved into the office, pushing past me
> and evoking in me the feeling that my space was being invaded.
> Then, lying on the couch and speaking in tones of easy cordiality, he
> revealed in what he said that he was an angry, vengeful person.
> *Through enactments of my own, expressed in bodily posture and vocal
> quality, I was responding to him not only with protective vigilance, but
> with an unconscious need to appease this menacing figure.* This latter
> reaction I recognized through my manner of interpreting. Ratio-
> nally, I understood that beneath his anger, behind the wish to strike
> back and hurt others, was a wounded man. Physically and mentally
> brutalized by a disturbed and vicious older brother, he had been left
> unprotected by troubled and ineffectual parents. Unable to defend
> himself, he had also been sexually used by this brother. Hating him
> and yet drawn to seek his approval, Mr. V. sought desperately to
> wrench from his heart and mind the image of the man who had
> tortured him and to whom he felt hopelessly attached. [p. 34, italics
> mine]

Jacobs then goes on to describe how Mr. V.'s parents did not
protect him from his older brother's emotional and physical
attacks.

When, in time, I understood this aspect of Mr. V.'s history, I sought opportunities to bring to the fore not only the anger that smoldered beneath his surface charm but, more specifically, the feelings of hurt that fed it. When I spoke in sessions, my voice was calm, its tone soothing as I tried to convey my understanding of the trauma that Mr. V. had experienced. *Such an approach to someone who was responding to life with the rage of a wounded animal was, perhaps, not inappropriate.* But as I listened to myself, I realized that my voice contained more than simply an effort to convey empathy. It contained a familiar undertone of fear; an attempt to appease and mollify which concealed an unconscious and *encoded* response to an angry man. It was the protective reaction I had, as a child, to my father's rages. [p. 35, italics mine]

Finally:

Recognizing this piece of countertransference helped me gain an under-standing of just how menacing I experienced Mr. V. to be and how anxious he made me. What I was not yet fully in touch with was the extent of the anger that his behavior mobilized in me. This reaction surfaced in response to a series of enactments carried out by both patient and analyst in the course of treatment. [p. 36]

One cannot imagine an analyst more sensitively in tune than is Jacobs in this circumstance. His reminiscences about his own father, who could express rages, had become activated, initially out of Jacobs's awareness; but then, with increasing self-analysis, these reminiscences became not only conscious but available for a countertransference realization.

However, notice the way Jacobs uses the terms *transactions,* *enactments,* and *countertransference* interchangeably. Also, while he does not do so in this material, Jacobs would, I believe, as easily use the term *communication* to describe the interplay of these influences between Mr. V. and himself. The title of Jacobs's (1991) book on this subject contains the subtitle *Countertransference and Communication in the Analytic Situation.* Notice also that Jacobs states that his calm and soothing voice tone "to someone who was responding to life with the rage of a wounded animal *was perhaps not inappro-*

priate" (p. 35, italics mine). Perhaps it was not inappropriate. But then, that it was a countertransference experience suffered (ego) passively by Jacobs I am not inclined to believe. Jacobs's calm and soothing tone need not necessarily be countertransference, even though he had similar fearful experiences with his own father, who exposed Jacobs to rages. Put another way, a calm and soothing tone could achieve a secondary, functional autonomy (Hartmann 1939) and become, simply, part of an analyst's work style. On the other hand, Mr. V., manifestly, in expressing himself in a "modulated constrained voice" was isolated from his own rage and fear. Countertransference could be considered *if* Jacobs's calm and soothing tone obviated interpretation about the emotional isolation (or splitting). But since this did not occur, according to Jacobs's description, what is gained by using a concept of countertransference? Jacobs's own reminiscences simply facilitated interpretation. And what would be added by the terms *enactment* or *communication?* What has transpired initially is that Jacobs and his analysand have influenced each other by a nonverbal symbolic means, as well as by subsymbolic effects, a physiognomic apprehension (Werner and Kaplan 1963, Bucci 1994). I do not believe these considerations to be irrelevant minutiae. It then becomes the task of Jacobs, as analyst, either to reconnect or to transform this nonsymbolic and nonverbal expressiveness into that higher physical organization (Freud 1915e, p. 202; and see Loewald 1960) enabled by language.

Actually, Jacobs (1991) does describe incidents that occurred in the analysis of Mr. V. that pertain to my use of the concept of an enacted symbol. I must cite Jacobs at length to do full justice to the productive clinical process enabled by the way in which he deals with these enacted symbols.

> Both enactments involved magazines and both contained important aspects of memory as well as being expressions of current conflict. One evening after work, when I was straightening up the waiting room of an office to which I had recently moved, I came across

something unusual. I noticed that the mailing labels on two magazines had been torn off. Investigating further, I realized that the magazines from which the labels had been removed were ones that had been forwarded from my old office. Several other magazines which contained the correct mailing labels had been left untouched. [p. 36]

"One day," Jacobs continues,

as I opened my office door to Mr. V., I saw him rolling a small piece of white paper between thumb and forefinger. Quickly he put the scrap into his pocket and, as usual, charged into the office. I said nothing to him then, but after his hour checked the magazines. The label from another magazine, one that had recently been forwarded through the mail, was missing. Now I had my man. It was Mr. V.

I was puzzling over how best to raise this sensitive issue with my patient when still another unusual event took place. A subscription to a magazine I had not ordered arrived at my office. This was a special interest publication devoted to a topic about which I had little knowledge. While it is not unusual for me, like many physicians, to receive unsolicited mail, including occasional throwaway magazines, this, clearly, was not one of those offerings. Casually, I scanned the pages, read through the table of contents, and realizing quickly that I had neither sufficient time nor interest to do more than that, I left the magazine in the waiting room for others to enjoy.

I then returned to my office and reviewed some notes while waiting for my next patient, Mr. V., to arrive. It was no more than thirty seconds before he rang the bell that the flash realization hit me: it was Mr. V. who had sent me this subscription. The topic that the magazine covered was one of special interest to him and represented one of his few avocations. He had spoken of this interest only a few times in analysis and on each occasion, quite briefly. When he did, however, I had noticed an enthusiasm for the subject which in other aspects of his life was notably absent. Quickly I retrieved the magazine from the waiting room and that night, after work, set myself the task of attempting to understand what I could of the interplay of enactments between Mr. V. and myself that, suddenly, had taken the center of the analytic stage.

It soon became clear that the episodes involving the magazines were connected and that each was a beacon signaling the presence in both analyst and patient of affects and fantasies that were being actualized in treatment but had not reached the consciousness of either. From time to time in analysis Mr. V. had mentioned the fact that his father's business had folded when he (Mr. V.) was an adolescent and that, as a result, the family had fallen on hard days. While he spoke of the shame he felt about his father's business failure and the wide reverberations it had on his family, Mr. V. never described exactly what had happened. In fact he avoided specifics, and when this omission was pointed out to him he claimed that the details of that troubled period were lost to memory. In fact, Mr. V. had managed to drive out of awareness much that belonged to that turbulent time. And what he did recall he found difficult to reveal.

Now as we discussed Mr. V.'s behavior in removing the mailing labels and explored its meaning, memories surfaced which had not appeared before. *The fact that his "crime" was dealt with not punitively but with an effort to understand it may have helped him to become more open.* In any case, Mr. V. spoke of the discomfort he felt when he noticed that some of the mailing labels contained my old address. Seeing unfamiliar faces in the waiting room and concluding I must have some new patients who did not know that I had moved from another address, he felt a sudden impulse to remove the mailing labels that would reveal that fact. Such information was private, he thought, and was no one's business. In acting as he did, Mr. V. imagined he was protecting my privacy.

As he described his feelings and the action that he felt compelled to carry out, Mr. V. recalled two other occasions when he had behaved in a similar way. The first incident occurred in adolescence and was connected to his father's loss of his business. What Mr. V. had not mentioned in his initial description of this event was that his father's decline was the result of his having been convicted of a white collar crime. It was this situation and its consequences that forced the closing of the business and precipitated the family calamity. For several years Mr. V. was shielded from the truth and it was only when he inadvertently came across some old legal papers in a desk drawer that he learned what had happened. So shaken was he by the discovery and so angry at being kept in the dark, that he tore the papers to shreds. He then disposed of the fragments and said nothing to anyone about what he had done.

The second incident occurred some years later when Mr. V. was working in a government office that dealt with criminal matters. One evening after work, when the office was empty, Mr. V. went to the files, removed the folder containing records of his father's case, and destroyed them. He felt a need to obliterate all traces of the crime.

In removing the mailing labels Mr. V. was not only enacting an old scenario and reliving pieces of history in the transference, but was expressing both his fantasy that I possessed shameful secrets that I was loathe to reveal and a wish to keep hidden certain impulses and fantasies of his own.

Sending me a subscription to a magazine he valued was also a complex and multidetermined act. On one level, it represented an apology and an atonement for Mr. V.'s behavior in destroying the mailing labels. As a youngster he had been tortured by feelings of guilt for having destroyed the legal papers, for secretly regarding his father with contempt, and for the realization of a childhood wish to see him go down in defeat.

In a similar way, Mr. V. felt guilty for having tampered with my property, but as was true in childhood, his guilt had deeper sources. Secretly he disparaged my new office, my clothes, and my speech. He regarded himself as superior to me and in his *fantasies* he often defeated me in contests of one kind or another. Regarding my new office as a stepdown from the old one, he saw in this change evidence of my decline and experienced a sense of triumph. Thus for Mr. V., sending me a subscription was an effort to atone for all of the unacceptable feelings toward me that he harbored. In addition, Mr. V. wanted me to know that he was a man of broad interests. Believing that I shared those interests, he wanted to let me know that we had much in common. Indirectly he also wished to let me know that in addition to the negative feelings that he harbored toward me there were also some positive ones, and he wanted me to like him. These positive feelings embarrassed and frightened Mr. V. and it was only through an enactment that they could be expressed.

For my part, I was aware, as I have noted, of a certain feeling of tension as I worked with Mr. V. and of a vigilance expressed in my posture and mode of listening. The extent, however, to which the undercurrent of violence in him and the subtle ways in which he conveyed his competitiveness and hostility had evoked in me a counterreaction of anger and a wish to strike back had not surfaced until my behavior in leaving the magazine in the waiting room made clear that I, like his parents and brother, was acting in a rejecting way toward him. [pp. 36–39]

Notice, Jacobs's consideration that the fact that Mr. V.'s "crime" was not dealt with "punitively" but only with an effort to understand, *to analyze*, "may have helped him [Mr. V.] to become more open" (p. 38). Can anyone doubt this? These enactments by Mr. V. were treated by Jacobs exactly as an analyst would treat manifest verbal free association. Jacobs simply and naturally situated himself within the psychic reality of his analysand. Then, together, Jacobs and his analysand came to analyze a critical panoply of reminiscences with respect to the analysand's experiences with his father, conjoined with love-hate in the current transference. For his part, Jacobs now came to believe that in his returning the analysand's "gift" magazine subscription to the waiting room, he was enacting a rejection toward his own ambivalently experienced father via countertransference toward the analysand. I agree with this assessment inasmuch as Jacobs knew—but had momentarily forgotten—that the magazine content was of special interest to the analysand. Transference-enacted symbols, understandably, can "pull" in this way for countertransference-enacted symbols, if countertransference is going to occur.

But something has happened here that is so transparent that its clinical significance can be overlooked. First of all, these "magazine" symbolic enactments were just that: symbolic vehicles through which critical reminiscences and current transference were being represented. Second, these enacted symbols were now—had become—connected and transformed into a "higher psychical organization" (Freud 1915e, p. 202; and see Loewald 1960). Third, in his initial acceptance and eventual desire only to understand these magazine enactments, Jacobs expresses, I believe, the only viable analytic attitude an analyst can possess in such a circumstance. If, however benignly, or without countertransference, Jacobs had expressed any sort of negative assessment toward the analysand over his actions, a productive clinical process would have become damaged.

In the next two sections, I will develop this framework. One can conceive the analysand's psychic reality in such a circumstance of enacted symbolism to be like that of a pre-oedipal or oedipal-aged child. This kind of mentality is especially made evident by the young child at play. Consequently, I consider (conceive) that a transference experience so organized with this kind of mentality is a kind of "pathological play." I use the term *pathological* because the organization of this kind of transference experience altogether, and enacted symbols in particular, are an attempt to construe the actual psychoanalytic relationship *to be* the transference experience (positive or negative). Jacobs describes Mr. V. to have "fantasies . . . [in which] . . . he often defeated me in contests of one kind or another" (p. 39). I do not dispute that an analysand who uses transferential enacted symbols, as did Mr. V., can also possess a capacity for such a fantasy. But only with some analysands will such fantasy suffice, and it is this condition for which psychoanalysis was classically conceived.

TRANSFERENCE AS PATHOLOGICAL PLAY

A transference organization that involves enacted symbols could not have escaped the notice of the person who initially conceived of transference. In Freud's (1915a) third paper on technique, devoted to transference love, he first describes the working through of transference, together with genetic reminiscences, as it occurs in an analysis, ordinarily conceived. Then, Freud states:

> There is, it is true, one class of women with whom the attempt to preserve the erotic transference without *satisfying* it will not succeed. These are women of elemental passionateness who tolerate no substitutes. *They are children of nature who refuse to accept the psychical in place of the material,* who, in the poet's words, are accessible only to "the logic of soup with dumplings for arguments." With such people one has the choice between returning their love or else bringing down on oneself the full enmity of a woman scorned. One

has to withdraw, unsuccessful, and all one can do is turn the problem over in one's mind of *how it is that a capacity for neurosis is joined with such an intractable need for love.* [p. 167 italics mine][1]

Freud does not describe details of this kind of analysand transference experience and behavior. But I think his implication is clear when he talks about how the analyst can experience a forced "choice" between "returning their love" versus "bringing down on oneself the full enmity of a woman scorned." Stated differently, and in terms of the framework developed here, there is a "class" of transference—I would say shaped neither like neurotic nor schizophrenic organization—in which the analysand may provoke the analyst into a struggle over transference construals of experience. The women Freud describes want to make out of agreed-upon observation—that Freud's response to them is only with language and only to use language to interpret transference experience—that Freud in fact is repeating the love rejection of the transference experience. Also important, and I believe implied by the overall context of the paper, is that these women "who refuse to accept the psychical" are in possession of some kind of enlarged psychic reality as it concerns the transference experience. This is to say that such a woman's transference construal that Freud is rejecting her love occurs together with a meaningful awareness of reminiscences pertinent to the transference dynamics of the rejection experienced with Freud in the psychoanalysis.

It is worthwhile to repeat certain of Freud's comments. First, he notes how the analyst has to "withdraw" and remain "unsuccessful"; second, how the analyst must puzzle over how such a "capacity for neurosis is joined with such an intractable need for love" (p. 167). Jacobs (1991), whose productive clinical work with Mr. V.'s "magazine"-enacted symbols I have just described, neither withdrew nor responded with a prohibition (however benign). He simply analyzed Mr. V.'s transference experience now organized with enacted symbols. However, here Freud is meeting the (so-called) eroticized transference, and without doubt this is a more difficult circumstance for a psychoanalysis. I suspect that Freud erroneously diagnosed these female analysands as neurotic, their problem simply some "intractable need for love" (p. 167). I suspect as well that these women were either narcissistically disturbed or borderline analysands, and the clinical problem centered on the organization of their transference construals of the reality of the psychoanalytic relationship. I say "suspect" because I agree with Blum (1973) that such eroticized transference can occur among neurotic women, or men. At the same time, Blum himself, and others, understand that intractable eroticized transference can also express an "altered" sense of reality (Dickes 1965). This special, altered state is what I will go on to develop as a transference experience organized as pathological play. Also very important is Blum's (1973) report that dynamically unconscious sadomasochistic dynamics can underlie eroticized transference.

Weiss (1942), 25 years after Freud, dealt with this same problem about "patients in analysis [who] often act out emotional situations which they have already remembered" (p. 490). I believe Weiss made an important contribution to this matter, and this was his use of certain of Federn's (e.g., 1926) ideas about the ego, and "ego feeling." Specifically, for Weiss, "ego feeling must be distinguished from analysand consciousness" (p. 481). And Weiss states further, "Ego feeling is an additional feeling to consciousness and only those *functions* invested with this feeling are felt to be normally with the ego" (p. 481). Where this leads us is to a realization that only if reminiscences pertinent to a transference experience occur with a certain organization of consciousness (enabling a certain type of ego feeling) can an analysand come to possess a transference in a way that, at least potentially, enables a working through in a psychoanalysis, classically conceived. If not, what can occur is another type of enlargement of psychic reality, which includes a sense of conviction that the transference experience is not just similar to reminiscences but really being relived by virtue of the analyst's actual relationship to the analysand.[2]

Obviously, this is not the classic analysis conceived by Freud (e.g., 1914c). In the classical conception: (1) What occurs at first is only transference repetition. The analysand has experience of the analyst-as-a-person that is not informed—which is to say such experience is not consciously realized into some larger psychic reality related to reminiscences—and such experience is admitted into the psychoanalytic relationship as in a "playground" (Freud 1914c). (2) What was at first only repetitious transference "material" changes into something "psychical"—that is, informed and informative for a larger, more complex, analysand psychic reality—but this by virtue of the, actually, only verbal interpretive relationship extended by the analyst to the analysand, enabling (3) the possibility of working through all that is meant by transference neurosis. Of course, all of this is relative for any particular analysand–analyst relationship, but it is nevertheless important and valid to describe the array of events because it is just such a process that is considered to be clinically normative in a classically conceived psychoanalysis; indeed, it was the absence of this kind of unfolding that caught Freud's (1915a) early attention when he spoke about a type of transference love that did not follow such an expectable line of development.[3] Put another way, and in a way stated by Sedler (1983), what does not occur are those clinically normatively expected "complementary" forms of memory expressed by transference repetition versus transference recollection. I return again to Freud's (1914c) simile of transference-as-playground. I can say that, contrary to clinically normative expectations, what occurs here is that the enlarged psychic reality obtained by the analysand through the psychoanalysis serves only to further support a sense of conviction that what transpires in the transference playground is something real that occurs because of the actual psychoanalytic relationship; and this prevents a working through of transference experience (a clinically normatively expected resolution of the transference neurosis).

Shortly I will propose and examine the proposition that it is language—language-mediated experience of both the real and unreal transference psychoanalytic relationship—that makes such a clinically normative progression so problematic for certain individuals. But first let me provide two examples from my own practice of what I call pathologically playful transference; these examples illustrate how language can acquire a problematic status in a psychoanalytic relationship. One example involves action per se; the second involves language that has become recruited into action.

First example:[4]

A young woman in psychotherapy employed massive splitting and denial in order to avoid a profound ambivalence conflict with me. She harbored enormous hate and a desire to destroy me. But this was directly evident only in two kinds of very occasional, conscious thoughts: first, she could have the thought that my "penis is on fire," and second, that a pipe pick, almost always in view, was pushed into the opening of my penis. She always became quite disturbed by such thoughts, and any attempt I made to discuss why the thoughts would occur was vigorously resisted. She simply refused to discuss it. Treatment almost exclusively was sitting up, and this had been her choice. She expressed anxiety about how overwhelmingly disorganized she expected she would become if she were to lie down on the couch. Also, she said that for her to even think about lying on the couch produced a feeling of such intense humiliation and degradation that she could not "submit" herself to it.

One day the patient announced, as she walked into the room, that she wanted to sit on my desk while she talked. I offered no objection but asked if she had any idea why she wanted to do this. She responded, immediately, with no smile or any other expression that might indicate embarrassment, "Then I'll be bigger than you."

The patient then described an experience that she later said would have felt too humiliating to talk about without benefit of the change in the physical relationship between us. We discussed the experience itself, which involved the loss of her own separate viewpoint (existence) in the physical presence of her mother, and her use of this kind of illusionary rearrangement of our bodies to avoid intense humiliation over telling me about the incident. The humiliation she expected to feel would be another kind of merger experience, now with me, but me as a derisive father transference figure who would belittle her lack of separateness from her mother. This would occur if she only talked to me about the incident in her usual chair. Therefore, she wanted to believe she was separate and bigger than I by physically elevating her body in relationship to me. After this discussion the woman returned to her chair of her own accord.

Second example:

This illustration is not a case of mine but one I supervised. The analysand, who continuously used the couch, is a 31-year-old woman, an editor and published poet, from a lower-middle-class Irish Catholic background, whose early education was in parochial schools. The analysand made a serious suicide attempt just before the first summer vacation break, that is, prior to her first extended separation from her analyst.

After a year of treatment, the analysand produced the first poem she had been able to write in several years, and about this she said, "The words are there; all I have to do is find them." It was the session after this that the analysand suggested that the analyst should not "say a god-damned thing, for a week maybe?" And she also said, "Why don't you shut up and let me be the boss." The analyst did not respond, actually feeling nonplussed and not sure whether or not to agree. The analyst already had remained silent for three sessions, at which time I saw her for supervision, and we agreed that her already established silence amounted to tacit consent for the remainder of the week.

After a week, the analysand asked to continue the arrangement. The possibility of such a second request had been considered in supervision, and we concluded that the analyst should speak at such a time and say she would agree to a continuation of the arrangement. However, I also suggested that the analyst add that she would speak if she believed there was an important reason to do so, and that she would explain the reason. After five more sessions, the analysand herself asked for the arrangement to stop.

Examples of transference material expressed in this period: "All of these years being silenced [i.e., she felt this to be true at home as a child] and now I'm silencing you. Why? . . . wanting control . . . I don't know if turning the tables will help. Amazing feeling to do this . . . so much in this room connected to everything else. Getting my own way like a terrible two-year-old . . . I feel omnipotent . . . feel as if a lot of what I'm doing is childish. Worried about going too far." This last statement was followed by the analysand's elaboration of a lesbian, sadomasochistic scene she had seen on television. An example of transference material connected spon-taneously to some personal school history and what is probably a screen memory: "They didn't give me a gold star in the first grade because I talked to a little boy. Never talked at the wrong time again. Silenced! At the end of the month going to give you [i.e., the analyst] a gold star."

The analysand indicated there were two events that made her want to stop the special arrangement: Her sister "pooh-poohed" an outburst of rage directed at her by the analysand by sending a Christmas card to the analysand saying "Merry Christmas anyway, silly." Also, the analysand's immediate boss, a woman, forgot that the analysand went to Boston on business; this was a trip the analysand felt she submissively had agreed to make, although her own belief was that the trip would not be worth the effort. The analysand, herself, interpreted how these two events had crushed her belief in her own omnipotence and control, so that this special illusionary transference arrangement also could not now be maintained. The analyst agreed with this interpretation.

It is instructive to examine these two vignettes for similarities and differences. The "desktop" incident was an occurrence in an ongoing intensive psychotherapy relationship that (selectively) focused on problematic areas of adaptation arising out of this woman's early and profound conflicts over separation-individuation. What should be stressed is that this incident, while it obviously involved the analysand's making of an illusion, nevertheless was used by the analysand to articulate a more realistic perspective about herself and her relationship with significant other people. She used this illusionary incident to investigate what had happened to her in the presence of her mother and to consolidate the real separateness of her experience and needs from those of her mother. What also could be observed was the patient's use of the illusion to maintain with me a collaborative, rational examination of her experience with her mother and to not allow the therapy experience to succumb into an unreal, crushing, humiliating experience with me as a sadistically critical father. Most important also, in this connection, was the patient's language. The language with which she expressed herself throughout the desktop incident was focused in form and problem solving in function; it was more effective than her usual rambling way of talking (rambling not to be confused with free-associational language, for which she had absolutely no tolerance).

The second, "enforced silence" circumstance, in which the analysand entertained an illusion of omnipotent control over the analyst, I regard as an incident in an ongoing psychoanalysis. The analysand's free-associational language was not just evident but became increasingly expressive with respect to sadomasochistic material. What is also important is to notice that such free associations spontaneously ramified into the patient's present and past life, as well as into the transference, something we consider favorably inasmuch as it enlarges psychic reality and lays down an optimal experiential basis for eventual integration and working through. Looked at from still another angle, the relationship between reality considerations and this illusion of enforced silence is different than occurs with the desktop illusion. With enforced silence, considerations of reality are increasingly left aside, and indeed, the influence of reality events on the illusion ultimately destroys it. In the desktop incident, the patient's considerations about reality became the important substance of the session.

Yet, notwithstanding what I take to be important differences between them, with respect to facilitating the analytic process and ego support in a psychotherapy context, these incidents do share some important similarities: in both circumstances there is clearly something that goes "beyond language" in the therapeutic relationship, and this something touches on a sense of action on the part of both patient and therapist. Put another way, and once again to make use of Freud's (1915b) metaphor, I can say that this idea of transference as a playground has moved and become recentered some place away from language and more toward action. It is to these matters of language and action in a psychoanalytic situation that I now turn.

LANGUAGE CONCRETIZATION AS
ENACTED SYMBOL

In classical psychoanalysis, language increasingly becomes the contemplated subject of its own investigation.[5]

And it is just here that certain working assumptions about classical analysis become clear. These assumptions are two: First, that language as a vehicle will suffice for that aspect of the relationship we conceptualize as the working alliance (Greenson 1967), which I equate with Stone's (1961, 1967) mature (love) transference and Freud's (1912b) unobjectionable transference. Second, for an (always relative) transference neurosis to occur, it is only necessary for the analyst to maintain a steady, rational, verbal interpretive examination of the analysand's increasingly expressive psychosexual and/or aggressive associations, or other analysand language that replaces such associations (resistance). These two points could be combined in this way: in classical psychoanalysis, free-associational language and its verbal interpretation, together with language that facilitates the emergence and contemplation of free associations, is assumed to be not only a suitable vehicle for communication but a completely satisfactory basis for the realization of meaning, including (and especially) transference construals of the psychoanalytic relationship.

The expression *realization of meaning* has a nice, catchy sound, but what exactly does it signify? The root *real* in the word *realization*, in addition to saying something about objective existence, has another connotation that pertains to what we have in mind when we use the word *meaning*ful, that is, meaning about something we experience as genuine, serious, or authentic with respect to ourselves. In Chapter 1, I discussed an analysand who once said to me, crying miserably, "I can imagine saying words, but they're so disconnected to feelings, I'm afraid you won't believe me." This state of affairs involved a depressive (and possibly masochistic) relationship to language as a symbolic vehicle for anything the analysand could experience as genuine, vital, or authentic about herself. We began to understand that this occurred when circumstances created a breakdown in the analysand's perfect-in-the-sense-of-grandiose experience of herself. It was not only that she could not believe that her words would be believable to someone else, she herself did not believe that any significant psychic reality for herself was realized at that moment with her language. It would be a mistake to call such a condition isolation of affect. First of all, the analysand could feel. And with isolation of affect language is experienced as believable by oneself and another, whereas what was occurring here was a profound alienation of language from the analysand's psychic reality. Put another way, the analysand's language, at that moment in the treatment, lacked ego feeling (Weiss 1942); and to the extent that we conceive the term *ego* to mean a vocal-auditory organization (Edelheit 1969), we can also say that no ego organization was available for the analysis. While we might describe the analysand's experience of language as ego-alien, it is important to distinguish the particular significance of the term *alien* in this context. It wasn't that she experienced language as an alien disruption of (ego) systemic organization, like a phobic anxiety or a compulsion; it was that no language, as a matter of principle, could realize her psychic reality. Her ego organization, we might say, had no voice.

A case reported in the Goldberg *Casebook* (1978) provides another type of example of how language can become, in principle, unsuitable, impossible really, as a vehicle with which to examine or express one's psychic reality. Here what occurs is not a basic alienation of language from psychic reality; rather, the use of language, dynamically and unconsciously, signifies a sort of extraordinary, sadistic, painful, narcissistic injury. I will refer to this as one sort of pathological concretization of language into the status of an enacted action.

In the case recorded, the analyst believed herself to be in some kind of empathic rapport when she stated to the analysand that her yearly Christmas vacation interruption of treatment "was indeed unfortunate" (p. 149). The analysand interrupted and said, "Such clarifications don't bring solutions, *these are words*" (p. 149, italics mine). He then said he would "look for a girl to fall in love" (p. 149). The analyst then interpreted that the analysand would be attempting in this way to prove his independence from her. To this, the analysand replied, "You're *tying me down* by saying this. . . . this is childish. It is a problem enough to see my anxiety related to your leaving; when you *talk about it*, it just becomes more disgusting" (p. 149, italics mine). The analysand alsostated that he intended to grow a beard in the analyst's absence.

A number of points are important here. First, the analysand recognized himself to be anxious about the separation. Second, his recognition of anxiety caused, in turn, a narcissistic injury ("this is childish"), and interpretive language at this time only seemed to augment such injury ("when you talk about it, it just becomes more disgusting"). Third, and unlike the analysand just described, this analysand immediately developed urges to recover both the lost object and self-esteem ("girl to fall in love with"), and he would become unlike a child by growing a beard. This experience of sharp, sadistic, narcissistic injury is congruent with the *Casebook* (Goldberg 1978) assessment of the analysand as a narcissistic personality disorder. It can be considered (conceived) to be an illustration of those relatively circumscribed incidents of narcissistic rage that occur in the treatment of narcissistic disorder but that do not impede the overall development of a grandiose and/or idealizing transference (Kohut, e.g., 1973, 1977).

Another type of language concretization, which makes language problematic for the classical psychoanalytic situation, involves what one might describe as a "collapse" of language as communication into concrete language as an enacted symbol signifying libidinal gratification. An example of this comes from Eissler's work with delinquents and his thought about the changes of procedure necessary to do psychotherapy with such individuals. In one paper, Eissler (1950) describes how he gave money to a male patient; in another case, Eissler told a promiscuous female patient that he was sure a love affair with her would be enjoyable but that he was convinced he would be of greater assistance to her as a therapist who only would talk to her. Eissler describes these changes as necessary because of the patients'

desire for "concreteness" (p. 116); "only the concrete becomes emotionally meaningful to him [her]" (p. 117).

Now, one can understand how giving money to a psychotherapy patient intuitively is describable as concrete. However, what is concrete about Eissler's verbalizing to the
female psychotherapy patient that he is certain that a love
affair with her would be pleasurable but that he is convinced
that he can be of still greater service to her as a therapist who
only talks with her? Allowing a patient to sit on top of a desk
and so become "bigger" than the therapist, also, intuitively,
is in some sense describable as concrete; but this also is
different from only talking to a patient. One can also sense
that agreeing to a sadomasochistic illusion of enforced silence is intuitively in some way concrete; but again, this also
seems different from only talking to a patient, however
gratifying may be the content of such language.

So, what do we really mean by concrete? And how can
language become concrete whatever the content of such
language? To begin with, this idea of concrete must be
separated from an idea of libidinal or aggressive gratification,
which may or may not be concrete. Giving money, or
lovemaking, is concrete libidinal gratification; but we would
not describe as concrete the gratification experienced over
the elegance of a mathematical proof. Physical assault is
aggression we would call concrete and perhaps concrete
sadistic, libidinal gratification as well. But a well-written
literary criticism, however barbed, we would not consider
aggressively or sadistically concrete. While such taxonomic
considerations about the term *concrete* have some use, they
do not produce any satisfying sense of clarification. I believe
this sense of obscurity will remain about whether or not an
individual's psychic reality is concrete so long as we labor
exclusively within only a descriptive and drive gratification
kind of classifying framework—concrete versus abstract pleasure and satisfaction. Another comparison we can formulate
is how either language or action can function dynamically as

symbolic vehicles, and I use the term *symbol* here in the psychoanalytic sense of the word.

When action functions, in the psychoanalytic sense, as a symbolic vehicle, we are inclined to think something is occurring we would describe as a concrete psychic reality. But notice that a conscious intention to symbolize in the psychoanalytic sense is not usual or necessarily present in either verbal free associations or what I have called language concretization as enacted action, which I believe also can perform a symbolic function. Actually, any conscious intention to use actions of any sort as creative symbolic vehicles will involve us in a performing art form, mime or ballet, and we do not experience such activities as concrete. I will shortly pursue more generally this matter of enacted actions as unintended symbols, but first I want to take up language concretization as a special case of unintended enacted action.

Theoretically, we can contrast symbolic meaning-in-language with symbolic meaning-in-action. But it is important to understand the interpenetration of such symbolic vehicles. Behavior such as smiles, frowns, and so forth occurs in the daily life of anyone and will interact in various congruent or contradictory ways with a person's ongoing language output (see, e.g., Rosenfeld 1982). All of these nonverbal behaviors are subject to interpretation in the psychoanalytic situation as enacted symbols, and such phenomena are included in what Freud (1905b) referred to as the dynamic unconscious "ooz[ing] out of . . . every pore" (p. 72) of the analysand. At the same time, and the other way around, language itself can become concrete, that is, it lends itself to interpretation as an enacted symbol. Many sensory attributes of language as an auditory experience, pitch, tempo, and so forth, are subject to such interpretation in everyday life as well as in the psychoanalytic situation (see R. Steiner 1987, Scherer 1982). Evidence for language as a physiognomic experience (e.g., Werner and Kaplan 1963) further supports this kind of observation (and see also

Edelson 1975). At the same time, having said this, I must
return to my earlier thoughts about a need to differentiate
the kinds of influence two people can exert on one another,
including analysand and analyst in the psychoanalytic relationship. It may be that certain attributes of language (or
behavior) were, initially, connected to dynamically unconscious fantasies and now have become functionally autonomous (Hartmann 1939). Or it may be that what oozes out
of every pore has remained connected to dynamically unconscious fantasies. In these two circumstances, a psychoanalysis either interpretively reveals this dynamically
unconscious fantasy directly or first interpretively reconnects
nonverbal expressiveness to dynamically unconscious fantasy. And there is another possibility—that what oozes out
has *never* become represented in the analysand's dynamic
unconscious, has always remained a physiognomically apprehended experience, felt and expressed as such. In such a
circumstance, we might say (conceive) that what a psychoanalytic interpretation accomplishes is to provide a symbolic
structure for the unconscious experience. I think, for example, what a psychoanalysis accomplishes for psychosomatic
ailments of one sort or another may be just such a symbolic
vehicle never before realized in the analysand's overall
(including dynamically unconscious) psychic organization.
This may also be a way of understanding what Freud (1915d)
meant by "primal repression" (p. 148), which has always
remained, for me, a somewhat enigmatic concept.

In any event, now we can see a way in which the term
concrete applies when Eissler (1950) verbalizes to his female
patient that he would enjoy lovemaking but believes he
would supply a better response by only talking to her as a
therapist. What I suggest is that language in this therapy
became significantly altered, and this alteration properly
remained unanalyzed to suit the purposes of the therapy.
Language now took on an important, significant meaning as
enacted symbolism. Language itself became lovemaking. As
enacted symbolism it is not only the pitch, tempo, and

related physiognomic experience of language between Eissler and his patient that are important but also syntax (e.g., Steingart 1977), as well as semantics and discourse qualities that relate to turn taking in therapy conversations (see, e.g., Kendon 1982). Two people can say to each other, "We had a *good* conversation"; the "good" in such a description includes, I believe, in addition to the semantic, this entire sensory, pleasurable experience generated by linguistic intercourse when language operates as a symbolic act. With respect to Eissler and his patient, one can say that all of this is a longwinded way of describing an unanalyzed sexualization of language dialogue that suited the purposes of the psychotherapy. But this perspective about how language can become an enacted symbol at least makes comprehensible how such a sexualization of language can take place. It should be clear that a similar set of statements, as I have just made for libidinization of language, could be written about the aggressivization of language (see, e.g., Dahl et al. 1978).

It is important to realize in such a circumstance what has happened to language; and this can include free-associational language uttered by an individual in psychoanalysis, or more problem-focused language stated in a psychotherapy, as was the case with Eissler. In such a circumstance language does not function essentially as a vehicle for communication but as a verbal *adornment* for whatever concrete transference psychic reality is being enacted.[6] And I believe, to put it another way, that it is the term *enactment* that is appropriate here to describe the use of language in such a circumstance. One has only to think a moment about how a child at play will utter language about something he or she is, really, totally uncomprehending— say, the language of an astronaut in flight ("main boosters jettisoned" . . . "apogee 100 miles," etc.). The function of such language is simply to adorn (along with costume, gesture, etc.) the child's playful enactment. Language in an adult psychoanalytic or psychotherapy situation can function in exactly the same way, and will regularly do so, in the type of transference I have described as pathological play. And, as I have indicated, this language enactment may subserve transference that involves libidinal or narcissistic gratification, or hateful release, or some oscillation between the two. In such a circumstance language obviously has become subverted away from the communicative interpretive purposes of psychoanalysis into a form of enactment.[7]

Language (unwittingly) can become subtly "tilted" toward enactment in a psychoanalytic relationship, and at the least is something to be considered constantly. Greenson (1965) has provided an example of how an analysand's (in this framework) witting enactment with verbal free associations was dealt with effectively, and seemingly only by authentic verbal means. The case involved a reanalysis, the original psychoanalysis being interrupted by the analysand. Greenson states that at this original interruption both he and the analysand realized there was "a great deal of unfinished business . . . unusual obscurities and difficulties . . . in trying to achieve a better resolution of her . . . sadomasochistic transference" (p. 162).

In the reanalysis it became clear to Greenson that the patient "at times consciously, at others preconsciously, and at still other times, unconsciously, blurred the real purpose of free association" (p. 164).

> It became clear that when the patient felt anxious in her relationship to me she would let herself slip into this regressive "sleep-talking" manner of speech. It was a kind of "spiteful obedience"—spiteful in so far as she knew it was an evasion of true free associating. It was obedient inasmuch as she submitted to this regressive or, one might say, incontinent way of talking. This arose when she felt a certain kind of hostility toward me. She felt this was an urge to pour out a stream of poison on me. [p. 164]

Greenson's "vigorous pursuit" (p. 164)—that is, steady verbal confrontation—of this analysand's misuse of her free associations for (in my terms) enacted symbolism of her sadistic hostility produced a second psychoanalysis with a "completely different flavor and atmosphere" (p. 164). Greenson uses this example to illustrate the creation of a significant (real) working alliance, relatively lacking in the first analysis, and with this I agree. And I do not question how such a steady verbal confrontation can occur and be needed in a psychoanalysis. But we might also wonder whether the significant use of verbal confrontation, in itself, is not also some (again, witting or unwitting) movement in the transference experience toward reciprocal sadomasochistic enactments between analysand and analyst. If so, this, of course, would also require interpretation at an appropriate later point in the treatment process.

All of this leads me to a further, more general consideration about this idea of acting out as an enacted symbol in the psychoanalytic relationship.

ACTING OUT AS ENACTED SYMBOL[8]

Freud (1905b) arrived at the concept of acting out from his work with Dora, specifically with respect to Dora's abrupt termination of the analysis:

> She [Dora] took her revenge on me as she wanted to take her revenge on him [Herr K.] and deserted me as she believed herself to be deceived and deserted by him. Thus she *acted out* an essential part of her recollection and fantasies instead of reproducing them in treatment. [p. 119]

I will spare the reader exhaustive details of the large literature on acting out. But it is worthwhile to outline the construct as it has evolved in the literature since Freud.

Central to Freud's concept of acting out are two features — the first is locale, and the second has to do with the (inferred) organization of consciousness that characterizes the analysand's transference at the time of acting out. About these two points Freud was clear: locale involves the psychoanalytic relationship, and organization of consciousness involves transference behavior and experience connected to reminiscences (fantasies) that remain dynamically repressed.

In subsequent literature Freud's term *acting out* has broadened to refer also to behavior and experience that is, characterologically, simply impulsive and/or antisocial (see, e.g., Kanzer in Panel 1957, Limentani 1966, Rexford 1966). And the locale for acting out has similarly broadened to include the manner in which an analysand conducts his or her life outside the psychoanalytic relationship (see Panel 1957, Rexford 1966). Frosch (in Panel 1957) and Blos (1966), among others, have pointed out that this twofold expansion of the concept of acting out has served only to create a measure of theoretical confusion, and thus has made the idea a less effective conceptual tool. Acting out, as Blos (1966) puts it, should retain properties that mark it as an "organized and structured mechanism. This is in contrast to the more primitive discharge process of impulsive behavior" (p. 120).

Still a third expansion of the concept has occurred in our literature, identified especially with work done by Greenacre (e.g., 1950, 1966), who emphasizes the dramatic play connotation of the term *acting out.*[9] The accent here is not that such an individual acts out instead of remembering (Freud 1905b). Rather, the analysand entertains the belief that "to make it *look* as if it were true is to make it true" (Greenacre 1950, p. 235). Greenacre also states that analysands who act out in this way have an "incompletely developed sense of reality" (p. 231). But the term *incompletely* conflates some idea of extent (or degree) of reality testing with what I believe is more usefully construed to be a special type of reality-testing disturbance (see Steingart 1983) that is neither neurotic transference fantasy, capable of realization in language-mediated experience, nor schizophrenic transference experience, realizable only through some outright reconstruction of reality.

With this pathologically playful transference, acting out occurs together with essential, important "remembering" (Freud, e.g., 1914c) pertinent to the content of what is being acted out.[10] I have already cited Weiss's (1942) observation about patients who act out "emotional situations they . . . already remember" (p. 490). And Greenacre (1966) similarly describes patients who act out in the transference even after "they have gained some genetic insight into conflict" (p. 145). Here the analysand has awareness—meaningful, acutely felt, emotional awareness of personal history—but awareness not enlisted into an organization of consciousness to function as a memory "grade" (Klein 1966) conducive to working through transference. Greenacre (1950) states, about such a condition, that the analysand has a "largely unconscious belief in the magic of action" (p. 227). And Kanzer (Panel 1957) has commented how acting out can be likened to "somnambulistic elements" of the dream state. Of course, strictly speaking, acting out is not an organization of consciousness as occurs in a dream state with its hallucinatory replacement of reality and a thought process transformed to perceptual experience (Freud 1900). But what occurs in this clinical context is, nevertheless, a significant departure from any normative view of memorial experience. If I return to Weiss's terminology, I can say that memorial experience is not invested with ego feeling, and the consequence of this is that there is no functional differentiation in awareness between intensely felt reminiscences and awareness of equally intensely felt transference experience. For the analysand, the transference is felt to be an actual repetition of childhood experience.

Thus, the first of what I see to be two clinical contexts for the concept of acting out is what evidently transpired in the case of Dora, whose action in leaving treatment can be conceived as an unintended, dynamically unconscious symbol, comparable to the production of verbal free associations.[11] Recall that Freud observed and quickly interpreted Dora's play with her reticule, something Freud believed to symbolize a desire to masturbate, about which Dora kept herself dynamically unconscious. Such expressions of other-than-linguistic enacted symbol are familiar, typified in the unwitting movement of the leg from the couch to the floor, in the forgetting of an umbrella, in the rubbing of an ear, and so forth.

Whether we interpret from verbal free associations, or from other dynamically unconscious, unintended enacted symbolism, the success of the psychoanalytic process depends on the recovery (construction) of dynamically unconscious experience. But with an interpretation directed at acting out as the enacted symbol, the analysis requires in addition a willingness on the part of the analysand to accept the conversion from unintended enacted symbol to the discursive language equivalent.[12]

But what if Dora herself was in conscious possession of reminiscences about Herr K. when she acted out? What if Dora said something like this to Freud:

> I was attracted to Herr K., and I wanted to believe he loved me, that he would divorce his wife to marry me. But then I realized he only wanted an affair with me just as he had with his children's governess. I hated him for that and wanted revenge. And you, Herr Professor Freud, I believe your behavior also shows that you will betray me should I allow myself to be drawn to you. I will not stay with you any longer.

What if Dora had said all this and still left analysis? Or what if Freud had made an interpretation to Dora along these lines, with which Dora genuinely agreed, but she still left treatment? Would we not now also conceptualize this to be Dora's acting out?

When acting out occurs in this second clinical context of what I call transference as pathological play, we can expect the analysand to be in conscious possession of pertinent reminiscences connected to transference dynamics. It is not a case here of acting out in place of remembering (Freud 1914c); rather, the analysand, with meaningful, conscious possession of reminiscences pertinent to transference psychodynamics (i.e., a meaningful, enlarged psychic reality), still insists that observations about the actual psychoanalytic relationship suffice as evidence that the transference experience is real. If Dora leaves treatment, even with such acutely felt reminiscences pertinent to her transference with Freud, it is because she refuses to treat the acting out as an enacted symbol signifying unreal, transference experience and chooses instead to treat it as an action reasonably related to some immediate actuality about her relationship to Freud.

Generalizing from this consideration, and adding some specificity to Weiss's idea of ego feeling, we can say that perception, memory, and so on, all the processes we conceive to be activities of the ego, will only possess ego feeling with respect to transference experience insofar as those processes are recruited into a type of symbolic function (Piaget, e.g., 1945) suitable for realizing transference as symbolic (of past) experience (no matter how intensely felt by the analysand).[13]

I say a "type" of symbolic function because it is important to distinguish ideas about different sorts of cognitive processing by which concepts are formed (e.g., primary process vs. secondary process) from symbolic vehicles with which (or through which) concepts are expressed (language, an action, a drawing, and so forth) (e.g., Werner and Kaplan 1963). Also, and of course of special importance for a psychoanalysis, we need to distinguish between dynamically unconscious, unintended symbolism and conscious, intentional symbolic activity. What is normatively idealized

(idealized in terms of an idea that a psychoanalysis embodies in some definite sense lawful process) is that what I call nonenactive language serves as the symbolic vehicle.[14]

Still another type of cognitive processing produces concepts (meaning) but resembles neither primary- nor secondary-process thinking. Our essential ideas about primary-process thinking are the ideas of extensive "displacement" and "condensation" (Freud, e.g., 1900); and the types of symbolism to which we connect these constructs include such things as the fantastic dream images produced by us all, the symptoms exhibited by neurotic individuals, and the thought (language) disorder and/or hallucinations expressed by persons with schizophrenia. However, the most illuminating referent for this other type of cognitive processing is not a dream image or a symptom or a thought disorder—it is the play symbol of a clinically healthy young child. Freud (1908) made the following comments about the child at play:

> The opposite of play is not what is serious but what is real. In spite of all the emotion with which he cathects his world of play, the child distinguishes it quite well from reality; and he likes to link his imagined objects and situations to the tangible and visible things of the real world. This linking is all that differentiates the child's "play" from "phantasying." [p. 144]

And, "The growing child, when he stops playing, gives up nothing but the link with the real object; instead of *playing* he now *phantasies*" (p. 145). What is crucial here is how to understand what it means that the young child "likes to link" his play with "tangible and visible things of the real world." Freud stresses that with development a playful linking pleasure is given up, and that another, developmentally more mature type of gratification, fantasy, which does not involve a linking pleasure, arises in place of play. But this conception omits what we see as a critical change in how one *thinks* as a young child contrasted with the later, mature kind of thinking we call secondary process. This development in cognitive processing has two intrinsically interrelated effects: first, a change occurs in the nature of thinking itself; second, a change occurs with respect to the relationship (status) between any particular, chosen symbolic vehicle and the idea (meaning) expressed through the symbol.

To begin with the second of these developmental changes in cognitive organization, symbolic vehicles (language, action, drawing, etc.) achieve an autonomy, a differentiation, in one's psychic reality from ideas (concepts) being expressed through such symbols (e.g., Piaget 1945, Werner and Kaplan 1963). With the young child, the manner and affect possessed by the symbols with which an idea is expressed retain a significance for the very meaningfulness (realization) of the idea itself. This is signaled in the singsong acoustical contours (pitch, amplitude, etc.) that characteristically imbue early childhood speech (and see Fónagy 1971). Versions of this kind of meaning organization can of course continue even with development. With such a psychic reality, a symbolic vehicle not only expresses meaning but also manifestly is invested with "magic" power to effect a pertinent realization of that meaning. Examples of language as a symbolic vehicle are the utterances of magical words in fairy tales—"Open, sesame," "Rumpelstiltskin," and so on. The point here is that the young child is naively magical in this way in his or her use of language (or dress or action) as symbolic vehicles to realize meaning for him- or herself. This leads us to question Freud's (1908) contention that the young child at play distinguishes such play "quite well from reality" (p. 144), since it is just this that does *not* occur. It does occur with the achievement of fantasy in later development, wherein symbolic vehicles are now differentiated in psychic reality from ideas expressed through such symbols. If a school-age child, or an adult, is expressing a fantasy, then his or her language is no longer magical; now language serves authentically only to communicate and not, in itself, to contribute to the sensibility of the fantasy experience.

My argument is that this entire framework for distinguishing a young child's organization of play experience from fantasy-structured experience can be used to comprehend a type of adult transference experience that deviates from expectations in a psychoanalysis. Put one way, and to connect this to Weiss's (1942) terminology, if an analysand's ego feeling about transference is organized like that of a young child (especially clear in play), then the transference is not readily influenced by verbal interpretations as a sort of symbolic repetition. Put still another way, it is with transference structured as fantasy that a nonenactive, linguistic symbolic function is "in place"; the ego feeling produced by such an organization is of a very different sort and renders transference much more susceptible to insightful, verbal interpretation as symbolic repetition. The important matter here is not any particular interpretive meaning for a verbal symbol, or whether the interpretation is agreed to by analysand and analyst, who are communicating with each other. In an analysis classically conceived, where, as I have put it, nonenactive language is experienced by both individuals as a satisfactory basis for the realization of meaning, it is commonplace for an analysand not to accept a particular symbolic interpretation about transference obtained by an analyst from verbal free associations and offered for consideration.

It is the operative influence of this type of symbolizing function that can be so tenuous in this second clinical context for acting out. Put another way, I believe essential to what we now often mean by acting out is not whether the analysand is in conscious possession of reminiscences connected to transference experience, but whether, with such an enlarged psychic reality, the unreal transference is still treated as real. We should conceive the action in such acting out to indicate a playful, I would say pathologically playful, type of disturbance for the notation (differentiation) of reality. The adjective *pathological* – pathological play – at this moment is pertinent in two ways: (1) The adult (or older child)—unlike the clinically healthy child at play—initially demonstrates a dynamically unintended use of enactive language (or acting out in general) to be symbols insufficiently differentiated from meanings expressed in such symbols. One can say there is no operative influence, no functional equivalent, to the way the clinically healthy young child at play spontaneously says "Let's pretend," "Let's make believe," and so on. (2) But then the adult (or older child)—and again unlike the clinically healthy child at play—will quite consciously and intentionally construe the pathologically playful transference experience so created to be the real psychoanalytic relationship.

For these reasons, acting out as enacted symbol will involve matters of gratification or rage or depression or whatever in connection with something I will call an *activity feature* of the psychoanalytic relationship. For example, the analyst's not talking, or the factual reality of a raise in fee, signifies the validity of a transference experience that the analyst doesn't care at all about the analysand's welfare, or the analyst is exploitative, and so forth. On the other hand, the regularity of the analytic schedule, the analyst's dependability, or the analyst's willingness to change an appointment schedule because of some real consideration signifies the analyst's real care for the analysand equal to exclusive, maternal devotion, and the psychoanalytic relationship is treated as if in actuality it is the realization of such a desire. It is important to note that when this activity feature of the analytic relationship is used as the symbolic vehicle for realizing transference, we can readily sense the connection between the symbolic vehicle (fee increase vs. schedule regularity and change) and the (unreal) transference that is being treated as real (not caring vs. exclusive, maternal devotion). Enacted symbolic vehicles in this clinical context do not operate with the same order of complex, disguised displacements and condensations that we see in dreams or, sometimes, even in verbal free associations. Rather, concrete enacted symbolic vehicles seem transparent, obvious. They are, one might say, natural, as is the case with the young child at play. But I use the term *transparent* for another reason. One connotation of the word is as I have just said, obvious, like the child at play. However, another connotation of the term has to do with something one readily sees through; that is, the symbolic nature of the acting out can readily get "lost," again, as naturally occurs with the child at play.

To return to Dora, I believe an element of prejudice figures in our conceptualization of such an action as Dora's leaving treatment, in the imagined circumstance wherein Dora acknowledges and feels in a meaningful way her equation of Freud with Herr K. And that prejudice takes the form of the analyst's (theoretical) unwillingness to consider that Dora's acting out also has the significance (status) of a pathologically playful symbol. Instead, we are prone to conceptualize Dora's action to be an instance only of a nonsymbolic drive gratification or instinctual release and the like. This kind of interpretation will only serve to collude with the analysand's subsequent, quite conscious intention to eradicate an experience of genuine symbol making (symbol differentiated from symbolic vehicle) with respect to the transference experience.

I turn again to Greenacre's (1950) comment that an analysand who acts out in this context has a "largely unconscious belief in the magic of action" (p. 85). It cannot be said that action, per se, in acting out is what produces magic. What creates magic is the analysand's desire to treat, that is, "misuse," such action to create a change of belief about what is real about the psychoanalytic relationship. An enacted symbol—acting out—in this context is intended to impact what is real about the psychoanalytic relationship in the manner of dramatic theater. But with theater—and unlike a psychoanalysis—the audience is involved in a willing surrender of what is real. We have in our language the saying *seeing is believing,* which is very much at the heart of this matter. An analysand desires to act out in such a circumstance because, like play, a symbolic expression through physical enactment makes the transference experience "look" more real, contrasted with only language expression. And regularly, in my experience, the analysand psychic reality I discover (Schwaber 1992) through further analytic investigation is the articulation of a struggle; this is a most intense sort of dynamically unconscious sadomasochistic struggle over who is to decide (analyst or analysand) what is to be considered to be real or unreal about the psychoanalytic relationship.[15]

Boesky (1982) has stated a view congruent with Greenacre's, and it is a concept about acting out similar in certain important respects to mine:

> The very fact that motor behavior is observable to others and even that it constitutes an event in the sphere of action heightens the reality force or reality quality of the event. Thus the shift to action creates an *illusionary reality* which serves the purpose of defense. [p. 48, italics mine]

But it is not self-evident that just because "motor behavior is observable to others" or that it is "an event in the sphere of action" it follows that what Boesky calls the reality quality of such action is enhanced. A reality coherence for compulsive hand washing is not enhanced because it is an action. The compulsive neurotic who suffers the symptom simply experiences an increased irrationality with respect to his or her behavior. The same would apply to avoidance behavior connected to neurotic phobias of one sort or another.

What is critical is the type of "thought structure" (Freud 1900) being represented consciously, or dynamically unconsciously, through action. We deal here with thinking in which meanings are produced by concepts whose defining

criteria consist of impelling attributes that inhere in a referent
(self, other, or inanimate thing): vividly experienced sensations that arise in a striking image, or salient smell, or taste,
kinesthesis, and so forth, *together with emotions and actions*
that arise in connection with the referent in the midst of the
impelling experience. A. M. Sandler (1975) has emphasized
that the production of this kind of meaningfulness should
not be conceptualized, and thus confused, according to the
concept of primary-process thinking that produces a dream,
but rather as meanings produced in the way a young child
thinks. And when a young child thinks, thoughts can only
be known *in this way*. Piaget's (e.g., 1947) term for this kind
of thinking is *preconceptual*, and Bruner (1956) calls it *ikonic*.
These terms have to do with an analogic, imagistic (Bucci
1989, 1994) encoding of experience built on subsymbolic
processing of experience. Recall, for example, my description of how a young child at play can "make" him- or herself
into an astronaut by vivid attire and an (uncomprehending)
expression of the language used by astronauts.

With a young child, this way of producing meaning will
occur whether the child is thinking as part of an effort to
adapt to some actuality in his or her life or as part of play.
And the boundary between play and actuality is not at all the
same kind of psychic reality as exists with a mature intellect
that differentiates real from unreal, fantasy experience. To
"mean" anger for a young child is to hit, or yell, or leave
another, and all the child who wants to engage in pretense
play at being angry need do is perform some such action
with another. To "mean" mother or father is to perform
tangible actions and/or to put on attire vividly connected
with the parental figure. As A. Freud (1936) has put it, a
young child is "insensible of . . . reality" (p. 80), and we can
understand this to mean that the psychic reality significance
of play experience (what we as adult observers might mis-
takenly call fantasy) in contrast to the child's actuality (what

we as adult observers call reality) is of an entirely different order than exists with the older child or adult.

But if I speak about a structure for knowing, I can also speak about a congruent structure for remembering. And here I must conceptually part company with Weiss (1942), whose explanation for why an analysand continues to enact transference experience, even with acutely felt reminiscences pertinent to the transference, is as follows: "One acts out instead of *remembering fully* with the appropriate attending emotions. It is because the ego cannot always regress to the corresponding state, or at least dwell long enough in it, that the rejection or acting out occurs" (p. 491, italics mine). This explanation at least suggests that it is not only possible but clinically normative that transference regression is somehow a getting back into the very same form (aside from content) of experience known and felt by the analysand as a child. But we know that this is not possible even with hypnosis (e.g., Weitzenhofer 1953), let alone psychoanalysis. Psychoanalysis, classically conceived, takes for granted a type of evocative memory (Piaget 1968). I believe this, in turn, presupposes that remembering can be authentically mediated—felt to be a genuine realization of a person's psychic reality—with language. Actually, we can say, with some irony, that the analysand who enacts a pathologically playful transference is more "fully" remembering childhood experience; such an individual's way of remembering is more "fully" like childhood experience in the transference inasmuch as the way his or her memory functions is closer in form to the only kind of knowing of which a young child is capable. Piaget (1968) conceived of a type of remembering, something he termed a "reconstruction" kind of memorial process, and this entails "imitating a model" (p. 14). I suggest that pathologically playful transference can be construed to be remembering via an imitative use made of the analyst serving as model; and a psychoanalysis, in such a circumstance, has the additional task of resolving conflict to enable the development of a new form of evocative, language-mediated memories (however intense the experience).[16] We can, then, add to Freud's (1914c) classic dichotomy of repetition and (evocative) remembering as alternative forms of reproduction in the transference this possibility of a third kind of imitation-with-model memory, the symbolic character of which applied to some present experience can readily get "lost."

I return, once again, to Dora. Why should we consider that an analysand in a negative transference, who for years endlessly vilifies an analyst, obtains less drive gratification, has less resistance, than a person who acts out by leaving treatment? It is a person's desires in concert with different ways of notating what is real or unreal (transference experience) that makes the difference. From another angle, were Dora to leave treatment with an intensely felt awareness that Freud was as untrustworthy as Herr K., she would also be forcing Freud to be a role model for her pathological play. Freud, of course, becomes Herr K., who now "really" is subject to (revengeful, role-reversal) abandonment and rejection.

I now have described three characteristics of pathological play as transference experience. (1) Experience authentically structured with language is not felt by the analysand to be either necessary or sufficient to realize transference. And language may be used as a kind of adornment (language as acting out) for whatever hostile or libidinal transference experience is being sought by the analysand. (2) Analysand enactments as symbolic expressions (ordinarily what is meant by acting out) develop as attempts by the analysand to control what is to be construed as real or unreal about the analytic relationship. (3) The analysand will, indeed, must, attempt to force the analyst to play a role in such enactments. Of these three characteristics, versions of the first two are easily recognizable in the play of clinically healthy young children. But this is not at all true of the third characteristic. A young child in clinically healthy play will, of course, at times desire adult participation. But the child does not *require* adult belief in the *actuality* of his or her play.[17]

It is usually not difficult to discern clinically healthy from pathological play in young children. A. Freud (1936), for example, described the case of pathological play in a young child who wanted to act as if he were his father.

> He used to put on his father's hat and walk about in it. As long as nobody interfered with him, he was contented and happy. . . . Whenever he was forced to take off the hat at meals or when he went to bed, he reacted with restlessness and ill humor. . . . The differences between him and the little boy who [in a clinically healthy way] plays at being a big man is simply that my small patient's play was for earnest. [p. 88]

The child's insistence that his significant adults rigidly accord his play a status of actuality is what marks his play as pathological. Certain comments by Piaget are relevant:

> Actually, play cannot (in the young child) be opposed to reality, because in both cases belief is arbitrary and pretty much destitute of logical reasons. Play is a reality which the child is disposed to believe in when by himself, just as reality is a game at which he is willing to play with an adult and anyone else who believes in it. [Piaget 1924, cited in Flavell 1963, p. 161]

And:

> At the level of early childhood there are two contrasting types of belief, the one connected with social, and especially *adult* behaviors, the other with spontaneous and egocentric individual behaviors. . . . When the child plays, he certainly does not believe, in the sense of socialized belief, in the content of his symbolism, but precisely because symbolism is egocentric thought we have no reason to suppose that he does not believe *in his own way* anything he chooses. . . . The . . . child does not consider whether his ludic (i.e., playful) symbols are real or not. He is aware . . . that they are

not so for others, *and makes no serious effort to persuade the adult that they are.* But for him it is a question which does not arise. [Piaget 1945, pp. 167–168, first and last italics mine]

What these comments by Piaget make clear, and I think the same is implied in A. Freud's remarks, is that the play of the young child ought not to be contrasted with "reality." What real means to a young child, contrasted with experience the child calls play, is of an entirely different order of knowing than what occurs later in development, when we can conceive of various forms of fantasy authentically differentiated (and integrated) with experience known as real. For this reason, I use a term like *actuality* to designate, in Piaget's words, the "social, and especially adult behaviors" the child knows on some basis to be different from his or her play. (See Steingart [1983] for a more extended discussion of this matter.) What is a critical marker for pathological play, as both A. Freud and Piaget indicate, is whether, or the degree to which, the young child will attempt to coerce significant adults into accepting his or her play as signifying some actuality about him- or herself.[18] It is this same element of coercion that is evident in the adult transference condition of pathological play.

This leads to a consideration, and issue, of a witting or unwitting participation on the part of the analyst in the situation of pathological play as transference experience (with either an older child or an adult patient). The "desktop" and "enforced silence" incidents I described earlier can be regarded as examples of an intentional participation by the analyst in pathological play, that is, volitional relocation of the transference into a shape further removed from a relationship centered on language as communication. If I now adopt Eissler's (1953) idea of a treatment parameter, I can say that both of these incidents are illustrations of a volitional use of an (eventually analyzed) treatment parameter. The use of this parameter ought to be conceived to support not only the unreal, positive transference but also the real, collaborative investigatory experience between analysand and therapist. It is intended to promote an eventual change from pathological play to the usual psychoanalytic relationship centered on language and verbal interpretations.[19]

Even unintended, an unwitting parameter can be introduced by an analyst that has beneficial, insightful effects, and that must be conceived, then, to involve a simultaneous useful realization of both real, collaborative and unreal (transference) experience. Certain incidents reported by Abend and colleagues (1983) in their work with borderline patients can be construed in this way. In three of four cases reported, a point was reached wherein the analyst expressed a serious possibility that the analysis might need to be terminated because transference appeared utterly refractory to insightful working through.

In one case, the analysand's initial reaction, to the analyst's consideration that the analysis should be terminated, was to become enraged and leave the office. She then returned and asked if she could "in essence have another chance." Then the analysand very much in the sense of a confession told of her shame and guilt about masturbation and "for the first time her secret bulimia and self-induced vomiting. From that dramatic moment, which appeared later in retrospect to signify unconsciously a *magical* undoing of the crushing abandonment by her father, and a wished-for 'second chance' with him, the analysis took a different course." [p. 43, italics mine]

With the second case, the analysand's initial response was " . . . one of victory." The analysand stated, "I never thought I'd hear you say that." He then began to cry and plead with his analyst not to discontinue. He acknowledged that his wish to humiliate his analyst was stronger than his desire to change, but he felt that if he stopped he would lose the one friend he had. Subsequent to this he did not experience the terrible humiliation he had expected, nor did he suspect his analyst of deceiving him by threatening him.

There was, however, no dramatic change in the work, but a gradual and significant one. He began to acknowledge painful longings to be loved and cared for. He felt, for the first time, wishes to be cuddled, caressed, and loved by a woman which he did not have to project onto her. Now oedipal wishes and memories became pronounced, and with them, intense fears of being attacked by other men. Fears of castration for masturbation were experienced. [pp. 59–60]

The third analysand's response was "surprise, incredulous that her analyst could give her up and stop trying to 'control' her. This transference was clearly connected to her father, who had had to be the only omnipotent, controlling force in her life."
    The analyst's countertransference feelings reached a crescendo during this time, certainly contributing to his raising the issue of consultation. . . . There was no question that the analyst was . . . experiencing what the patient had felt at the hands of her father.
    The transference crises finally softened, and there emerged clearly for the first time in her analysis transference feelings which were associated with her mother's critical attitudes. She felt the analyst had quietly disliked her throughout treatment. [pp. 71–72]

What has happened here? An analyst's suggestion that treatment might need to be terminated, itself a product of both realistic consideration and perhaps countertransference, which typically can be stimulated by borderline patients, has been responded to by the analysand with a similar but insightful productive amalgam of transference and realism. Put in terms of the framework developed here, an *unintended* willingness by the analyst to "play along" (enact) with pathologically playful transference enabled the analysand to be willing to take on a more realistic view of his or her experience. Buie (1985) considers that what has occurred here is only analysand compliance, and thus a false improvement.[20] I do not agree. Why should analysand compliance lead to expressions of *new* clinical material, previously withheld? I take this to implicate a working through of anal-rapprochement, sadomasochistic dynamics, something I will take up in the next chapter.
    If I am correct, an analyst must first react to an analysand's urge for some kind of enactment in such a way that the

analysand will experience what is occurring to be more than only talk. Otherwise, the analysand will feel that his or her experience about the psychoanalytic relationship (both real and transferential) is not understood, and this, then, must result in a sense of rejection, or humiliation, and so on. Language uttered by an analyst that is immediately structured as an interpretation will be so experienced by the analysand as only talk and completely awry with the playful status (form) of any language at such a moment of enactment urgency. Freud (1909) once described psychoanalytic interpretation in the following manner:

> We endeavor . . . to enable the patient to obtain a conscious grasp of his unconscious wishes. And this we can achieve by working upon the basis of the hints he throws out and so, with the help of our interpretative technique presenting the unconscious complex to his consciousness *in our own words*. There will be a *certain degree of similarity* between that which he hears from us . . . and which, in spite of all his resistances, is trying to force its way to consciousness, and it *is this similarity* that will enable him to discover the unconscious material. [pp. 120–121, second and third italics mine]

But language in such circumstances functions as it does in a play experience. That is, language in itself is not felt by the analysand to be sufficient realization of any (real or transferential) aspect of the psychoanalytic relationship. Enacted symbolic expression becomes critical, and the analyst must (intuitively or willingly) use words to "tilt" language toward enactment. It is in this kind of circumstance that Freud's (1915a) comments apply about analysands who "refuse to accept the psychical in place of the material" (p. 167). And with respect to Freud's (1909) comments about psychoanalytic interpretation just cited, an analyst first must somehow achieve a "similarity" in (playful) form with language before authentic verbal interpretation can be effective.

The crux of this matter is a kind of symbolic (sense of enactment) provision brought into a psychoanalysis with language; it is not essentially an issue of psychic gratification or pain and can involve either sort of experience (or admixture). Bird (1957) has described a case of an analysand who began to act out by missing sessions "whenever feelings about me [the analyst] were on the verge of becoming conscious" (p. 642). Initial straightforward interpretation about the acting out only produced its intensification. Then Bird began to comment about the analysand's acting out in a "joking way" (p. 642), what Bird described as "baby talk" (p. 643), although I might call it play talk. He talked about the meaning of the acting out to the analysand in the third person:

> I think that man is here again—the doctor who intrudes on a certain patient's thoughts, tempting her to think about him. He's disguised as his own office, and he looks like trouble. Now I have a hunch that if we can find out what it is this certain patient thinks about this certain doctor, we can stop trouble before it starts. [p. 642]

Bird himself certainly realized that this manner of speaking is just like how an adult and child, together, might address interactions taking place among play figures being effected by the child. Bird's use of language in this way led not only to a diminishment of the acting out but to the recovery of critical childhood reminiscences.[21]

A borderline analysand in psychoanalysis with me was quite conscious and insistent that our relationship should extend into her life outside our sessions. At the end of each hour she wanted me to leave the session, go through the door with her, and especially be present to help her deal with colleagues and superiors at work. Work, especially, was a stressful and bitter experience for her; she constantly experienced humiliation, intrigue against her, and so forth. This associative material was often suffused with a quality of bitter complaint toward me about her mistreatment. Her work problems she attributed to her relationship with her father. A very successful physician, he fully expected, according to my patient, that a younger son could follow in his footsteps, but this was not true for the analysand because she was a female. In one session, she bitterly described how when a son is born, a Jewish father will go to synagogue proclaiming gratitude to God for the male heir and the productive life expected to be forthcoming. But nothing like this happens to a girl baby born to a Jewish father. At this point, I said something like this to the analysand: "So, if I were your dad, and you were my little baby girl, we could have it different. I would go to synagogue and say to God how happy I was at your birth. And I would say, 'Listen God; what interesting and exciting kind of work will she do—physician, lawyer, what will it be?'" and so forth.

It was with this analysand, and just prior to my making this transference interpretation, that I found myself imagining Frank Sinatra singing the ballad "My Boy Bill" from the Soliloquy of the musical *Carousel*, and as I have indicated, this daydream involved both intense auditory and visual experience. I believe, in hindsight, that it was the dramatic quality of my daydream that caused me to make the interpretation *in this form*; that is, instead of simply saying again to the analysand that she wanted me to be her wished-for father, in some degree, I *playacted* such a father and made the interpretation in such a manner. I spoke in this way perhaps for as long as 1 minute. But the analysand already had begun to sob after my first few words.[22] Then there was a period of silence. After this, I emphasized to the analysand how she would accept nothing less than the realization of this, and more, I said she was prepared to destroy the psychoanalysis to produce another bitter repetition with her father unless I complied. Her bitter, verbal complaints toward me were not genuine discourse but enacted actions with language to make me feel remorse as her father, and to force me as her father to lovingly protect her in her life outside the treatment relationship.

I believe some alleviation of the analysand's work problems did follow this incident. But, certainly, much more work of this sort had to be done. And this, in turn, developed into uncovering the analysand's rage over what she felt to be her physician-father's dismissal of her oedipal sexuality as a little girl. The father functioned as physician for his children and was conducting examinations on his daughter until her preadolescence. What enraged my analysand was how her father could maintain such emotional detachment in touching her body, while, of course, exciting her tremendously. She also revealed a repetitive masturbation fantasy in which she was naked, with her clothed father, and making him excited. She never could allow herself to have an orgasm with the fantasy because as she approached orgastic excitement, it all felt "too real." At this point, I interpreted to the analysand that she needed to maintain a (transference) experience of frustration with me because she expected she would become very anxious otherwise; a (transference) experience of security and pleasure with me she would (wishfully) make "too real" as she did her masturbatory excitement as she approached orgasm. But my point here is that all of this further important clinical material was enabled by an initial playful-enactment experience.

By my willingness to allow myself to talk this way, I played along in a definite manner with the analysand's desire to alter the reality of the psychoanalytic relationship. What if I had not done this? What if I had only interpreted or confronted her? I believe that had I done so, she would have continued to experience only an interaction in the transference with her distant and aloof father, and we would have gotten no further.

Acting out in the transference—especially in what I have described to be this second clinical context in which enacted symbols are meaningfully felt to be connected to reminiscences with significant others in childhood—is related to the saying *actions speak louder than words*. However, psychoanalytically we should understand there to exist a psychody-namically driven conflict between actions and words. With actions, the patient wants to change, really coerce a change, about how experience will be indexed for both patient and therapist, so that transference content will now be treated as something real about the treatment relationship. I believe the therapist makes a mistake if he or she immediately becomes invested in a return to the parameters of a classical psycho-analysis and advocates this by explaining - the need for prohibition (however benignly and sincerely felt). In my experience, two other sorts of responses by a therapist will be much more likely to be useful. First, the therapist may need to find a way to play along with the patient's enacted symbol so that the clinical process is safeguarded for even-tual verbal analytic implementation. And second, of course, is just that—analytic interpretation. At first the intervention may begin only with questions and clarification about what has produced the patient's urgency for enactment. But, ultimately, interpretation must be made about the psychody-namics of the acting out, and this in my experience always includes the patient's sadistic desire to control what is to be considered real. My listing of what comes first, and what second, is deliberate, as I have found this sequence to be most useful in my own clinical experience.

But loose talk about a willingness on the analyst's part to play along requires further clarification. First, and this is by way of repetition, when I say "play along," I mean to emphasize a form, or shape, to how an analysand is orga-nizing the knowing of experience in the psychoanalytic situation, and this applies both to the real, collaborative relationship that is a psychoanalysis as well as to the transference. The term *play* is intended to emphasize a position away from authentic, language-mediated meaning toward action-structured, enacted symbols, including a pos-sible use of language concretization as an action symbol. I can conjecture that the borderline analysands described by

Abend and colleagues (1983) were already expressing enacted symbols in their analyses, that action symbols always
produce a provocation for the analyst to respond in kind,
and that the analyst's actions regarding possible termination
of treatment were a composite of realistic considerations,
together with a shaping of countertransference experience.

I certainly do not mean to imply that matters must always
reach such an extreme point of transference-countertransference as pathological play. In my experience enacted
actions sometimes occur around the issue of consultation for
a possible termination. However, it obviously matters much
whether an analyst feels, countertransferentially, "driven" to
such an action or not. Also, development into this more
extreme type of enactment can often be mitigated, first, by a
(conceptual) recognition of the other-than-neurotic organization of both the transference and real, collaborative psychoanalytic relationship, and second, by accepting into the
treatment process playful enactment without initial interpretation.

But of course the psychodynamics (content) of pathologically playfully shaped transference also must be considered.
In a following chapter I will discuss psychodynamics in
greater detail, together with etiological considerations. However, for now, note that in all three cases *new* material is
reported by Abend and colleagues to occur following the
treatment crisis produced by a consideration of termination.
In one case the analysand revealed for the first time her
"secret bulimia" (p. 43); in the second case, wishes to be
"cuddled" as well as sexual desire for a woman became
expressed, together with castration anxiety imbedded in
masturbation (pp. 59–60); in the third case, the analysand
"clearly for the first time" (p. 72) revealed transference
feelings that the analyst had always quietly (secretly) dis-
liked her just as she felt to be the case with her mother.
These treatment crises evidently facilitated working through
a withholding of important analytic material. The psycho-

dynamics at work here are decidedly pre-oedipal, although without doubt these pre-oedipal psychodynamics enter into, and complicate immensely, oedipal psychodynamics. But, most immediately, it is narcissistic and instinctual drive-related, anal-rapprochement psychodynamics that are critical. And in my experience, this is to be expected when a desire for such transference enactments appears to become urgent in a psychoanalysis (or psychotherapy).

To return to the cases reported by Abend and colleagues, I can say that the treatment crises produced by the analysts' consideration of termination was an anal-rapprochement crisis. These analysands had now obtained real confirmation from the analyst of their capacity to produce an effect or impact. But transferentially they had now "succeeded" in a sadistic assault on an intensely loved-hated analyst. And to whatever extent the analysts' consideration of termination may have expressed (ego passively suffered) countertransference anger, we can also say that these analysands had produced hate (Winnicott 1949) in the countertransference. The working through of the consultation–termination crisis is a transferential working through of profound and split love–hate urgencies toward the object. Desire for reparation (e.g., Winnicott 1955) of the destructive effects on this loved-hated object produces either new analytic material or a general improvement in the workability of the transference experience. All of this, of course, would need to be interpreted to the analysand. But such interpretation can only occur at a clinically useful time *after* this enactment first, simply, has been admitted and accepted *as is* into the playground (Freud 1914c) of transference (as well as the real psychoanalytic relationship). This later occurrence of verbal interpretation generally will apply to a circumstance in which an analysand experiences an urgency for one or another sort of enactment in the clinical process.

Another example of unintended, playful acts between analyst and analysand, and something whose symbolic meaning is initially not understood, is provided in an important paper by Sandler (1976). Sandler prefers the term *role-responsiveness* (p. 43) to *acting out*, as illustrated in his example of a female patient who, from the beginning of treatment, cried in each session. Sandler routinely passed her a box of tissues, although it was not what he would ordinarily do, which would be to take up with the patient why she was not bringing her own tissues or handkerchief to the session. "Now I did not know why I did this," states Sandler, "but, having begun the practice, I did not feel inclined to change it without some good reason" (p. 46).

As the analysis progressed, many determinants of this analysand's constant crying emerged, but especially her intensely felt loss of her mother's attention because of the birth of her brother. The analysand recalled how at about 2½ years she was relegated to playing by herself in the backyard while her mother attended to her new baby brother. At this time the analysand was also sent to a nursery, where she remembered herself as very withdrawn; she later learned that the report of the school psychologist included a description of her as being very regressed as well as subject to uncontrollable rages and temper tantrums. At this point in the analysis, says Sandler, "we were able to get at the repetition in the present of her fear of soiling and disgracing herself, and her need to control her objects as she had to control her sphincters" (p. 46).

A moment came in a session when Sandler's patient began to cry silently, but Sandler did not respond to her need for tissues. The analysand became "quite panicky and began to accuse me [Sandler] of being callous and uncaring" (p. 47). Sandler's response was that he did not know why he did not now pass her the tissues, but if the analysand would continue talking, perhaps this could be understood. What developed was the analysand's realization that her great anxiety was not simply that she would soil herself but *"there would not be an adult around to clean her up"* (p. 47). The recognition and working through of this fantasy marked "a crucial point in her analysis" (p. 47).

> I believe that this patient had forced me into a role, quite unconsciously on her part and mine, a role corresponding to that of a parental introject in which I enacted the part, first, of the attentive mother and then suddenly that of the parent who did not clean her up. . . . Within the limits set by the analytic situation he [the analyst] will, unless he becomes aware of it, tend to comply with the role demanded of him, to integrate it into his mode of responding in relating to the patient. Normally, of course, he can catch this countertransference in himself, particularly if it appears to be in the direction of being inappropriate. However, he may only become aware of it through observing his own behavior, responses and attitudes *after these have been carried over into action*. [p. 47]

I would understand Sandler's give-tissue–stop-giving-tissue behavior with the analysand to be an unwitting playful enactment; it is unwitting both in the sense of its being unintended as such, that is, a playful tilting of the transference experience toward reality, and because the meaning of the playful enactment was not initially understood. It is important to notice how Sandler uses the word *forced*—"forced me into a role"—which I think correctly alludes to a countertransference origin of the analyst's behavior.

The transference incidents I characterize as pathological play are neither descriptively nor conceptually the same as transference circumstances that Gedo (1979) calls beyond interpretation—"pacification," "unification," or "optimal disillusionment." These circumstances involve interactions in which the analyst supplies some aspect of a holding environment (e.g., Modell 1976) by providing, with words, regulation for an overstimulated (prerepresentational) state, or integration for a fragmented self, or a necessary realistic perspective on the analysand's grandiosity or idealization. Gedo sees these circumstances as matters of developmental deficiency (arrest) repetitively suffered by the analysand and therefore beyond any kind of psychodynamic (conflict) interpretation.[23] He has also called these circumstances enactment, but it is clear that his use of the term is only loosely metaphorical. The essential interaction between analyst and analysand during one of these incidents beyond interpretation is decidedly not beyond verbalization in any sense; the interactions made by Gedo at such moments are conventionally verbal, as is any response by the analysand. Gill's (1981) commentary that such interventions as Gedo advocates amount to suggestions that remain unanalyzed as to any psychodynamic, transference significance is of course rejected by Gedo inasmuch as he believes there is nothing of psychodynamic conflictual significance to analyze. On the other hand, Gedo (1981) would accept a term like *management* as appropriate to such a circumstance.

Gedo (1979) does describe an incident with an analysand that could be described as a witting participation in a pathologically playful transference experience, but it would also have to be described as a kind of forced, witting participation. An analysand began to insist that the light from a floor lamp, placed behind the couch, was shining too brightly into her eyes and that it was like a light "at a police station where prisoners were subjected to the third degree" (p. 86). Immediate verbal efforts to interpret this analysand's experience in terms of exhibitionistic and masochistic needs proved to no avail, and rather quickly a power struggle ensued.

> As time went on, whenever she found lights on when she came into the office, she refused to lie on the couch, either sitting on it in scowling silence or stomping out altogether. No attempt to *talk* about the issue was acceptable to her *as long as she did not get her way*. [p. 88, italics mine]

After some (unspecified) time, Gedo ultimately agreed to the analysand's request to be in control of the light source,

saying to the analysand that this was a "therapeutic conces-
sion," the meaning of which would have to be understood at
a later time. The analysand then rather quickly acknowledged that she was deliberately (consciously) withholding
her associations because of the struggle over the lighting in
the room. This in turn led to her further acknowledging
lifelong conscious manipulations of silent, stubborn resistance, and ultimately a forced and profoundly disturbing
separation she had had to endure with regard to a house-
keeper she had loved deeply as a toddler.

Further comments by Gedo (1981) about this light-in-
the-room incident as well as remarks by Rangell (1981) are
intriguing. Gedo says: "With people whom I have analyzed
with success, this was the *sole instance* in which I was unable
to deal with such a situation through *verbal means* alone" (p.
117, italics mine). To which Rangell responds: "In my
experience, such a statement coming from an average,
classical analyst is overly strong. Nonverbal empathy is
entwined even with the classical analytic stance more freely
than that" (p. 256). "Well," counters Gedo, "I am a flinty
character, and I am used to storms of rage in my office. If
anything, then, I may be excessively reluctant to depart from
verbal treatment methods" (p. 296).

In this disagreement Gedo and Rangell are both in some
measure correct and incorrect. Certainly, empathy is involved and required from the analyst. But when is this not
the case? It is the particular *nonverbal form* of empathic
response the analysand wants from the analyst that is
distinctive about this episode. And my argument is that the
analysand at such a moment can only *know* through enactment that there exists a real, cooperative working attitude
between analysand and analyst, as well as a positive transference experience. But, and included in this view, I believe
Gedo is correct about what he construes and senses. The
analysand also sadistically wants Gedo to feel forced to

believe that her transference experience of being tortured is due to some reality about the psychoanalytic relationship.[24]

It is also important to distinguish this idea, that there exists an experience of the psychoanalytic relationship that is structured like a kind of pathological play, from certain theoretical and praxis innovations proposed by Ferenczi (esp. 1929, 1931), who, correctly, I believe, recognized the importance of analysand "[psychic] material in the *shape* of action" (1931, p. 131, italics mine). And it is clear that Ferenczi was attempting to revise our theory and practice with respect to analysand acting out in the transference in the face of importantly felt reminiscences pertinent to just such acting out, something I have termed enacted action of one sort or another. (Ferenczi [e.g., 1931] used just this term *acting out* in his comments.) But Ferenczi also considered that analysand enacted action (acting out) should be conceived to possess *only* a positive therapeutic significance, a "benign regression" as Balint (1968) would later describe it. I believe this is incorrect, and I have presented a more complex perspective. Analysand enacted symbols (acting out) that occur together with importantly held reminiscences present the treatment relationship with what could be called a special condition for analytic loving and knowing that is other-than-language used as a genuine symbolic vehicle. And this special condition for analytic loving and knowing, so long as it remains critical for a psychoanalysis, applies both to the real, collaborative and transference experience of the treatment relationship. But I have stressed throughout *patholog-ical* play. I conceive, unlike Ferenczi, that enacted symbols also always implicate coercive attempts by the analysand to make the analyst believe that the treatment relationship has been, is, or should be something in reality it cannot be, whether this be psychically pleasurable or painful.

From another angle, Ferenczi (1931) emphasized, in his idea that procedures from "child analysis" be introduced into adult treatment, that this should be done because the adult analysand had suffered trauma requiring concrete gratification by the analyst serving as a mother figure. Ferenczi (1929) developed, logically enough, what he called a principle of indulgence, which came to include such things as extending sessions by as much as 1 or 2 hours, visiting and analyzing analysands in their homes, stroking an analysand's head, affectionately kissing an analysand, and so forth (also see Bergmann and Hartman 1976). Freud (see, e.g., Bergmann and Hartman 1976) predictably argued that the analyst's provision of such a relationship made a psychoanalytic relationship impossible and questioned its morality. However, while I hardly minimize the moral issue, I think that to focus on it exclusively only more subtly continues to place a matter of libidinal gratification always in the foreground of our theory and praxis about acting out, and this is what I believe is sometimes misconceived.

Put another way, Ferenczi's praxis could only enhance confusion and conflict over the interplay of real and unreal experience. It was his conception, and intention, to use his praxis to *replace* (he believed) early, actual maternal trauma with a treatment-created nurturance experience of equal psychic significance for the analysand. But this kind of praxis can never succeed in any literal sense. The psychoanalytic relationship cannot realistically be a relationship of mother and child, and no amount or type of provision by an analyst can make it one. Finally, Ferenczi's idea of pathogenesis is an ancestor to the more contemporary notion of developmental arrest (Stolorow and Lachmann 1980). But with Ferenczi, the trauma that produces the arrest was conceived exclusively to be a matter of inappropriate or excessive libidinal frustration, with no conception of either the vital role of narcissism (Kohut 1977) or a necessary condition for early executive (ego) functioning (Winnicott, e.g., 1955). A more detailed consideration of etiology[25] of necessity will involve me in a consideration of mind emergence in psychic development.

NOTES

1. Obviously, this "class" of analysand includes men as well as women. Segal and Britton (1981) also use these very same comments by Freud to consider that there is a type of analysand who experiences, and can cause the analyst to experience, a special type of strain on an exclusively verbal psychoanalytic relationship.

2. I will say something more later about different kinds of memorial organization and connect this to Piaget's work.

3. And, essentially in the same way, any formulation of a physical law is such a normative idealization involving planes with no friction whatsoever, perfect vacuums, and so forth.

4. I have elsewhere (Steingart 1983) used this material as part of an examination of the concepts of splitting and denial.

5. But I mean here a *sort* of what Mahoney (1979) calls aesthetic discourse. An analysand, comfortably and productively free-associating, is most certainly not (ordinarily) a poet or writer who *intends* to create meaningful symbols.

6. I take the term *adornment* from important comments by Greenacre (1971) about acting out: "speech becomes an infantile adornment" (p. 68). I will shortly examine Greenacre's ideas in more detail. McDougall (1980) has also commented about this matter.

It might be argued that what I have called language as enactment is an example of regressive primary-process thinking such as produces dreams. According to this argument, the way in which a child uses noncomprehended language in play is an example of a displacement of meaning as, indeed, can occur with verbal material in a dream. But this does not square with how clinically healthy children actually play. Two such children dressed up in their Sunday best, seated at the back of the church, would never believe they could play at being astronauts simply by talking like astronauts. They do not *look* like astronauts and they are not *acting* like astronauts. And a child at play being an astronaut would never treat his or her laser gun as a penis, which, of course, can happen in a dream.

7. Of course, even in a psychoanalysis in which language essentially remains a communicative-interpretive process, influence of language concretization is normally and naturally present; but in such a context it only serves to "enrich" language with "background" influence. Further, one can consider (conceive) that language as genuine discourse normatively develops out of a period in life in which words function psychically as a transitional object (Winnicott 1951). One thinks here of the typical wordplay enacted by the young child who is just beginning to acquire language.

8. I used some of this material in my organization of a case seminar entitled "Acting Out in the Transference," at the midwinter meeting of the Division of Psychoanalysis of the American Psychological Association, Ixtapa, Mexico, February 18, 1986.

9. There is also an interesting use of this connotation of dramatic-play action in a concept of playacting devised by Ekstein and Friedman (1957) in the treatment of an impulsive, antisocial 13-year-old. This child enacted, over many therapy sessions, an elaborate play that involved himself and the therapist as members of a criminal gang. But what these authors mean by the term *playacting* is quite different from the concept elaborated by Greenacre.

Except for problems that arise in not using customary terminology, I believe it would better clarify the situation of this child's action in the transference if the action were not conceptualized as acting out. Such a transference circumstance is better understood to be an example of denial. Perhaps Jacobson (1957) comes close to making the distinction when she comments that acting out "appears to be regularly linked with a bent for denial" (p. 136). My argument is that such a clinical phenomenon as is described by Ekstein and Friedman (1957) is an expression of a type of denial, really the same as what A. Freud (1936) meant by "denial in [enacted] fantasy" (and see Steingart 1983).

10. Again, when I use the term *remembering* in this context I am not concerned about the veridicality of such reminiscences.

11. Stated in terms of what analysts call (at least at times euphemistically) the "academic literature," my argument is that there is no fundamental difference in operational definition between verbal symbol and symbol as such an enactment. Further, I believe the same is true initially for action as enactment in what I will in a moment describe as a second clinical context for acting out.

12. In this first clinical context for acting out as enacted action, what one is attempting with an interpretation, such as Freud made to Dora about her fingering her reticule, is a conversion of analysand psychic reality simultaneous with a drive content enlargement of analysand psychic reality. This leads to questions about interpretive technique for acting out with respect to timing and content, something I will discuss, but not extensively, later in this work.

However, aside from specific questions about interpretive technique, there are conceptual issues that deserve at least brief mention. This matter of a conversion from action as enacted action into some language equivalent relates to an idea of acting out (enacted action) as resistance (or defense). Mahl (e.g., 1977) has observed and investigated what he calls an "A" (motor act)–"B" (verbalization) phenomenon wherein symbolic action is sooner or later spontaneously (without interpretation) converted by the analysand into verbal free associations. This could be construed to be an event sequence that represents a giving way of resistance (or defense), but Mahl suggests that such a sequence may (also) be regarded as a clinically normative process for the recovery (construction) of dynamically unconscious experience.

There is also a question of a conceptual boundary for this idea of acting out as enacted symbol. It is clear that I have sought to give this idea of an enacted symbol specificity. I believe my use of the term *enacted symbol* is essentially similar to what Kanzer (1966) already has described as "enacted experience," which occurs in the "motor sphere of the transference":

> It is important to construct in detail the actual situation *represented* by the acting out—the compulsive masturbatory substitutes of the anal phase with its regressive relationships to sphincter control; the avoidance of the phobic reactions; the dramatizations of the hysteric. [p. 153, italics mine; see also Kanzer 1961]

I agree with Kanzer that actions as symbolic enactment in this first clinical context can represent diverse psychosexual and aggressive dynamics. But I will argue that a conspicuous presence of enacted symbols in what I will in a moment describe as a second clinical context for acting out implicates in particular a certain anal-stage psychodynamics. See also, in this connection, Stein's (1973) comments about the necessity to bring acting out into the transference.

13. Freud (1923) stated: "For the ego, perception plays the part which in the id falls to the instinct" (p. 25). I am modifying this statement to read: "For the ego, symbolic representation plays the part. . . ." But this revision is congruent with a comment by A. Freud (1936):

> This intellectualization of instinctual life, this attempt to lay hold on the instinctual processes by connecting them with ideas which can be dealt with in consciousness, is one of the most general, earliest, and most necessary requirements of the human ego. We regard it not as an activity of the ego but one of its indispensable components. [p. 163]

But I have emphasized how any symbolic vehicle for thoughts and feelings must be felt to be a meaningful way of expressing one's psychic reality, and most certainly this must be so for language, which is genuine discourse in a psychoanalysis.

14. The use of this term *nonenactive* relates to my previous discussion as to how language can become an acting out.

15. Clinical material reported in the literature, already cited, can also be conceptualized in this way: Freud's (1915a) commentary about

"bringing down on oneself the full enmity of a woman scorned"; Dora's (Freud 1905b) desire to obtain "revenge"; the Goldberg (1978) *Casebook* analysand who stated to his analyst, "You're tying me down by saying this." I believe further case material I will cite shortly in connection with work done with borderline and narcissistic pathology described by Abend and colleagues (1983), as well as work by Gedo (1979) and Greenson (1965), also supports such a viewpoint; Bach (e.g., 1985) especially has described such dynamics with extensive clinical material.

16. Piaget applies this notion to certain behaviors of birds and bees, whereas I have in mind remembering occurring in humans, which I assume involves representational processes not existent in such animals. Also, see G. S. Klein (1966) with respect to complexities about the memorial process as well as Rapaport (e.g., 1951) in connection with the more general question of varieties in the organization of human consciousness. Loewald (1976) is especially responsive to the fact that every psychoanalysis involves a significantly new form for the differentiation and integration of experiences indexed as past versus present in one's psychic reality; but I believe Loewald conceives of this issue within the classic psychoanalytic situation of evocative memory mediated by language.

17. With this description of the three characteristics of clinically healthy versus pathological play, I am attempting to respond to questions raised by Drs. Anni Bergman and Steven Ellman about my use of the idea of pathological play.

18. My depiction of pathological play in young children—that what is critical is its dysfunctional relationship to the actualities of the child's life—is a different emphasis from that of Galenson (1971), who stresses whether an age-appropriate repertoire of skills is available to the young child at play. A striking persistence of immature play skills in a young child who is neurologically intact and not culturally deprived must indicate some sort of pathology. But how this may or may not relate to what I have here described as pathological play is, I suspect, complex. And I agree with McDevitt (1971) that any attributes about the play of a young child turn out clinically to have a complex relationship to the child's adaptation, treatability, as well as capability as an adult for creative output.

19. In this sense a nonverbal, parametric (according to Eissler [1953]) interaction with an adult can be likened to a play technique with a young child. But this analogy can easily lead to misunderstanding. In the case of the very young (oedipal, pre-oedipal) child, an actual developmental immaturity exists with respect to verbal symbolic activities, whereas with the adult, the condition is instigated and maintained because of psychic conflict that engenders a desire to do away with a genuine verbal symbol-making experience.

20. The final case reported by Abend and colleagues evidently did not involve such a critical moment in which possible termination was suggested by the analyst. But certainly there was enacted action by the analysand intended to force on the transference experience the status of a reality. For example, this analysand "moved to an apartment near her analyst's office, announcing that he was now the 'center of my life' " (p. 83). At least it is clear that such analysand enacted action was "accepted" by the analyst in the sense that the treatment was not stopped because of it. There also is a possibility that these instances of analyst-initiated consideration of consultation about a possible termination of treatment are examples of what Winnicott (1949) means by "truly objective countertransference" (p. 195).

I am aware that Singer (1985) has reported only two rather than three such parametric incidents in his review of this work; he also describes these incidents as planned. But this kind of assessment actually minimizes the taxing nature of the work done with the analysands, and thus insufficiently appreciates the magnitude of success achieved. Buie (1985) considers these to be cases in which a point is reached where the analysis was "threatened with consultative intervention or termination" (p. 379), that the crises only "seem to mark a turning point toward improvement and resolution" (p. 379), and that what occurred is better understood to be analysand compliance in order to prevent abandonment by the analyst. And I have said that I do not agree with him: Why should compliance lead to new and *unexpected material*? Also, I believe it is a mistake to construe an analysand's experience about the analyst's consideration that treatment would have to stop to signify, simply and only, a threat to be abandoned. These incidents were not planned "strategies" employed by the analyst, but an expression (and I include whatever countertransference elements may have been operative) of a *genuine* sense on the analyst's part that he felt stymied and unable to be of further help. This circumstance actually can promote in borderline patients a critical experience wherein the analysand feels that he or she can exert a real, significant effect on a significant other (in addition to whatever unreal transference is also experienced).

21. In this connection Weinshel (1988) has provided an interesting example of how his refusal to treat a (strictly speaking) unlawful act on his analysand's part as pathological play experience intensified negative transference. The incident involved the analysand's crossing a road against a red light on her way to a session.

22. When I presented this material to a seminar dealing with work with the "more difficult" analysand, it was suggested to me that this Frank Sinatra fantasy illustrated male chauvinism. I still find this mind-boggling. Certainly, the song "My Boy Bill" is chauvinistic, as is the 1940s culture

that produced it. But this song obviously connected with experiences with my own father, and to consider my fantasy at this moment to be chauvinistic shows no understanding of how the dynamic unconscious operates. It surely would have been chauvinistic to have been unable, smoothly and easily, to use my fantasy to facilitate the expression of this female analysand's complex of feelings about her father.

23. But Gedo does state that such developmental deficiencies may become enmeshed in conflict and require some sort of psychodynamic interpretation.

24. Gedo (1979) understands the analysand's need for such control to be a matter of her "being entitled to impose her subjective needs on our transactions without being made to feel unreasonable as a consequence" (p. 88). But one can see how sadomasochistic struggles have become caught up in the determination of what is to be construed as real or unreal about the psychoanalytic relationship. Gedo himself at least alludes to this issue in his description of his own experience before he agreed to give the analysand control over the lighting. "On my side, it was an effort to safeguard my own boundaries; the demand that I conduct an analysis in the dark (or acknowledge bizarre motivations for my manner of lighting it) had made me feel that I was being absorbed into the patient's system of volition against my will" (p. 88). I would emphasize in particular, and distinctively, a struggle over one's own *belief* system, as to what is real about oneself as an analyst and what is real about what one is doing as an analyst, that can threaten one's boundaries.

I should distinguish the kinds of transference and countertransference experiences I classify with the term *pathological play* from the work described by Little (1981). While Little does speak about special transference difficulties with "borderline states," she evidently construes the idea of borderline to be descriptive of a type of psychosis; thus, while Little has a chapter in her book entitled "Transference in Borderline States," she also speaks in this same chapter about this "question of technique in the analysis of transference psychosis" (p. 142). Little entitles her book *Transference Neurosis and Transference Psychosis*.

I do not conceive this condition of transference experience I call pathological play to be a psychotic transference; and I believe the reality-testing disturbance it represents to be a stable type of personality structure (Steingart 1983), neither neurotic nor psychotic organization. Also, and this probably has much to do with Little's equation of the terms *borderline* and *psychosis*, Little considers that the basic dynamic issue for her analysands is one of wishes for merger and threat of separation. The anal-rapprochement, sadomasochistic dynamics I have emphasized (and see esp. Bach 1980) presuppose the establishment of differentiation, which is the matrix for psychopathology. Finally, Little describes actual *manage-*

ment procedures on her part that involve the analysand's outside life; for example, Little makes a referral to a surgeon for one of her clients and talks to the surgeon about the psychological implications of the upcoming surgery. Such management is quite unlike what I conceive and describe to be an analyst's intention to relocate a transference experience into a place somewhere away from a relationship to be realized exclusively with language, and it has two paradoxically (but understandably) opposite effects: what the analyst actually does with it has such a significant, real effect on the client's life that the unreal, transference experience (meaning) that occurs surely will be extremely difficult, if not impossible, to analyze.

Segal and Britton (1981), who claim to speak for a Kleinian viewpoint, also consider this light-in-the-room incident, and state that Gedo's agreement to give the analysand control of the light only served to "collude" with the analysand's psychopathology. But if, in fact, collusion occurred, why is it that (according to Gedo's report) what followed was an outpouring of sadomasochistic material with respect to transference, genetic, and contemporary life experience of a sort that impresses us as productive and enabling insight? Segal and Britton might argue that what occurred was gratification for the analysand of some primitive, omnipotent power illusion about herself. But at least we can be clear that in fact what followed was notably lessened demands for control. Clinically, this is not what is expected with a straightforward gratification experience for needs that remain pathological, hence insatiable, and it is difficult to see what sort of evidence would convince Segal and Britton that the use of this pathologically playful interaction was an analytically useful parameter (as defined by Eissler [1950]). For that matter, it is also difficult to see what evidence would convince Gedo that his initial unwilling use of an analyzed nonverbal parameter is to be preferred to unanalyzed verbal commentaries considered to be "beyond interpretation." Segal and Britton are also confusing on this point because they allude, with evident approval, to Rosenfeld's (1966) work, and response, to the acting out of obviously much more disturbed psychotic individuals. Rosenfeld, for example, describes how he allowed a patient to touch his tie and stroke his hands. An analyst also can "play along" with such a transference condition verbally, but it is not a conventional form of verbalization such as occurs in a psychoanalysis, classically conceived. In this connection I have described Bird's (1957) interesting use of "baby talk" with a patient inclined to act out.

It should be clear that what I conceive to be acting out as enacted symbol is not at all the same idea as what McDougall (1985) means by "action symptoms" (p. 109) or "acting out phenomena especially when phenomena take a psychosomatic turn" (p. 112). McDougall is very much working with an economic idea of acting out as discharge; and she also considers that the dynamic function of such discharge is "psychic repudiation or foreclosure" (p. 111) of the development of any meaningfully felt psychic reality. For McDougall, an important clinical example of such "foreclosure" occurs with alexithymia—a condition in which individuals have "no words for emotions or are unable to distinguish one emotion from another" (p. 114). Etiologically, she considers this kind of acting out to foreclose any meaningfully felt psychic reality to be located in early separation-individuation psychopathology.

While I consider McDougall's comments about such psychopathology extremely valuable and pertinent to certain of my clinical experiences, it is not what I have in mind in this book. The people I describe as using enacted symbols experience meaningfully *felt* psychic reality, indeed, insist that their intensely *felt* psychic reality be recognized to be *the* reality of the psychoanalytic relationship, and have no particular inclination to psychosomatic manifestations. Shortly, I will elaborate further what I consider to be an anal-rapprochement etiology for this psychopathology.

25. We can also question Ferenczi's ideas about what constitutes a treatment process with children, but this is beyond the purpose of this discussion. However, what still must be appreciated is Ferenczi's early attention to pre-oedipal factors in pathogenesis. And there is also Ferenczi's intuitive realization that an excessive demand by an analysand for action (acting out) in a psychoanalysis is something that can usefully (at least initially) be approached by means other than exclusively language.

5

Etiology of Pathological Play as Transference

Inasmuch as the location of the psychopathology I have described as pathologically playful transference is in this area of the notation of actuality versus not-real experience, it is to the origin of such notation that we should look for etiology. My comments will relate to Eissler's (1950) statement, I believe insufficiently appreciated, that we must distinguish between consciousness and self-awareness. As I understand Eissler, and with respect to the development of consciousness, this means an examination of the development of such processes as attention, concentration, thinking, remembering, emotionality, and so forth, all of which, of course, affect self-awareness. But the development of self-awareness has its own terms and history.[1]

Pine (1982) has used the expression "crystallization of the self" (p. 151) to characterize certain changes in self-awareness that occur in the "first two or three years of life" (p. 152), a period that encompasses the individuation subphases of both practicing and rapprochement (Mahler et al. 1975). The practicing subphase is instigated by the toddler's desire and physical capacity for independent locomotion. There are three critical observations about the practicing toddler: (1) The toddler has an extraordinary "investment in practicing motor skills and in exploring the expanding environment, both human and inanimate" (p. 71). (2) Also, with a toddler we see

a "relatively great imperviousness to knocks and falls and
other frustrations" (p. 71). And (3) "substitute adults within
the set-up of our nursery are easily accepted" (p. 71). Of
course, the mother remains important—but now as a "home
base"—to which the toddler returns periodically "for refuel-
ing through physical contact" (p. 69). What are we to infer
from these observations? Mahler and colleagues say it suc-
cinctly: "narcissism is at its peak" (p. 71). To elaborate: the
practicing toddler is "exhilarated by his [her] own abilities,
continually delighted with the discoveries he [she] makes—in
his [her] expanding world, and quasi-enamored with the
world and his [her] own *grandeur and omnipotence*" (p. 71,
italics mine). One should add that the mother in this practicing period is, in complementary fashion, experienced as a
perfect, ideal facilitator for the toddler. Together, mother and
practicing toddler form a "dual unit," a symbiotic entity that
has acquired "feet"; it is capable of expansion through the
toddler's locomotion, and this naturally and normally involves enormous narcissistic satisfaction for both partici-
pants.[2]

The desires and cognitive capabilities of the anal-rapprochement child will spell an end to this euphoric dual-unit
experience for both mother and toddler. Again, three types
of critical observations are reported by Mahler and her
colleagues: (1) Ambivalent behavior toward the mother is
characteristic; "shadowing" of the mother, that is, incessant
watching and following, together with a requirement that
she share every experience, will alternate with vigorous
physical rejection and "darting away" from such closeness.
(2) Substitute figures for the mother are not easily accepted,
and anxiety over separation from the mother is obvious.
(3) There is a "noticeable waning of the toddler's previous
imperviousness to frustration" (p. 76). From all of this we
theoretically infer a new status for self-awareness. The
toddler and mother "no longer function effectively as a dual
unit—that is to say, the child can no longer maintain his

delusion of parental omnipotence, which he still expects at times will restore the symbiotic status quo" (pp. 78–79).[3]

But there is something implicit in all of this change from practicing to rapprochement that deserves theoretical acknowledgment in its own right; it represents an emergent status for self-awareness not ordinarily connoted by a construct of individuation that emphasizes the achievement of boundary setting between self and object representation(s). It is, we might say, the achievement of an "interior" differentiation with respect to self-awareness. Systematic observation of young children clearly and consistently indicates the emergence of a capacity for pretense during the anal-rapprochement period (see, e.g., Ungerer et al. 1981). The reason the younger, practicing toddler is noticeably oblivious, unbothered, and unaffected by knocks and falls, frustrations of all kinds, is that an actuality that is psychically, narcissistically painful is not yet *held together* with playful, unreal experience that is narcissistically pleasurable (grandiosity and idealization), so that one type of experience will not really influence the other with respect to self-awareness.

Another way to say this is to make use of certain of Winnicott's ideas. Winnicott (1967) talked about "babies' *legitimate* experience of omnipotence" (p. 112, italics mine) and also stated (1953) how the young child's unreal transitional object creations must not be "challenged." What I am saying is that in the anal-rapprochement period the young child must deal with illegitimacy and challenge to self-awareness that is unreal experience because of desires and capabilities that arise naturally out of the child's own emotional and cognitive development. Now the child will face "grades" of experience in self-awareness not only about him- or herself but about significant others as well. Unreal self-grandiosity and object idealization will be known and felt in significant contrast from actual (real) representation about self and other, especially what is actual about limits with respect to *control* of life events. And this awareness about actual (real) limitation can itself easily be changed into a "negative" grade of unreal self-awareness, that is, into experiences of self-humiliation and object degradation (and see Hanly 1982).

From here it is but a short step to realizing that anal-stage ambivalence conflicts, with which we are so familiar, will act as a special but natural stimulus for emergent, complex grades in self-awareness. The process also operates the other way around: the full articulation of anal psychosexual dynamics in themselves is in part enabled by this emergent growth of complex actual (real) to unreal experiences in self-awareness. The anal child is not just rewarded but praised, really idealized, for his or her production of stool. But the product of what is so ideally produced, the stool itself, the child is to notate as something that possesses no value. Further, this stool itself, and the stool maker, can easily become notated as something, and someone, that is negatively unreal, degraded, insofar as the stool is considered not just without value but repugnant. In other words, the anal-rapprochement child is not just making stool, and not just through stool making negotiating vital matters of space and control between self and mother. Also, separated from all of this, and embedded in all of this, is the child as a maker-of-meaning, especially as someone who can make transitions between grades of actual (real) and playful experience in self-awareness with respect to him- or herself and significant others (Steingart 1983).

But to say that the clinically healthy, anal-rapprochement child will achieve some appropriate manner and degree of control over actual (real) to unreal fluctuations in self-awareness does not mean we have a "crystallization of the self" (Pine 1982, p. 151), wherein crystallization includes a connotation of integration as we ordinarily use the idea. All that we need—indeed can assume (e.g., Piaget 1947)—is simpler. It is that the clinically healthy, anal-rapprochement child is now someone who can tolerate and thus hold such

experiences sufficiently together—that is, who has a sufficient sense of a changed quality in self-awareness—between
what is actual and what is playfully unreal (Steingart 1983).
However, there is as yet no self-awareness that is itself a
patterned realization of fluctuations in grades of experience,
actual and playfully unreal. The fact that the rapprochement
child does not possess such psychic function and structure is
one powerful reason for the extraordinary but expected mood
swings and negativism of the anal child. This is especially
pertinent as the child must negotiate his or her actual limitations, as well as the actual limitations of the mother, with
playfully unreal awareness about his- or herself or the other.

It is, I suggest, psychopathology centered in this meaning-
making aspect of anal-rapprochement life that is the etiological source for transference as pathological play. Language,
under these circumstances, must become problematic. This
does not have to do in any simple way with the overt,
intense interest in words that occurs during anal-rapprochement life (e.g., Vygotsky 1934) together with a dramatic
increase in a child's vocabulary. But it has much to do with
the explosion of grammatical competence, which begins
during anal-rapprochement life (e.g., Brown 1973), and how
this implicates a new order of regulation for the child of his
or her experience (e.g., Freud 1915e, Luria 1981, Vygotsky
1934). In short, a new organization of consciousness is now
enabled by language (for better or worse). Stated the other
way around, and I believe indicated by clinical observation,
psychopathology centered in this actual versus unreal
meaning-making aspect of anal-rapprochement life affects
the child's (and adult's) sense of whether language serves as
an adequate vehicle for the realization of his or her total
psychic reality.[4] In this etiology it is not a matter of
something so evident as gross neglect, or gross indulgence,
in the relationship between the anal-rapprochement child
and its mother. Rather, it is a matter of whether the anal-
rapprochement relationship is such that the child experi-

ences him- or herself to be in some clinically healthy degree of control over the creation of these fluctuations of actual to playfully unreal self-awareness.

It is important for the child to feel and know adequate control over both narcissistically, playfully self-enhancing experience as well as experience that is narcissistically depleting. Here again, the idea of libidinal gratification must be more finely examined. A child may experience enormous playfully narcissistic satisfaction, which from one point of view is intensely libidinally gratifying, but if not sensed sufficiently to be the child's own unreal creation is pathological and will instigate anal-rapprochement ambivalence conflicts. I understand Kahn (1968) to have this in mind when he distinguishes the term *idealization* from a concept of *idolization*, which implicates narcissistic gratification that is felt as imposed. This, of course, also relates to Kohut's (e.g., 1977) theory with respect to narcissistic trauma of the young, anal-rapprochement child. Obviously, too, unresolved anal-ambivalence conflicts thus insinuated into meaning making about what is actual versus unreal about oneself or the other must affect the child's stance toward the unreal oedipal drama as well as the oedipal realities that are to come. Here a line of investigation would extend into acting out and perverse psychopathology, which is an attempt to deny certain oedipal realities. I will not pursue this further here (but see Spiegel 1954 and McDougall 1980).

What I do emphasize here is that when, or to the extent, anal-rapprochement ambivalence conflicts are insinuated into this process of meaning making, a special sort of anal struggle for control ensues in a psychoanalysis that amounts to insisting that the transference be regarded as real. Analysand acknowledgment of what is unreal, in other words, to accept the unreal character of the transference, will be experienced as a masochistic surrender, or passive compliance, or mortification with respect to the analyst as an anal authority figure, and will be resisted. At the same time, and in anal, "opposition" fashion, the analysand will fasten on certain realities about the psychoanalytic relationship in order to rebelliously or sadistically destroy, and so deny, the psychic reality and significance of the transference. What then can be insisted on is that the psychoanalytic relationship is "only" one of the professional who offers a client a service for a fee, that it "only" involves several hours a week, and so forth. What the analysand is not willing to do is hold together in some fashion what is real and unreal about the experience of the psychoanalytic situation because to do so is felt to involve either, or both, profound narcissistic injury and exposure to sadistic mistreatment.

Bach (e.g., 1977, 1980, 1985) especially has illustrated how, clinically, such sadomasochistic dynamics regularly reveal themselves in adult narcissistic pathology. As Bach (1980) puts it, "The object line of rapprochement overlaps the instinctual level of anality" (p. 194); Bach also considers that rapprochement is a critical period for "working through both the self/object differentiation and re-integration and the subjective self/object self differentiation and re-integration" (p. 187). What Bach has in mind here, with his use of the term *subjective,* is a Piagetian view of the development of experience about oneself that, indeed, will eventuate into an objective, that is, nonegocentric (e.g., Piaget 1947) viewpoint about one's experience and the experience of others, and for which a term like *realistic* (reality) is appropriate (see also Steingart 1969). But though the anal-rapprochement child is working through a situation in which physical individuation between self and mother now exists as an objective aspect of psychic reality, this same young child's social experience is nevertheless markedly egocentric (Steingart 1983), and for this reason the child's play experience cannot be contrasted with terms like *objective* or *real.*

Imagine, for example, a 2½-year-old child who now stands, for the first time, on the top step of a sliding pond and then completes a successful slide. We understand that what has transpired in the child's playful (unreal) psychic reality is extraordinary bravery, which naturally supports the child's narcissistic grandiosity; or it is a heroic feat performed naturally for an idealized maternal love object; or, more usually and naturally, it is a larger-than-actuality occurrence that facilitates both self-grandiosity and object-idealization experience. But now imagine that this same child does not execute a particular slide successfully, falls to the ground in an uncoordinated heap, and incurs a physical hurt. This kind of occurrence is inevitable because of the actualities related to the child's size and skill, as well as actualities with respect to the limitations of his or her caretakers.[5] It will be in some manner held together by the anal-rapprochement child and felt to be in significant contrast with other, playfully enlarging grandiose and idealizing experience produced by a successful slide. But this toddler will naturally assume that his or her own belief and experience about the unsuccessful slide (e.g., "The slide is no good anymore" or "I no slide anymore") will be worked through with the significant other. This kind of example is simple and commonplace; congruent examples that ramify throughout the toddler's life can easily be cited by anyone. But such repetitive contrasts in playful, psychically "enlarging" experience versus actuality-centered experience are no less significant for their ordinariness. Everything depends on how these are to be negotiated by both child and parental figures, especially with respect to the initiation of movement toward both actuality- and play-centered experience.

And with respect to actuality-centered experience, comments by Winnicott are pertinent, although his use of the term *reality* in what follows is, I believe, better re-read as *actuality*, as I have described the psychic reality of the young child. Winnicott, of course, is readily identified in our literature with a theoretical position that some type of unreal, playful experience is critical for clinical health, and that this holds true for an individual's entire life. For example:

> The task of reality acceptance is never completed . . . and . . . relief from this strain is provided by an intermediate area of experience which is not challenged (arts, religion, etc.). . . . This intermediate area is in direct continuity with the play area of the small child who is lost in play. [Winnicott (1951), pp. 240–241]

But Winnicott (1945) also stated:

> We often hear of the real frustrations imposed by . . . reality, but less often hear of the relief and satisfaction it affords. There are no brakes on fantasy, and *love and hate cause alarming effects*. External reality has brakes . . . and, in fact, *fantasy is only tolerable at full blast when objective reality is appreciated as well.*[6] [p. 153, italics mine]

With this perspective, only to describe the trauma of anal-rapprochement life as a "too sudden deflation" (Settlage 1977, p. 814) of childish omnipotence and idealization does not stress enough the child's equal need to hold on to experiences centered about actualities and, especially, feel a reasonable control in the regulation of experiences between such actualities and playful enlargements of his or her life. Loewald (1975) considers that the "two year old hardly distinguishes between dream and actual life occurrences. The distinction between confabulation and objective truth has little or no meaning for him" (p. 363). The position that I have taken here is that this is, paradoxically, both true and false. In one sense, with respect to the play versus actuality experience *boundary* being of a different order of psychic significance than exists with an adult or latency fantasy versus objective reality distinction, this is true. But we can also say, loosely, that the differentiation between actuality and play about him- or herself and significant other is *too* vivid to the 2-year-old because the child is just beginning to acquire such grades of experience in his or her self-awareness. The anal-rapprochement child, then, is at some special, one might even say exquisite, point of vulnerability with respect to this critical differentiation in self-awareness; it is, in part, for this reason that actuality-centered life can so easily be made "negatively" unreal into experience of self or object degradation.

MIND EMERGENCE

But there is still a deeper question related to the emergence of symbolic play—pretense—in the second year of life. Leslie (1987) puts the question this way:

> Pretending ought to strike the cognitive psychologist as a very odd sort of ability. After all, from an evolutionary point of view there ought to be a high premium on the veridicality of cognitive processes. The perceiving, thinking organism ought, as far as possible, to get things right. Yet pretense flies in the face of this fundamental principle. In pretense we deliberately disturb reality. How odd then that this ability is not the sober culmination of intellectual development but instead makes its appearance playfully and precociously at the very beginning of childhood. [p. 412]

A psychoanalyst, perhaps, initially will see no serious problem here. After all, the psychoanalyst will say, exactly from an evolutionary point of view, this emergence of a capability for play—pretense, make-believe—so early in development enables the young child to bear the manifold narcissistic and instinctual frustrations involved in anal-rapprochement socialization experiences. One thinks again of Winnicott's (1951) comment that "reality acceptance is never completed" (p. 240), and that playful, enacted symbols can bring "relief from this strain" (p. 241). Interestingly, a psychologist like Furth (1987), who works very much with a Piagetian perspective, makes a similar statement:

> Why are spontaneous symbols *at first* used in a playful man-
> ner? . . . I would answer the above question by saying that unless
> children *first* assimilated reality to their desires, they would never go
> to the trouble of constructing a symbolic world and—for good or
> evil—suffer its consequences. [p. 40, italics mine]

And notice Furth's belief how it is play that is first used for
symbolic expression. I will return to this comment in a
moment.

But to answer the question in this way is to miss the point
of Leslie's (1987) question. What he wants to understand is
why (so much) play thinking doesn't cause "abuse" to the
young child's thinking about the actualities of his or her life.
Leslie's insight involves the recognition of a "striking similarity between . . . properties of pretend play and the logical
properties of sentences containing *mental state terms*" (p.
416).[7]

> The emergence of pretense is not seen as a development in the
> understanding of objects and events as such, but rather as the
> beginning of the *capacity to understand cognition itself*. It is an early
> symptom of the human mind's ability to characterize and manipu-
> late its own attitudes to information. Pretending to oneself is thus a
> special case of the ability to understand pretense in others (someone
> else's attitude to information). In short, pretense is an early mani-
> festation of what has been called *theory of mind*. . . . Pretend
> representations, by contrast, are *opaque*, even to the organism who
> entertains them. They are in effect not representations of the world
> but representations of representations. For this reason I shall call
> them second order, or borrowing a term from Pylyshyn (1978),
> *meta-representations*. [p. 416]

Now, I simply want to say that it is during the anal-
rapprochement phase that we can conceive of the child
coming to a sense that he or she possesses a mind, and, of
course, that significant others also have minds. Prior to this
point in development, we obviously can conceive that the
young child has awareness, but not a mind, not awareness
that may or may not be reordered so as to be "opaque" with

respect to reference to actuality (reality). Kagan's (1981) extensive research into the development of self-awareness in the second half of the second year of life also supports such a viewpoint.

Something else adds to this significance of early play as a manifestation of mind experience. Furth (1987) argues a case that it is the *earliest* manifestation of mind experience in normative human development. At about the second year of life, intentional communication with language begins to emerge. But Leslie points out it is not at all clear whether such verbalization should be conceived to be an effort simply to change some situation or behavior or whether it implicates a child's cognizance and intention to influence someone else's mental state. It is not until about the third year of life that the child demonstrates an appropriate, grammatical use of mental state terms in his or her language, terms like *know*, *think*, *wonder*, and so forth. (Bretherton and Boeghly 1982, Shatz et al. 1983). If play is regarded as the first manifestation of mind usage for a young child, then all our familiar anal-rapprochement, sadomasochistic control dynamics (e.g., Erikson 1950, 1962, Freud 1917) will extend, also, into an area of mind control.[8] Or, better stated, into an area of mind control having to do with fluctuations between playful, unreal representation and thinking and feeling involved in adaptation with the actualities of the young child's life. From this perspective I can say that these adult borderline and narcissistic transferences I have termed pathological play represent a pathological continuation into adult life of a fundamental disturbance in a person's sense of mind control. Other considerations about mind development (see, e.g., Hartmann 1939, Stern 1985) suggest that mind-symbolizing activity is not initiated in development only in pretense play. Still, one can conceive early pretense play to involve a mind-symbolizing capability on a kind of "holiday." Piaget (1945) employed such an idea when he used Bleuler's concept of functional pleasure (p. 62) in connection with early pretense play—that is, functional pleasure in the use of the mind's symbolic function.

Other important issues follow on this point. But I will focus here briefly only on one. The issue is how we will want, now, to relate a concept of self to this matter of coming to possess an experience of mind in the anal-rapprochement period of life. As a philosopher Cavell (1985) has interesting things to say on how most productively to understand or deploy a concept of the self with respect to an idea of mind; and now by mind I understand a term conceptually equivalent to Freud's (e.g., 1900) notion of a "psychic apparatus." First, for Cavell the idea of self, throughout, is nothing more than a status of organization of mind, and such organization, of course, undergoes development (and see Steingart 1969). I believe Cavell could understand the pretense capabilities of the anal-rapprochement child to indicate (at least) the beginning emergence of a new organization of mind, and thus a new type of self, in which, as she puts it, "reflexive self-awareness is more specifically grounded" (p. 12). Cavell calls this a "second sense of self" (p. 12); it is a "self as subject" (p. 13). What I have simply called earlier infantile awareness, Cavell conceives to be a "self in sense one" (p. 11); it is a "self in a weak and general sense . . . a structure of awareness . . . the being whose structure it is (i.e., no sense of self as subject)" (p. 10).

> There is no reason in principle [Cavell says] why there need be only one substructure, or one concept of self in sense two; though, of course, since they are substructures of the same larger structure, self in sense one, there will be interplay and overlap. But to the extent they are different, they will pick out different events and actions as ones from which one can speak or one can lay claim. Such a split subject will be, by definition, a *vacillating and unreliable* one; like the self prior to the stage of subjectivity in which one's self as subject was more an object for another. [p. 22, italics mine]

This, structurally speaking, vacillating and unreliable self is what I argue we must conceive with respect to the anal-rapprochement toddler just beginning to experience his or her mind with pretense play.[9]

COMPARATIVE PSYCHOPATHOLOGY

I turn now to some comments about comparative psychopathology with respect to language, action, and the idea of reality in the psychoanalytic situation. Over 30 years ago Eissler (1950) conjectured that the delinquent is someone who protects him- or herself "against new and surprising internal content; he does not want to expose himself once more to traumatic experience which he incurred when he was on the verge of discovering his ego" (p. 112). If we re-read Eissler's statement so that ego means self, then this verge of discovery point is nothing else but the young anal-toddler, first euphoric in the practicing period and now moving into anal-rapprochement dynamics with the inevitable consequence of a grade in self-awareness between actuality with respect to self and object limitation and playful (unreal) representation about self and significant other. I thus suggest that an individual who massively acts out, who is impulse ridden, and so on, is someone who desires to regress—and dynamically misuse—an earlier practicing stage of life where actions amount to a pathologically maintained, playful illusion that one is in perfect harmony with an omnipotent other as facilitator, the way one briefly felt as a toddler who had just acquired expansive locomotion. It is, then, an attempt to return to the practicing period of life in which pathologically enlarged grandiosity and idealization experience is not held together in an individual's psychic reality with any sort of painful self-awareness that derives from actual limits for oneself or some significant other. Pathological, substance-addictive conditions can be taken to represent a similar point of genetic fixation; and indeed, it is often the case that individuals who represent themselves clinically with massive acting-out tendencies also show inclination for substance abuse.

In my experience, adults assessed as having narcissistic personality disorders need not (relatively) resort to such massive acting out in the transference. Instead, they will seek to establish pleasurable, object-idealizing and/or self-grandiose transference experience by concretizing language as an enacted symbol in the psychoanalytic relationship. That is, language expression, including free associations, can serve essentially as an adornment for pathologically playful, narcissistically gratifying transference. From my discussion about the etiological disturbance for such pathologically playful transference, it should be clear that I think Kohut (e.g., 1977) has made an important contribution to praxis with his advocacy of a prolonged acceptance of such transference. An appropriate and therapeutically needed sense of control over the making of unreal experience is thus afforded the analysand without premature interpretation, which would only serve to repeat original trauma. But it should also be clear that I agree with Kernberg (e.g., 1975) that adult narcissistic pathology is no simple arrest of a healthy child's self- and object-enhancing play, but is, rather, a pathological formation that implicates profound anal-rapprochement, sadomasochistic conflict over control of reality, and that such a struggle at an appropriate time must be brought out and worked through in the psychoanalytic relationship. However, and in contrast to both these authors, I do not see how terms like *cohesion* (e.g., Kohut 1977) or *integrated* (e.g., Kernberg 1975) are usefully applied to *rigidly* maintained grandiosity and/or idealization. Because we have rigidity rather than integration, any felt departure from self or object perfection will result in "narcissistic rage" (Kohut, e.g., 1973) over a felt *total* decompensation of the idealization or grandiosity.

With this eruption of rage, the way in which individuals who have narcissistic personality disturbance experience (feel) language is abruptly and vividly changed. Now language is experienced as enacted, hostile activity; language has become in itself an aggressive assault on the analyst's and/or analysand's self-esteem. However, and as Kohut has made clear, with interpretation of an experience of empathic failure, these incidents of rage can remain relatively circumscribed and not impede the overall development of a grandiose and/or idealizing transference. Put another way, if I say that a female delinquent uses massive sexually promiscuous actions to promote a magical illusion that she is in a perfect practicing harmony with an omnipotent significant other who completely facilitates her wishes, then I can also say that a person with narcissistic personality disorder is someone who is pathologically and playfully "promiscuous" with language, but now in a "rapprochement" (Mahler et al. 1975) transference experience in the psychoanalytic situation. But I repeat that narcissistic rage implicates the dynamically unconscious existence of extraordinary, sadomasochistic struggles for control over reality; and in fact, an experiential centering by the analysand only on his or her narcissism equilibrium is intended to obscure such psychodynamic drive experience, which naturally will be carried forward into oedipal life (and see Hanly 1982). Kohut's (e.g., 1977) argument is that we should regard (conceptualize) such drive experience only to be a matter of some sort of epiphenomenal fragmentation. But how can it be that this sadomasochistic (and oedipal) drive experience regularly appears and reappears in pathological narcissistic transferences, over diverse life histories, unless the psychodynamic experience itself is a constituent of narcissistic trauma and not merely a nonetiological by-product?

But I have used the word *constituent*. Something only can be a constituent of something more complex than itself. What I call mind emergence, or Kagen (1981) calls self-awareness, or Cavell (1985) calls reflexive self-awareness, Freud (1915c) can be understood to have called "total ego."

This idea of an overall more complex organization–total ego–connected to the developmental acquisition of a capability for love (and hate) emerges out of libidinal and aggressive drive experiences toward emotionally significant objects. But Freud (1915c) conceived that in, as he put it, "sadistic-anal *organization* . . . love . . . is hardly to be distinguished from hate in its attitude toward the object" (p. 139, italics mine). I think this is not correct. Even casual, let alone systematic clinical observation (Mahler et al. 1975), demonstrates that the anal-rapprochement toddler is working through extremes of love and hate toward ambivalence (Winnicott 1955). However, the important point is this: from the perspective of the total ego of the anal-rapprochement toddler–as well as adult narcissistic and borderline disturbance–sadomasochistic expression *is* a fragmentation phenomenon. In the same way, neurotic symptoms are another sort–really another order–of fragmentation phenomenon. I can believe this, and still, in my more-or-less-usual Freudian praxis, understand how critical it is to analyze constituent drive experiences of various sorts. I can adopt for my purpose here Freud's (1933) well-known metaphor of how a piece of crystal will shatter: *certain kinds* of fragments will be produced by the shattering of a crystal according to *certain kinds* of faults.

Finally, with respect to comparative psychopathology, I believe individuals we conceive to be borderline (Kernberg, e.g., 1975) are people who characteristically concretize language in the psychoanalytic situation to be an adornment for pathologically playful transference experience that is aggressive and painful, or who will generally rapidly oscillate between painful transference and a concretization of language in the service of some gratifying, unreal, transference experience. Kernberg makes clear, in distinction from narcissistic pathology, that throughout such transference the analyst experiences him- or herself to be emotionally "fully there" for the analysand as both hated and loved object.

Also, if I understand Kernberg correctly, I am in agreement
with him, and not Kohut (e.g., 1977), in considering that
there exists a similar point of developmental disturbance for
both adult narcissistic and borderline psychopathologies.
But Kernberg also considers (conceives) that this common
point of genetic disturbance chiefly has to do with oral-stage
dynamics, especially envious experience, and oral-sadistic
impulses intended to destroy the envied significant other (or
projectively identified, envied other). I believe that my
experience, and that of others cited from the literature, is
more usefully conceptualized (clinically interpreted) to involve sadomasochistic experiences that are regressively
caught up with autonomy dynamics at the anal-rapprochement stage over what is real and unreal about oneself
and significant others. Strictly speaking, an envious experience presupposes the existence of a grade in one's psychic
reality, so that a significant other is elevated in an unreal way
to possess attributes in comparison with which oneself is
unrealistically degraded. It is, I think, more tenable to
conceive of such complex representational activities to be
occurring with the advent of anal-rapprochement-stage dynamics; envious experience, I believe, becomes regressively
(orally) caught up and condensed into these anal-rapprochement, sadomasochistic dynamics.[10]

PROJECTIVE IDENTIFICATION

This idea of pathological play, which I have coupled with
anal-rapprochement-stage dynamics, immediately provides
a framework for understanding the projective identifications
that characteristically occur in the transference of both borderline and narcissistic patients; and this is especially pertinent to how such projective identifications in the
transference of (certain) borderline patients can rapidly fluc-
tuate in contradictory (conflictual) fashion. As Kernberg

(1975) puts it, with such projective identifications analysands "can still [feel] identify themselves . . . with the object onto whom aggression [or some other experience] has been projected" (p. 31). All we need do is consider (conceive of) the situation of very young children at play and the organization of their self-awareness when they assign play roles to each other. The roles easily—characteristically—are reversed (irrespective of sexual anatomy), indicative of how the young child maintains an empathy (Kernberg 1975) with whatever projected identification is occurring at the moment. This is a description of the natural, clinically healthy play of very young children, and no undue anxiety is evident over these role reversals. We can infer (conceive) that an immature organization of self-awareness must mediate such play; a self-organization might be said to exist, but I think it more useful to state that what exists is a panoply of self-representations (Steingart 1969) that have not yet achieved any mature coherence. And, with respect to psychopathology, imagine the situation of a Dr. Jekyll (Stevenson 1886) who does not have the benefit of a drug that enables disassociated experience. Jekyll can only projectively identify all manner of "evil" impulses onto a Mr. Hyde; consequently, Jekyll now experiences an ongoing empathy with the evil Hyde, not, of course, an empathic realization in which the "ego . . . [is] . . . enriched" (Freud 1921), and passively suffers intense anxiety over his own evil impulses as well as those of Hyde. (Further, as Kernberg [1975] points out, complementary projective identifications may be instigated within the analyst as a consequence of such analysand transference.) But in none of this, neither the clinically healthy psychic reality of very young children at play nor the context of conflictual psychopathology with adults, need one conceive that a complete dedifferentiation occurs with respect to boundaries between self versus object representations. Rather, what I think is more usefully the case is the operation of an insufficiently cohered self (system)—naturally due to immaturity in the very young child and the result of conflict in the adult—such that splitting rather than repressive processes are dominant (Kernberg 1975).

Paradoxically, but understandably, it is just this "ready availability" of diverse conflictual experience possessed by borderline and narcissistic analysands, both in their representations of themselves and significant others, that makes these analysands potentially so gifted in their psychological mindedness. It also makes clear why they may be creative notwithstanding their emotional disturbances. The special problem for the psychoanalysis of these analysands is how to make both the real and transference psychoanalytic relationships productive. With this idea of experience structured as pathological play, I have argued a case that it is in the enacted (mis)use of language that psychoanalysis can become so problematic in borderline and narcissistic cases. An important clinical difference between these two types of psychopathology thus can be conceived to be different kinds of (mis)use of language in the transference, wherein anal-rapprochement-stage, sadomasochistic struggles become enmeshed in control over what is actual or playfully unreal experience about self and significant others.[11] I trust that the way I have just put this—different kinds of (mis)use of language—will indicate that I do not reduce our total psychoanalytic comprehension of borderline and narcissistic psychopathologies into a simplistic behaviorism, to be only a matter of language behavior. But I do conceive that such (mis)use made of language constitutes a significant, initially dynamically unconscious means for the expression of narcissistic and borderline disturbances that consequently requires interpretation at appropriate moments in the treatment process.

NOTES

1. Another way to say this is to say that the history and functioning of a gestalt (self-as-organization) requires concepts that are different from

terms used to describe part processes and functions (and see Steingart 1969).

· 2. Is there a kind of evolutionary wisdom in all of this for the development of our species? Would any of us have the audacity to venture to stand upright, and be urged to do so by our mothers, without benefit of some such protective, "dual-unity," narcissistic bond?

3. It is outside the scope of this work to assess, and argue against, Stern's (1985) recent criticism of the concept of a normal symbiotic phase. But work by Leslie (1987) and Cavell (1985), which I will cite shortly, is certainly relevant.

4. It is amazing to me how Freud (1915e), who evidently only had available associationistic, theoretical concepts, nevertheless still centered his thoughts on this relating-regulative capability enabled by language. Consider the following statement, in which the italicized term is Freud's:

Moreover, by being linked with words, cathexis can be provided with quality even when they represent only *relations* between presentations of objects and are thus unable to derive any quality from perceptions. Such relations, which become comprehensible only through words, form a major part of our thought processes. [p. 202]

Related to this, and still using energetic terms, Freud also spoke about a "hypercathexis," which consists in a "thing-presentation . . . being linked with the word-presentations corresponding to it. It is these hypercathexes, we may suppose, that bring about a higher psychical organization" (pp. 201–202). Loewald (1978) makes the important point that in such an integration *both* ideas and language are now changed and constituents of a new psychic organization. It is intuitively easier to get some sense of how language is changed now that words are experienced as symbolic vehicles. But it is not as easy to sense the experience of change the toddler has about ideas that now have become some kind of verbal thought.

5. For further discussion of this term *actuality* see Steingart (1983). I deliberately chose a hypothetical, but plausible, example with a 2½-year-old. Ogden (1986) describes an incident involving playful pretense, versus the actuality of being washed in a bathtub, that involved a toddler who, "after being frightened by having his head go under water while being given a bath, became highly resistant to taking a bath" (p. 206). Several months later, the child's mother was able, with "gentle but persistent coaxing" (p. 206), to persuade the child to be placed in 4 inches of bathwater. However, the moment the child was in the tub, "his entire body became tense" (p. 207), and it was clear that he felt himself to be in great danger; the child repeatedly said, "My not like bath" (p. 207). He

would not allow himself to be bathed. The mother, sensitively, engaged the child in a make-believe experience in which she requested tea from him. Immediately, the child relaxed; he then used cups and an empty shampoo bottle to provide tea for his mother that would have enough milk and be "not too hot" (p. 207). However, when after a few moments of such pretend play, the mother reached for a washcloth, the play immediately stopped, and the child once again was extremely resistant to being bathed. The mother, once again, requested tea, and the play resumed.

Ogden offers this as an example of an adaptive and creative use of play by this toddler, something Winnicott (e.g., 1971b) referred to as a concept of "potential [psychic] space" (p. 107). I do not. I would understand this incident to be an illustration of the child, still traumatized by the actuality of being bathed, using tea play to deny the existence of this actuality. Such incidents of traumatic experience undoubtedly are part of every child's development, and produce circumstances of use of (I would say) pathological play.

Three other points worth considering are: (1) It is important to realize in terms of diagnostic assessment that in such a circumstance the impetus for pathological play is actual, experienced trauma and not some inner developing psychopathology. (2) The way in which this child stopped his play when faced with the reality of a bath is just the way a young child in treatment will stop playing when the therapist has made an ill-timed or too-direct interpretation (Erikson 1950). (3) I would place much greater stress than does Ogden on the mother's sensitive realization that this tea play could provide the child with *control*. The mother asked for tea from the child, and the child could actually safeguard the mother from danger by insuring that the tea was "not too hot."

6. Incidentally, I take these comments by Winnicott to be his identification with a philosophical position of some kind of realism.

7. It is worthwhile to cite Leslie (1987) at some length about this:

Philosophers have long recognized that from the logical point of view, propositions behave strangely when placed in the context of such terms.

Three properties have commonly been identified. First, the reference of terms in such embedded propositions becomes *opaque* (Quine 1961). For example, "the prime minister of Britain" and "Mrs. Thatcher" refer at the time of this writing to the same person. Therefore, anything asserted about the prime minister of Britain, if true, must be true of Mrs. Thatcher as well (and, likewise, false for one, false for the other). If it is true that the prime minister of Britain lives at No. 10 Downing Street, then it must be true that Mrs. Thatcher lives at No. 10 Downing Street. But put this proposition in the context of a mental state term and this no longer holds. Thus

"Sara-Jane believes that the prime minister of Britain lives at No. 10 Downing Street" in no way entails the truth (or falsehood) of "Sara-Jane believes Mrs. Thatcher lives at No. 10 Downing Street." In a mental state context one can no longer "look through" terms to see what they refer to in deciding such issues. The mental state term suspends normal reference relations. Quine (1961) calls this *referential opacity*.

Second, propositions involving mental state terms do not logically imply the truth (or falsehood) of propositions embedded in them. Thus "John believes the cat is white" says nothing about whether or not the cat really is white. Again, one cannot look through the embedded proposition to the world.

Third, assertions involving mental state terms do not logically entail the existence or non-existence of the things mentioned in the embedded proposition. Thus "the King of France is bald" is a strange statement because it logically implies or presupposes the existence of a French King. It is just as hard to say it is false because that would still entail the King of France's existence. But "Jacqueline believes the King of France is bald" has no such problems. The existence is not entailed.

Thus for each of these semantic properties of mental state expressions there appears to be a corresponding basic form of pretense: (A) referential opacity—object substitution (deviant reference pretend); (B) non-entailment of truth (or falsehood)—attribution of pretend properties (deviant truth pretend); and (C) non-entailment of existence (or non-existence) imaginary object (deviant existence pretend). I suggest that these connections are not coincidental. [pp. 416–417]

8. More recently, Hobson (1990) has criticized Leslie's (1987) work, and Leslie and Frith (1990) have responded to the criticism. The crux of the argument has to do with different theoretical perspectives brought to bear on this matter of mind emergence in development. Leslie's approach is avowedly "computational"; he stresses the coming "on-line" of a cognitive process (mechanism) for producing metarepresentations that enable pretense play in the anal-rapprochement period. Hobson's perspective is emphatically interpersonal, one could say, psychoanalytically object relational. He stresses the evidence for the infant's built-in sensitivity to the responsiveness of the significant other, and the continuation and development of such (especially affective) attunement (e.g., Stern 1985); he argues that it be taken to mean the maintenance by the young child of multiple perspectives about experience and that it is the child's internalization of his capability for multiple social experience that produces a multiple stance toward his or her representations, that is, metarepresentations that enable pretense play.

I should emphasize that whichever theoretical perspective is utilized, what is of interest to me, and psychoanalysis, is the emergence in the child's development of his or her own mind in the anal-rapprochement period. And by mind I mean what Cavell (1985) calls "reflexive self-awareness" (p. 12), to which I will refer shortly.

In their rejoinder to Hobson's critique, Leslie and Frith (1990) acknowledge a possibility of the presence of metarepresentational capability for pretense play in the anal-rapprochement period. But they argue that there is no present evidence to suggest that infant *attunement* to a significant other is anything more than just that—"mechanisms that are simply sensitive to social and behavioral factors [the 'orientations' of others]" (p. 123). I agree with Leslie and Frith and I do not believe that future research will support an argument for the emergence of a metarepresentational capability prior to the anal-rapprochement period. Hobson, and Leslie and Frith, in their debate with each other, utilize comparative data about cognitive development with respect to normal versus anomalous children, especially autistic children. A psychoanalytic contribution to this issue would involve close attention to the clinically healthy (normal) development of *negativism* during the anal-rapprochement period, worldwide. Instances of oppositional *behavior* between infant and caretaker are evident, of course, from birth. But if we restrict negativism to mean a clash of a *mind's* intentions between child and caretaker, then I believe this becomes evident only during the anal-rapprochement period, notwithstanding what I assume would be notable differences in child-raising patterns cross-culturally. As far as I am aware, such cross-cultural study is not now available.

9. Cavell (1985) also has some important things to say about the notions of will and responsibility that interrelate with self (mind) development—and how these terms are appropriate or not appropriate to an immature being whose self (mind) development has not yet reached a certain stage of organization. (See also Cavell 1991.)

10. This way of putting it—"regressively (orally) caught up and condensed into anal-rapprochement dynamics"—is a change in my own thinking (Steingart 1983).

Kernberg (1975) might object that I am describing only a special subgroup of borderline and narcissistic individuals, that is, those who are analyzable. This may be so. But it in turn at least raises a question about what will constitute a productive psychoanalytic process with such individuals and especially, I think, with respect to analysand (mis)use of language and acting out.

11. I cannot, now, make any more specific statements about either the description or the conceptualization of these events. But at least the focus I place on language use (and misuse) points in a direction for clinical child observation as well as research.

6

A Clinical Episode

A female patient began to reveal a morbid and angry conviction that I wanted to "mold" her mind with my interpretations so that she would be left with no mind of her own.[1] This patient's mother had committed suicide, slitting her wrists, after the patient (then a recently graduated college student) firmly told her mother that she would no longer talk to her each day. The patient's father had died in an auto accident when she was 9 years old. The mother had been hospitalized for agitated, depressive episodes. A younger brother was idealized by the mother, if anything, more so after the father's death, so that the brother became a repository of all the mother's projectively identified grandiosity. The patient became the incessantly needed and possessed repository for all the mother's projectively identified self-debasement: the patient's hair was "wrong," she lacked sufficient intelligence, and so forth.

Interpretation was felt by the patient, with intense conviction sometimes, to be the expression of a malevolent need on my part to bind her to me as a debased object. This had to do not only with what I said in interpretation but, even more, with *how* I said things to her. My language was too vague, or too general, and in particular I did not use words with sufficient precision. For example, the patient once was talking about the characteristics of a new man she had met and used the word *repulsed* to describe some of her reactions to him. A few moments later, I used the word *revolted* to

allude to this emotional reaction. The patient angrily pointed
out that I had not used her word (repulsed), that I had
substituted my word (revolted), and that this was an example of my lack of precision in the use of language.

My countertransference at this moment was intense,
taking the form of a kind of clinical stupidity that created, in
turn, a sense of clinical helplessness. I felt that no matter
how much I tried, I often seemed to be making matters
worse between us. I always was "putting my foot in it."

Before I go on to describe how I ultimately interpreted to
the patient, I want to say something more about qualities
relating to this women's anger. Also, I want to say something more about my countertransference.

The patient's anger was not a typical sort of anger. It was
not that her anger was frequent—stretches of time would go
by where everything felt (to her and to me) fine between us.
In fact, she would sometimes say, during such experience,
that she felt helped and understood by what I said. But then
the angry outbursts would occur, like sudden violent thun-
derstorms. Indeed, we came to understand that such explo-
sive outbursts were necessary in order to prevent a sense of
sustained, good connection.

But her anger, when it exploded, was unusual. She
screamed at me as loudly as she could. And she screamed at
me so loudly that, in the midst of the screaming, she would
suddenly become concerned that someone in the waiting
room would hear her and conclude she was crazy. Clearly,
she was mortified that she was now being like her mother,
and projectively identified with me as a child, in her position—as a child with her mother.

There was something else about her screaming. As much
as I felt terribly beleaguered, and had painful doubts about
my abilities as a therapist at such times, I always felt a
desperate quality in her rageful screaming. I think this also
had to do, at least for her, with a mentality of projective
identification. No matter how angry she felt, no matter how

demeaned I was supposed to feel, she remained equally desperate in her rage to obtain something from me she felt was lacking at such times. Put another way, she never could (never wanted to) completely rid herself of intense, early pre-oedipal wishes to be a child, attached, loved, and well connected with me as a mother. She never rid herself completely of her desire for me even when she was screaming at me for not being well connected to her. Put still another way, she had not developed in the structure of her psychic reality from projective identification to projection (Kernberg 1987).

With regard to my countertransference, something happened to me in my psychic reality that never had happened up to that time, or since. Following the patient's sudden eruption—one of her screaming fits—over my not recalling the use of her word (repulsed), I began to have trouble remembering what she was telling me. I don't mean that I literally and grossly forgot all of the major themes she presented. But I could not remember, for example, for maybe a moment or so, the name of the new man in her life who "repulsed" her, which was John, say, and not Bill. What I was suffering here was not even countertransference experienced directly and immediately, but a *symptom* produced by my countertransference. I do not believe my forgetting symptom was "obviously" (Gill 1984a) expressing my countertransference to the patient. This went on for two sessions, after which I (finally) allowed myself to feel the full extent of my countertransference hatred.

With this, my forgetting symptom disappeared and never returned. Obviously, I was "killing" my patient by not fully remembering what she told me, as I am accustomed to experience with any patient. Shortly after this, in what I felt to be an appropriate clinical context that included a now benign experience with me (see Pine 1985), I made certain comments to the patient. First, I acknowledged to the patient that one can make a case for a subtle but important difference in connotation between the words *repulsed* and *revolted:* in fact, *repulsed* only connotes a self *actively* pushing away a disagreeable experience; *revolted* may connote either a self *passively* being made to turn away from a disagreeable experience or a self in retaliation against such experience. Needless to say, such an issue of experienced activity versus passivity was critical for this woman's psychodynamics. In fact, what she did as a young adult was express an intention to repulse her mother absolutely in order to escape her mother's utterly irrational need to possess her.

The repetitious nature of my patient's transference experience was obvious to both of us, but this did little to modify her conviction that I was out to possess her mind. Very much in keeping with comments described by Kernberg (1984), I told the patient firmly, but not (I believe) sadistically, something like the following: that our relationship was at such times in jeopardy; that I understood she believed sincerely in the truth of her conviction that I had a dangerous need to "mold" her with my characteristically (i.e., characterologically) less precise use of language compared to hers. Each of us, as Kernberg has put it, "lived, at this moment in two incompatible [I would prefer to say psychic] realities, as if one of us were crazy. . . . if it were true that we were living in mutual incompatible realities, both of us must be having an experience similar to that of a normal person faced with madness" (p. 305).

This had nothing to do with genetic interpretation, obvious to both of us, and of little use at that moment. I spoke to her about her disturbance with my language. This had more to do with how I used language than what it was I said with language. I explained that, on further consideration and study, I discovered that I understood the word *revolted* only to have the same connotation as the noun *revolution.* Revolution is an act of aggression against someone felt to be an oppressor. I did not know, before such study, how the word *revolted* could change connotation between active and passive. She was a person who would not make such a mistake with language; I was such a person. I then added: If she believed that awareness and respect for all of a word's particular meanings was a real index of my appreciation for the individuality of a person, I could understand her disturbance and mistrust of me. Further, this (relative) lack of precision with the words *repulsed* and *revolted* was one she also believed indicated I had a kind of "mushy" mind, insufficiently discrete and bounded. Consequently, she believed herself and her conscious, highly articulated, linguistically precise mind to be in danger of being turned into "mush" if she allowed my interpretation to have effect. Also, I interpreted that she desired, with her relentless attacks on my language (mind), to make me feel, with her, the same valuelessness she felt with her mother.

What the patient then emphasized to me, now in a gentle voice, was that she felt not simply misunderstood but, even worse for her, *vaguely* understood, not seen as the distinct person she was, as she so often felt with her mother. Notice that the patient could here have begun to scream at me again, about my not understanding that her feeling of not being "seen" was the right way to describe her experience. But she did not. There was, then, for this woman, a "thinglike" quality attached to language; not a thing as Freud (1915e) conceived in his theory of what produces schizophrenic thought disorder, but a thing after the manner in which young children at play employ and use language expression to enhance a certain pretense belief. In this instance, a person's mind *is* structured and discrete, or is "mushy" and unbounded, depending on whether or not that person uses words extremely precisely.

I made clear to the patient that I considered her beliefs about myself as a person to be unreal (transferential); and these experiences obviously had to do with her need to be both intensely attached and disengaged from me as her mother. In my experience, this kind of approach to such a structure for transference experience is helpful. My patient and I were able to find what Freud (1939) would term a "material reality" we could share, which entailed, exactly, that we could not find any common psychic reality: each of us experienced the other as mad.

NOTES

1. The reader may wonder why I refer to this woman as a patient rather than analysand, which is the term I have used largely (and prefer) in the rest of this book. This is because this woman was in twice-a-week psychotherapy. If she had been in analysis, my handling of what I am about to describe would have been no different; however, other aspects of my work with her were indicative of our work being ego-supportive psychotherapy.

7

On the Comprehension of Psychic Reality

So I come back to psychic reality, always to psychic reality, which is "decisive" (Freud 1916–1917). It is by this time no secret that I urge for psychoanalysis a position that regards an analysand's manifest and dynamically unconscious psychic reality to exist, in some definite and essential sense, as it is. This is so irrespective of the analyst's work style or theory of mind (which, wittingly or unwittingly, informs his or her interpretations), as well as the manner in which the analyst carries out a clinical psychoanalytic process. Now, I just used the phrase "theory of mind." On another level of discourse, what I urge for psychoanalysis is that it posit the existence of a human mind that is objective the same way a (forever) not-observable electromagnetic field is real for physicists. This human mind, then, operates in ways so that each of us, and of course each analysand, can use his or her mind to produce his or her particular conscious and dynamically unconscious psychic reality, which then also exists as it does in some definite sense. Freud, of course, believed this, and he elaborated different theories—models—of the human mind throughout his writing (e.g., Freud 1900, 1915e, 1923).

Psychoanalysts and philosophers of science who do not accept this position for psychoanalysis are of two sorts. One sort (e.g., Gadamer 1977, Heidegger 1927, Ricoeur 1970, Rubovitz-Seitz 1991) believes that other-than-human nature can be conceived with such objectivity, whereas the "mind stuff" (James 1890) of psychic reality (meanings, reasons, beliefs, desires, however these emergent properties are conceived) cannot be so objectively conceived; we only involve ourselves with interpretations, hermeneutic renderings about human mentality that make it narratively intelligible in one way or another, and have neither relevance nor reference to any idea of a human mind that arises as it does, independent of our efforts to understand it. The other kind of rejection (e.g., Putnam 1981, Schafer 1991) is more radical. This viewpoint is that not only is psychoanalysis not in any way a science that presupposes some objectivist, existent reality; here, all scientific theory is "theory of description," and truth an "ideal coherence of beliefs" inasmuch as there are no "mind independent states of affairs" (Putnam 1981, pp. 49–50). Devitt (1984) argues against both positions on the premise (with which I concur) that they put the "epistemic and semantic carts before the ontological horse" (p. 194).

I want to elaborate this by using the work of such philosophers of science as Bhaskar (e.g., 1975) and Harré (e.g., 1970). At issue is what Bhaskar calls the epistemic fallacy, conflating, or assuming, that ontology is reducible to epistemology, and a scientific law is no more than a description of our perception of a conjunction of events. In other words, this constrains, really equates, any idea of reality to the means with which we obtain knowledge about reality. This kind of idea is that of an empiric reality, and it is the sort of idea of reality maintained by the logical positivists in the early part of this century. But it is, now, for many realist philosophers, an antiquated realism, producing absurd, counterintuitive conclusions: that, for example, in a world without humans, the natural laws of, say, physics, would no longer exist. This empiric or, I would like to say, naive realism is not the nature of reality to which scientific constructs and their laws refer. Scientific constructs, and laws, are attempts to represent a nonobservable, transcendental reality (and see Manicas and Secord 1983, Will 1980) that involves entities and processes with causal powers. What I have just said applies, if anything, in the extreme for an idea of an objectivist reality for the human mind. We experience (perceive) our own subjectivity, or one (an analyst) empathically realizes the subjectivity of another (the analysand). This perceived (experienced) psychic reality of feelings, sensations, ideas, and so forth is the means (epistemology) by which we conceive a transcendentally real human mind— and about this mind we can theorize with respect to its nature. When I have used an idea of a correspondence doctrine of truth in this book, I mean by it my belief that a Freudian (or any other) theory of mind is an attempt to represent something that I take to exist and to be a part of a "world that exists independently of cognizing experience" (Manicas and Secord 1983, p. 401). But Freudian theory about the nature of human mentality (Hartmann 1939, Rapaport and Gill 1959) is a complex, conjoined "subjectivist" and "externalist" accounting (Cavell 1991). I find in Steiner (1992) a viewpoint sympathetic to mine, and I continue to believe that Erikson's (1950) *Childhood and Society*, together with Loewald's (1971a) "On Motivation and Instinct Theory," are the best examples we have of an attempt to begin to systematically work through to a Freudian conception of mind.[1] But controversy, or ferment, about the nature of theory now is characteristic in science and philosophy of science and mind (Bechtel 1988a,b). Although I think it accurate to say that while Freud never completely freed himself of a mind–body reductionistic inclination, the degree to which he did, and then proceeded to produce a theory about human mentality that can be understood to derive from a position of a transcendental, mind realism, is extraordinary and a tribute to his creative genius. A good example of this comes from Freud's (1914a) paper on narcissism:

Since we cannot wait for another science to present us with the final
conclusions on the theory of instincts, it is far more to the purpose
that we should try to see what light may be thrown upon this basic
problem of biology by a synthesis of the *psychological* phenomena.
[p. 79]

And it is pertinent here to cite a kind of summing up by
Freud (1940) about the scientific status for psychoanalysis,
which, I believe, makes clear his commitment to such a
position of transcendental realism for the human mind:

The processes with which it [psychoanalysis] is concerned are in
themselves just as unknowable as those dealt with by other sciences,
like chemistry or physics, for example; but it is possible to establish
laws which they obey . . . [and] to arrive at an "understanding" of
the field of natural phenomena in question. [p. 158]

This leads to another point.

Theory formation, whether it be about inanimate nature or
human mentality, is, as Polanyi (1958) put it, always "personal knowledge." One important meaning to Polanyi's idea
is that scientific theories are never naively realistic in the
sense of being some sort of inevitable induction of repeti-
tiously perceived conjunctions of events. For example: Freud
(with Breuer 1895), early on, observed hysterical symptoms
and later himself (Freud 1911b) considered paranoid delusions. Hysterics and paranoids dream, and dreams (ordinarily) possess fantastic visual features. What amount, or
kind, of induction could ever be sufficient to produce, for
Freud, his innovative theory (e.g., 1900, 1911b, 1915e) that
there exists a special sort of primary-process thinking, and
that it is this same out-of-the-ordinary thinking that, in part,
produces hysterical symptoms and paranoid delusions as
well as the fantastic visual features of dreams? By the same
token, consider this radical conception with respect to what
is termed ontological hermeneutics (e.g., Gadamer 1977,
Heidegger 1927). According to such a philosophy, if I under-

stand it correctly, Freud's concept, constitutive of an entirely new way of conceiving human mentality, would have to be somehow importantly grounded in the historical, cultural context within which Freud lived. I certainly am no historian. But I cannot find an influence in Freud's historical, cultural context (Gay 1988) sufficiently relevant to help me so contextualize his extraordinary reformulation of human mentality. I should think this would be the case with all creative genius.

Polanyi (1958) states about theory formation:

> In spite of the hazards involved, I am called upon to search for the truth and state my findings. To accept commitment as the framework within which we may believe something to be true is to circumscribe the hazards of belief. It is to establish the conception of competence which authorizes a fiduciary choice *made and timed*, to the best of the acting person's ability, as a deliberate and yet necessary choice. The paradox of self-set standards is eliminated, for in a competent mental act the agent does not do as he pleases, but compels himself forcefully to act as he believes he must. He can do no more, and he would avoid his calling by doing less. The possibility of error is a necessary element of any belief bearing upon reality, *and to withhold belief on the grounds of such a hazard is to break off all contact with reality*. The outcome of a competent fiduciary act may, admittedly, vary from one person to another, but since the differences are not due to any arbitrariness on the part of individuals, each retains justifiably his universal intent. As each hopes to capture some aspect of reality, they may all hope that their findings will eventually coincide or supplement each other.
>
> Therefore, though every person may believe something different to be true, there is only one truth. . . . This position is not solipsistic, since it is based on a belief in an external reality and implies the existence of other persons who can likewise approach the same reality. [pp. 315, 316, italics mine][2]

Here Polanyi is articulating a philosophy of science that emphasizes the inevitable, deeply *personal* engagement—no simple "reading off" from conjunctions of events or historical and/or cultural contextual influence—that is a scientific effort to represent a transcendental reality. I have chosen this particularly eloquent language because, at one and the same time, I can understand it to be not only a philosophy of science for the human mind that is the province of psychoanalysis but also a statement about the nature of the psychoanalytic treatment process. Each time an analyst interprets, he or she is involved in a personal engagement—an attempt to understand something about the transcendental reality of the human mind and the way the analysand has used his or her mind to produce a particular kind of psychic reality in a particular clinical circumstance.

I have, in accordance with my own position of a correspondence doctrine of truth for psychoanalysis, described psychoanalysis to possess two sorts of so-called observation statements. The first type has to do with the manifest, conscious experiences and actions expressed by an analysand, about which, it seems to me, consensual agreement can fairly easily be obtained. A second type of so-called observation statement involves my conviction that a "layer" (for want of a better word) of dynamically unconscious experience exists about which consensus can also fairly easily be reached. But I say "so-called" observation statements. The inevitable influence of theory on "observations" can be analogized to be a sort of "cultural" outlook, together with the actual culture within which we develop and live our lives. On the one hand, it is important to point to cross-cultural evidence for universal human experience, for example, to codify color experience in a similar way (cited, e.g., in Brown 1991) or to recognize facial displays of emotion (Ekman, e.g., 1980, 1992, 1993).[3] But there are people who do not "know," for example, our color orange (again, cited, e.g., in Brown 1991) or know our experience of sadness (cited in Lakoff 1987). However, I already have indicated that people who do not know our color orange, if trained to acquire more diversified color experiences, will acquire our categorical color experience of orangeness (Brown 1991). It so happens that Tahitians do not know our specific experience of sadness, and instead incorporate such experience into a general sense and meaning of physical malaise, that is, fatigue, lack of energy, and so forth. But this Tahitian thinking about sadness is not that far removed from our Western thinking. We understand a sense of chronic fatigue, poor appetite, and so on, to be physical so-called vegetative symptoms of depression, and indicate this in our *DSM-III* diagnostic manual (American Psychiatric Association 1980). Moreover, Levy (1973) states that the lack of a specific Tahitian term for sadness or depression "does not mean that such statements are unexpressable" (p. 306). Levy explains how a Tahitian man could say, "I felt *bad* because my *vahine* [woman] has gone on a trip, and there was no one else in the house, and my thoughts kept turning toward her" (p. 306, first italics mine). It is some kind of irony that, just as there is this increase of popularity among psychoanalysts for a deconstructionist hermeneutics as a basis for psychoanalysis, there has occurred a sea change among cultural anthropologists toward a perspective for human universals (see esp. Brown 1991). I do think it accurate to say that a kind of generalized psychoanalytic outlook is, now, so much part of our contemporary (at least) Western culture that something like a manifest slip of the tongue is selectively "sorted out" and possesses a kind of significance that was not the case before Freud.

In any event, I realize that the so-called database of interest to a psychoanalyst is no more or less infiltrated with theory than is the case with any science. The "tracks" left by microcosmic particles in a Wilson cloud chamber (see, e.g., Asimov 1966) are already theory laden, as is the cloud chamber itself. For an economist, a devised statistic like money supply is already theory laden and will be variously interpreted according to an economist's theoretical orientation. And so forth. But I can still maintain that a transcendental reality of a human mind exists, as it is, in some essential way. And I can believe that how an individual uses his or her mind to produce a particular psychic reality also exists as it is. That Freud (e.g., 1927) believed this to be the case is certainly no reason for anyone else to believe it. At the same time, it must be appreciated that the basis on which Freud did so much of his theorizing most certainly was not that of logical positivism, which conflated an ontology of mind with "immediate" perceptions (experiences) had with the mind. It was because Freud (1915e) made a decision (Polanyi 1958) to qualify—radically—the significance of consciousness altogether that he was able to devise a theory about a psychic reality of a dynamically unconscious mentality. On another level, belief in transcendental realism is current among a number of contemporary philosophers of science (e.g., Bhaskar 1975, Devitt 1984, Harré 1970).

But what difference, if any, does it make if a psychoanalyst holds to a correspondence doctrine of interpretation as opposed to a narrative theory of belief (Putnam 1981)? "If patients thought," muse Sass and Woolfolk (1988),

> that beauty and coherence are all that underlie therapeutic interpretations, many would probably demand some more traditional epistemological warrant. Even if patients were able to accept these new rationales, who is to say that such relativistic and aesthetic trends would not in the long run prove more demoralizing than liberating for them? In the case of some patients—and perhaps not only those with prominent schizoid or narcissistic traits—this relativistic attitude might contribute to an already-present sense of arbitrariness and alienation, or to a tendency to play with interpretations in a way that is less therapeutic than escapist. [p. 452]

Such a contention could be researched, though I find it unbelievable. I cannot imagine that the analyst who holds a hermeneutic rather than a correspondence doctrine somehow conveys less seriousness and conviction about the importance of an interpretation. Nor can I imagine that a certain work style, personality attribute, whatever, can be hypothesized *only* to be present with one or the other of these two positions. Consequently, to say that the analyst who holds to a correspondence doctrine is authoritarian or that the analyst who holds to a hermeneutic orientation is inclined to surrender interpretation to an analysand's resistance strikes me as what Freud (1910d) meant by wild psychoanalysis.

What I do believe is that whether an analyst holds to a correspondence doctrine aligned with a transcendental realism about human mentality, as opposed to a hermeneutic view of interpretive activity, has consequence for his or her vision of psychoanalysis itself (Schafer 1983). Specifically, I think it very likely that it has a consequence for an analyst's belief in the possibilities for controlled research into psychoanalysis. I mean psychoanalysis understood as a body of propositions about how a human being uses a transcendental reality that is the human mind to produce a psychic reality, together with psychoanalysis as a clinical process that purports to describe "real states of affairs" (Putnam 1981, p. 49) about an analysand's psychic reality. Many research issues exist, and any research program would presuppose (1) identifiable psychoanalytic orientations that can be reliably differentiated one from the other; with (2) identifiable and reliable consequences for types of clinical process; and (3) consensus within each psychoanalytic orientation with respect to clinical inferences (interpretation, judgment, assessment, etc.). I do not underestimate the difficulties of such research. But there is, already, I believe, sufficient controlled research evidence that this is possible. I can point especially to a recent survey of some of these research issues and findings reported by Caston (1993), and Caston and Martin (1993), together with their "manikin" methodology for dealing with the problem of clinical stereotypy with respect to clinical inference (and see an important paper by Meehl [1969]). Hamilton (1993) has recently reported research with respect to the reliable identification of theoretical orientation.

Together with this, there is an obvious growing emphasis in our literature on clinical vignette reporting that includes details of the analyst's subjectivity (e.g., Jacobs 1991).

But one has to appreciate Freud's (1895) "apology" for the narrative nature of his reporting about his work with hysterical patients, and at the same time appreciate the value of such narrative reporting. It is not the business of clinical vignette reporting to attempt to establish "unitary dimensions" and "unarguable operations" (Holt 1962), as is the case with controlled research investigation into personality and clinical process. Surely, one cannot remain content only with a *sense* of consensus among clinicians (as does Guntrip 1978), with respect to acceptance or refutation among our currently varied interpretive theoretical orientations and versions of clinical process. What Glover (1952) said some 40 years ago, I believe, still holds true: "So far no system exists whereby the scientific authority of research workers can be distinguished from the prestige of senior analytical practitioners and teachers" (p. 404). Is there a better way at least to attempt to disentangle alterations in clinical process and interpretation from transference influence other than through controlled research into psychoanalytic process? Until shown otherwise, it is reasonable to assume that the differences I have described make for differences in clinical outcome. Controlled research into clinical process (e.g., Weiss and Sampson 1986) at least offers a way to try and find answers; clinical dialogue, no matter how sincere, is no substitute for it (and for further discussion see Haggard et al. 1965). The issue looming over the possibility of controlled research is this: Can the important explanatory constructs of a psychoanalytic orientation be transformed into *variable* terms (Cassirer 1923)? This, really, is what makes "operations" for measurement so important (Holt 1962) and why, I believe, Freud (see esp. 1915e), throughout his writing, constantly stressed what he called the economic point of view. If this can be done, or to the extent that it can be done, a psychoanalytic theory (whatever orientation) can devise a "quantitative calculus" of desire (Davidson 1980) and aspire to the kind of lawfulness attributable to a science. If not, we will still possess what Davidson calls useful statistical generalizations, which would be valuable. A final point I want to make is this. Shapiro (1993) describes Freud as having provided "discoveries . . . in systematizing knowledge about the *how of remembering*" (p. 418); and Shapiro urges analysts who work in a more-or-less-usual Freudian fashion to "seriously test" this knowledge. In fact, I believe, as did Freud (1926b), that psychoanalysis provides us with systematized knowledge of great significance that is, at least, a part of all facets of human mentality (thinking, emotion, judgment, etc.). But how can we really seriously test this knowledge without controlled research into child development (see esp. Kris 1956)? The variegated theory of personality development Freud gave us, for example, his (1926a) theory of anxiety development, is not at all the same as adult reminiscences about development. Freud's anxiety theory is about taken-to-be-real "material" events (Freud, e.g., 1939) and how possible fantasies are engendered by these events in an interplay with psychosexual templates for organizing experience, which then determine our psychic reality as we develop.

The implications for psychoanalysis (psychology) of this fundamental difference in a concept of objectivity—this naive or empiric reality of logical positivism versus a transcendental realism that posits an existence of a mind not reducible to conjunctions of perceived events—has already been incisively stated by Will (1980) and Manicas and Secord (1983). I agree with Will that a philosophy of science (Popper 1959) that maintains a scientific theory is made credible *only* by testing refutable hypotheses is too narrow a basis. It makes such experimentation the only avenue into assessing scientific theory. It insufficiently appreciates evaluation of a theory with respect to its capacity to explain *afterward* an event not initially within the purview of the theory's network of prediction. And it negates completely the value of an accumulation of confirming instances for a theory (see also Guntrip 1978). Also, Will is certainly correct that clinical process is an "open," not-controllable system of events, therefore not identical to the classic experimental constraint of operative variables, hypothesized determining agent (s), and prediction of results. Further, even sciences for which classic experimentation is much more frequently achievable, say, physics, are not fully able to predict material and energic occurrences in their own "open," natural domains (see, e.g., Gleick 1987). As Manicas and Secord (1983) put it: "The past is, in a sense 'determined.' That is, what happened can be causally *explained*. But the future is *not* determined precisely because the complex related structures and systems of the world are constantly being reconfigured" (p. 403). Of course, the same is true – if anything, more true – for personality and clinical process.

Neither analysand nor analyst can know in advance what will transpire from one clinical circumstance to another. Neither should one expect that "serious" (Davidson 1980) psychological laws always be able to predict rather than, in hindsight, explain, as is true for any science. But in my attempt to develop a definition of psychoanalysis adequate to cover our present diversity with respect to interpretation and version of clinical process, I have emphasized how the psychoanalytic relationship is commonly used to illustrate and (always relatively) resolve analysand dynamically unconscious, inflexible, ordained, repetitious experience and action, in short, everything Freud (e.g., 1920b) means by the repetition compulsion. I can use the chess metaphor (Freud 1913) for a psychoanalytic clinical process of whatever "persuasion" (Schafer 1983): Each chess piece – knight, castle, king, pawn, and so on – has a fixed possibility of action on the chessboard. For me, this means that clinical psychoanalytic process is somewhere in between an "open," natural psychological domain and the stringently "closed" arrangement of classical experimentation. Consequently, I believe statistically controlled research procedures can be, in fact, have been, applied to psychoanalytic clinical process. Thus, critical determining agents can be identified and "tracked" in their natural clinical occurrence. And hypotheses can be formulated to explain the effects of these determining agents, comparing clinical phenomena associated with their presence or absence. Luborsky's (e.g., 1973) work on momentary forgetting in treatment sessions and its connection to conflictual, dynamic thematic content is an example of such research.[4] But with child development (i.e., longitudinal) research another situation obtains, because here we are in a completely "open" system of psychic events. To take an example from Manicas and Secord (1983), no one expects physical laws to predict that, say, a 23-year-old bridge that took 5 years to build will collapse, and so we have systematic, "firsthand" physical knowledge about the dynamics and structure only during the initial stages of construction. In the same way, no one can expect psychological lawfulness to predict academic failure of a college student if systematic, firsthand knowledge is available only for the first 5 years of the student's psychic reality. In both cases, intervening "data" would have to be collected, and some measure of reconstruction would be necessary. But still, different theories could be assessed in terms of their relative ability to explain, retrospectively, the later occurrence, be it physical or psychical; and this, I believe, is something more than narrative coherence. For example, once explanatory reconstruction has been made, replications might be performed or sought in "open," natural systems.

There will always be a fruitful, albeit at times disturbing, interrelationship between science and philosophy of science. But we do not notice biochemical or genetic research inhibited by the kinds of disturbing philosophical questions thrown up by philosophy of science. Certainly, those suf-

fering from cancer or AIDS would like to see controlled
research continue. The knowledge we can acquire from such
research produces what Sir Francis Bacon (1620), almost 400
years ago, called "power"—a "power" for the "endowment
of human life" (p. 120). Why should we not attempt this for
the kind of emotional suffering that is such an important part
of the subject matter of psychoanalysis?

But there is more to it than the contribution of psychoanalysis as a science for the alleviation of human suffering. There
has always been more to it. The words just cited from Bacon
come from his extraordinary work *Novum Organum*, which
heralded the era of the Enlightenment. An assessment of
Bacon's philosophy of science, together with his recom-
mended experimental methodology for obtaining findings
that could be socially useful as well as scientifically credible
assertions about the nature of reality, is not relevant to what
I want to say as I end this book. But I do want to emphasize
this: it is impossible, I believe, after reading Urbach's (1987)
analysis of Bacon, for anyone to continue to believe that
Bacon's method and philosophy were that of a naive, induc-
tive eliminatist with an equally naive (empiric) idea of reality.
And there is something else that animates Bacon's work.

Novum Organum is replete with references to how the
scientific experimentation Bacon recommends expresses his
love for God. What inspires Bacon is a wish to understand, to
know, God's creation—nature—and ourselves as part of his
creation:

> For that which is deserving of existence is deserving of knowledge,
> the image of existence. Now the mean and splendid alike exist. Nay,
> as the finest odors are sometimes produced from putrid matter (such
> as musk and civet), so does valuable light and information emanate
> from mean and sordid instances. [p. 132]

Now, compare this beautifully turned language with what
Freud (1914c) had to say almost 300 years later regarding
human emotional disturbance, especially the dynamic un-

conscious, and what a psychoanalytic treatment relationship entails for an analysand:

> He [the analysand] must find the courage to pay attention to the details of his illness. His illness itself must no longer seem contemptible, but must become an enemy worthy of his mettle, a part of his personality, kept up by good motives, out of which things of value for his future life have to be derived. [p. 152]

What else is this but Freud understanding himself as a true son of the Enlightenment, and psychoanalysis as an instrument to continue the work of the Enlightenment? Almost 20 years ago Erikson (1976) described Freud as someone who "founded the psychoanalytic branch of enlightenment" (p. 410). It was Freud who first extended this loving desire *only to know* the psychic reality of that which is "mean" or "putrid" about human mentality, that is, our variegated sorts of psychopathology: symptoms, perversions, delusions, irrational hates and loves, whatever, and of course, all that exists in our dynamic unconscious. And it was Freud who first insisted that such investigation produces "valuable light," which can be of benefit not only for the analysand but for our civilization.

On the occasion of Freud's death, W. H. Auden (1939) composed in his memory a poetic eulogy that was also about psychoanalysis. Lines from this poem illustrate Auden's incisive understanding:

> but he [Freud] would have us remember most of all
> to be enthusiastic over the night,
>   not only for the sense of wonder
>   it alone has to offer, but also
>
> because it needs our love. With large sad eyes
> its delectable creatures look up and beg
>   us dumbly to ask them to follow:
>   they are exiles who long for the future
>
> that lies in our power, they too would rejoice
> if allowed to serve enlightenment like him.

I will return to Auden shortly.

What especially riled Bacon in *Novum Organum* was what he called idols—actually, rigid dogmas (and see Urbach 1987)—that prevented a loving, flexible, open-minded pursuit of understanding nature through research. Of special relevance to psychoanalysis are what Bacon called idols of the theater. These were the speculative philosophies originated by the Greeks and especially (for Bacon) the excessively rational, insufficiently empirical philosophy of Aristotle: "He [Aristotle] did not introduce a wide impartial survey of experience to assist his investigation of truth; he brought in carefully schooled and selected experience to justify his pronouncements" (cited in Urbach 1987, p. 130). Bacon wrote these words in a somewhat earlier work entitled *The Refutation of Philosophies* (1608, cited in Urbach 1987). Again, Bacon had in mind Aristotle, especially Aristotle's physics. And we return to *Novum Organum*:

> There was a peculiar and proper motion in all bodies and if they shared in any other motion, it was owing to an external moving cause, and [he] imposed innumerable, arbitrary distinctions upon the nature of things; being everywhere more anxious as to definitions in teaching and accuracy of the wording of his propositions, than the internal truth of things. [pp. 113–114]

Thus, for Aristotle (see e.g., Asimov 1966 and Russell 1946) there were four fundamental kinds of matter, each of which had its "natural" place in the universe: the natural place for our familiar common solid materials on earth was the center of the earth (hence objects fell down); the natural place of water was around the rim of the earth (thus the oceans); the natural place of air was around the rim of water (the sky); and, finally, the natural place of fire was outside the area of air (lightning, interpreted as fire), and this was the explanation for why fire rises. But, of course, now we know this is not correct, and there is no such thing as this sort of natural place in physics. A fire set in a spacecraft shuttling around the earth will rise (air expansion, convection, etc.), but a stone most certainly will not fall. Psychoanalysts can, perhaps, more easily appreciate Aristotle's mistake. His physics, after all, was largely taken from previous Greek philosophers, and his biological research did advance zoology and botany, especially with respect to marine life (see, e.g., Downey 1962).

But psychoanalysts cannot so easily appreciate Aristotle's psychology. For Aristotle, human mentality also had a natural place—and this place was rationality (see, e.g., Downey 1962). Notwithstanding the glorious achievements of Greek culture, there is every reason to believe that irrational mentality was as evident then as it is now. Here, surely, Bacon (1608, cited in Urbach 1987) was correct that Aristotle did not conduct an "impartial" study of human mentality and conduct. Put another way, Freud as a descendant of the Enlightenment wanted to accomplish for human mentality what Galileo had accomplished for physical mechanics. What Galileo (see, e.g., Asimov 1966) brought to physical mechanics was a non-Aristotelian physics. It is always the physical *dynamics* in a given physical circumstance that determine the motion of a body, and not some Aristotelian natural place for it. In the same way, for Freud (e.g., 1915e) it is always the way in which *mental dynamics* operate in a given human circumstance that determines how (never completely) rational a human being will be, and it is not some natural human place to be rational.

I want to return to Auden, whose poetic eulogy to Freud conveyed to me such a sense of intimacy with the experience that I assumed he must have been in a Freudian psychoanalysis. I was wrong. But I did learn that Auden was an avid reader of Freud's writing all his life, and already at age 18 had his own collection of Freud's literature (Carpenter 1981). Auden lived openly as a homosexual all his life, when, at least relatively, it was more difficult to do so compared with our present time; and he clearly was using Freud's investigations into homosexuality not only to understand various fantasies that can enter into homosexual lovemaking but also to *accept* his own lifestyle (Carpenter 1981). This must be why Auden (1939) wrote as he did:

> If he [Freud] succeeded, why the Generalized Life
> would become impossible.

And:

> for one who'd lived among enemies so long:
> if often he was wrong and, at times, absurd,
>   to us he is no more a person
>   now but a whole climate of opinion
>
> under whom we conduct our different lives:
> Like weather he can only hinder or help.

What is Auden telling us with this beautiful and powerful language? He is telling us this: Freud, in creating psychoanalysis, produced not only a theory of personality, together with a treatment to alleviate human suffering, but as well, I believe, a real if utterly unique love relationship intrinsic to such treatment. Freud, Auden is telling us, also created a *social movement*: "Our civilization imposes an almost intolerable pressure on us and it calls for a corrective" (Freud 1926b, pp. 249–250). The point is that, as a science devoted only to understanding, in common and in concert with our other social sciences, psychoanalysis exerts a force for civilization that is humanizing in the best sense of the word.

Another great man of literature, Oscar Wilde, did not have Auden's good fortune to live in a time when a "whole climate of opinion" could be affected by the humanizing influence of psychoanalysis. In his novel *The Picture of Dorian Gray*, Wilde (1891b) relegates his (and our) homosexuality and altogether our dynamic unconscious into a hidden psychic place where it is portrayed only as ugly and repulsive, and so remains without light or love. Wilde's (Ellman 1988) homosexuality (bisexuality?) could only remain an unacknowledged element of his psychic reality, with consequent turmoil and anguish, and with no possibility of any sort of productive resolution for his personal life with significant others. But I have chosen to speak about Auden and Wilde for two other reasons. With my discussion of these two other matters, I can end this book.

The issue of homosexual lifestyle, in which I include a person's sexual identity as well as that of the loved other, is as old as it is contemporary, but we are all aware how in contemporary literature it is now an intensely discussed topic (e.g., Corbett 1993, Isay 1989, Socarides 1978). Questions are raised about etiologies (plural) of homosexual lifestyle and also about our concepts of male, female, active, passive, and so forth, with respect to psychic reality; and all of this can only be salutary for furthering our understanding. But why is it that these questions are raised in our contemporary literature as if Freud himself was settled on this complex matter of sexual lifestyles? Freud (1910c, 1920a) described different (pre-oedipal vs. more oedipally centered) etiologies for homosexuality. Further, any careful examination of Freud's *Three Essays* (1905a), including the footnotes added over the years, attests to his recognition of just how complex this matter of sexual lifestyle is. Corbett (1993) comments how Freud (1920a) alluded to "the mystery of homosexuality" (p. 170). Indeed, Freud did say this, just as he considered heterosexual lifestyle to be a puzzle. For example:

> Thus, from the point of view of psychoanalysis the exclusive sexual interest shown by men for women is also a problem that needs elucidating and is not a self-evident fact based upon an attraction that is ultimately of a chemical nature. [Freud 1905a, p. 146]

Or one can use another example from Freud's (1923) *Ego and Id* monograph. Here, Freud describes his conception of the "complete" Oedipus complex, with which we are familiar, and "which is twofold, positive and negative, and is due to the bi-sexuality originally present in children" (p. 33). But a few pages earlier Freud considers that perhaps "identification . . . [with the loved other] . . . is the sole condition under which the id gives up its objects" (p. 29). Consequently, if, in the resolution of the oedipal complex, the little boy *does not* intensify his identification with his mother, who is now given up as an erotically loved other, this is "not what we should have expected . . . since [it] . . . does not introduce the abandoned love object into the ego" (p. 32). Instead, the boy intensifies his identification with his father. Once again, heterosexual male lifestyle (as described above) is a puzzle; of course, this same puzzle applies to the emergence of a complementary female heterosexual lifestyle. Freud (1923) actually stated, "We are accustomed to regard . . . [this heterosexual outcome] . . . as the more normal" (p. 32). And we do not have to belabor Freud's (1905a) devastating critique of any idea of degeneracy applied to homosexuality.

So, most certainly, what also is not new (or should not be new) is a more-or-less-usual Freudian practice with respect to the psychoanalysis of a homosexual analysand that is to be without therapeutic ambition (Freud 1912b)—*either way* with respect to sexual lifestyle outcome—as it is for anything else about the analysand's way of life. And once again, in my opinion, Freud is revealed in theory and in practice to be a powerful, humanizing voice of the Enlightenment. But adult analyses, even conjoined with child analyses, will always leave us with insufficient knowledge about the development of sexual lifestyle (or anything else of significance for psychic reality). Analytic reminiscences about the acquisition of sexual lifestyle are simply not the same as the interplay of "material" (Freud 1939) events, with psychosexual schemas for organizing fantasies about real experiences, that Freudians conceive to be critical for determining psychic reality.

Suppose, for a moment, I am correct. And suppose, as a consequence of psychoanalytically informed, statistically controlled research, together with psychoanalysis of adults and children, we come to possess much more adequate understanding about the determination of sexual lifestyle, homosexual or heterosexual. Would we not, inextricably, also then possess more knowledge than we do today about what it is that determines which life is lived most productively and with the least suffering? Should we draw back from acquiring such knowledge out of a concern that it might be misused by society? Can we not trust ourselves, in such a circumstance, to be guided by continually assessed mental health values that transcend this issue of sexual lifestyle?[5] If this be our concern, and it actually prevents this (and other) research, then to this extent we consign ourselves to a kind of dark ages of mental health.

Finally, I want to return to Wilde because I want to consider two interrelated issues: the relationship between the creative artist and reality—and by reality I mean that version of objectivism termed transcendental reality (e.g., Bhaskar 1975)—and the relationship between the creative arts and interpretation in the psychoanalytic relationship.

How are we to understand Wilde's (1891a) famous dictum—and *dictum* is a word that occurs to me for good reason—"Life should imitate art" (cited and discussed, for example, in Kronenberger 1976 and, of course, Ellman 1988)? This statement is really a command. It is not simply the entire statement that illustrates this command but especially the word *imitate*. If we understand Wilde's use of the word *life* to mean not only that envelope of societal custom within which he lived but also reality, then Wilde is expressing, clinically, an unbalanced relationship between reality and the life of imagination. If we now imagine "reality" and "fantasy" to be two people in a relationship with one another, then Wilde is not even granting reality its own identity. It is a vital matter in every psychoanalysis, espe-

cially a more-or-less-usual Freudian clinical process, which
aims to bring to light all manner of psychosexual and
aggressive endogenous fantasy, that a clinically healthy
relationship exist between fantasy and reality (see esp.
Loewald 1975 and Winnicott 1951). Wilde's command that
life (reality) imitate art fractionates (splits apart) what otherwise would be a natural *coherence* between art and reality.
Wilde's statement intends art to have an imperious relationship over reality. That Wilde needed to make such a statement is entirely understandable, considering his travails and
suffering. But the clinician must nevertheless appreciate how
Wilde's own narcissistic disturbance together with (late)
Victorian society combined to produce his misfortune.[6] And
Wilde expressed both his awful suffering and his sense of
utter subjugation in his poetry. Here are a few bitter lines
from "The Ballad of Reading Gaol" (1896):

> But this I know, that every Law
>   That men have made for Man,
> Since first Man took his brother's life,
>   And the sad world began,
> But straws the wheat and saves the chaff
>   With a most evil fan.
>
> This too I know—and wise it were
>   If each could know the same—
> That every prison that men build
>   Is built with bricks of shame,
> And bound with bars lest Christ should see
>   How men their brothers maim.

But art—certainly great art—promotes what Keats (1818)
described in his epic poem *Endymion* as a "fellowship with
essence" (p. 108). It is clear (see, e.g., Thorpe 1935) that what
Keats means by fellowship and essence is not only a poetic
immersion into immediate, real life experience but also how
artistic rendering has something to tell us about humanness
beyond our immediate experience. Freud (1911a) put it this

way: "[The artist can] mold his fantasies into thoughts of a new kind which are valued by men as reflections of reality" (p. 224). Freud was not just a great writer but a careful writer. He does not say "reflections of a *new* reality" but "thoughts of *new kind* . . . valued as *reflections* of reality" (p. 224). This is in keeping with the objectivist, transcendental realism (Bhaskar 1975) Freud held to throughout his life.

Another way I can describe this is to adopt Polanyi's (1958) term *universal intent*. I can realize that great art also has a universal intent, as is the case with the theoretical construction of a scientific theory, although, and obviously, these two forms of expression are very different from one another. Nevertheless, the great creative artist and scientist are animated by this same loving desire and responsibility to express that which corresponds to something about a transcendent reality, both inanimate and animate. We have at our universities—and as far as I am aware this has always been the case—a (one) faculty of "arts and science."

This expression of a universal intent—perhaps better, universal appeal—is obviously not changed by the artist's medium. The *Mona Lisa* is not just about a woman: it is about something that is femininity, or even beyond femininity, something universal that involves the possession of a human mentality. The same applies to Michelangelo's *David*, or a Beethoven symphony, or whatever. The same applies to whatever style is used by the creative artist. The Roman playwright Terence (163 B.C.), can say:

I am a man: Nothing human is alien to me.

Or the Romantic Keats can emphasize how his subjectivism is such that he is a "chameleon poet" (cited in Bate 1963). But it is all the same. The creative artist always intends to use symbols for this universal appeal. Still, if the creative artist does have something of this kind to say to us, and if his or her creative symbols are not currently considered expressions of madness (Kris 1952), then the artist is also involved in a "love affair with the world" (Greenacre 1957, p. 490). The artist can, of course, have a love relationship with another; but insofar as his or her creativity is concerned, it is a love relationship with no particular other. Consequently, if I am correct in my understanding of what is meant by "ontological hermeneutics" (Gadamer 1977, Heidegger 1927; and see esp. R. Steiner 1992), the artistic creation in itself can be said to possess a kind of purely hermeneutic existence. But especially great art still must possess universal appeal, which is only possible because of our shared human existence (see, e.g., Brown 1991). Nevertheless, what a great work of art will mean to an individual can vary, endlessly, repeatedly, depending on that person's own changing life circumstance, as well as the work's cultural and historical contexts. It can even be that an artistic creation once thought of as madness can, at another time, be interpreted as a powerful comprehension of reality. Thus the impulse for ongoing critical reevaluation of art, which is, perhaps, as close as we can get to the experimental validation of science. This kind of hermeneutic existence for art is what Freud (1914b) meant by his remarks about the belief that a state of "intellectual bewilderment" is necessary "[for art] . . . to achieve its greatest effects" (p. 212), though as a descendent of the Enlightenment, Freud had the "greatest reluctance to believe in any such necessity" (p. 212).

Why? Well, in part, a great work of art considered now only in itself is, as I have suggested, something given to us by the creative individual for endless interpretation about the reality of our universal human condition—just the opposite of a system of logic that allows for only one way of reasoning. But a system of logic, or a great work of art, is still created by an individual and so must result from the "mental life" (Freud 1910b) of that individual. Put another way, "No one . . . [is] . . . so great as to be disgraced by being subject to the laws which govern both normal and pathological

activity with equal cogency" (Freud 1910b, p. 63). Freud
believed he had devised a method, the psychoanalytic treatment relationship, that enables us to understand a work of
art in terms of the creative individual's psychic reality,
especially, of course, dynamically unconscious mentality.
Let us consider how Keats's (1818) poetic sensibility fixes on
a nightingale's song and produces an ode that expresses
something about the transcendental reality of the human
condition (mentality). We are left with this moving ode,
which exists, as I say, purely hermeneutically. But suppose
Keats is in a psychoanalysis with me, and his associations are
about the poetic symbols of his "Ode to a Nightingale." And
suppose Keats associates to these poetic images. For example:

> Where Beauty cannot keep her lustrous eyes,
>   Or new Love pine at them beyond to-morrow.

Is it at all difficult to understand that for this "new Love"
Keats would either directly associate (or one could interpret)
Fanny Brawne, his great love, who had entered into his life
the previous year (Thorpe 1935)? Or take another example,
where Keats addresses this "immortal Bird":

> Fade far away, dissolve, and quite forget
>   What thou amongst the leaves hast never known,
> The weariness, the fever, and the fret
>   Here where men sit and hear each other groan.

Is it at all difficult to understand that for these poignant lines
Keats would directly associate, or one could interpret, his
serious, chronic physical illness? But this kind of psychic
reality understanding of the *content* of art is an altogether
different matter from an understanding of creative process,
and Freud (1910a) appreciated the difference: this *"artistic
gift . . . that is still a psychological mystery"* (p. 50). Even if
we believe we now have some glimmer of understanding
(Kris 1952, Nass, e.g., 1989) about creativity, how can that

possibly detract from our appreciation and gratitude for the awesome universal appeal of a great work of art (see, e.g., Colvin, in Thorpe 1935, p. 350)? At any rate, were thematic meanings to this great verse established, such meanings would be examples of what I have termed either our manifest or our dynamically unconscious database, no more or less than that of any other science. Equally important, Keats and I would be devoted only to understanding *his* psychic reality, no generalized other's, and Keats's psychic reality now would have the status of a loved object for both of us.[7] To be sure, I would seamlessly inform such meanings with an array of symbols, supplied me by my own Freudian orientation, if the psychoanalysis remained productive, to further "open" Keats's psychic reality (loss of love, anxiety and depression, perhaps illness as sexual impotence, and so forth). Another analyst, with another psychoanalytic orientation, would use another array of symbols, and we have barely begun the research necessary for evaluating these differences. I have urged, for psychoanalysis, a position that this great ode is enabled by the transcendental reality of a human mind that exists as it does. The nature of this human mind includes processes with causal powers that make possible the creation of great poetry to express one's psychic reality, and consequently, this psychic reality in a definite sense also exists as it does. Therefore, psychoanalytic interpretation, while artful (timing, tact, etc.), is neither creative expression nor hermeneutic activity.

In sum, Freud created in psychoanalysis a social movement for scientific enlightenment about human mentality and a consequent humanism; a scientific theory of personality; a procedure to investigate and ameliorate human suffering; and a unique but real sort of love between two individuals that is the psychoanalytic relationship. Indeed, there is no "prototype" (Freud 1915a) for this relationship, and it is "a thing apart" (Freud 1912b). There is no other experience like it for either the analysand or analyst.

NOTES

1. Steiner's article is extremely valuable for its informative over-view of the hermeneutic tradition in Western philosophy. Also, and in particular, Steiner clarifies how Habermas (1971) is to be distinguished, as a hermeneutic philosopher, from both Gadamer (1977) and Heidegger (1927). Habermas clearly retains a connection, as Steiner explains, to the Enlightenment perspective of nature (including human) to be understood irrespective of context. For example, Habermas retains a concept of "normal communication" (cited in R. Steiner 1992, p. 25); indeed, Ha-bermas conceives psychoanalysis to be a critical social force to promote just such "normal communication." And nothing could be clearer than his statement, "I defend an outrageously strong claim in the present context of philosophical discussion: *namely, that there is a universal core of moral intuition in all times and in all societies*" (p. 23).

Consequently, Steiner questions how it is that Habermas has been appropriated by psychoanalysts (e.g., Schafer 1983, Spence 1987) who advocate a hermeneutic positioning for psychoanalysis. But then again, Spence and Schafer differ altogether with respect to Spence's (1990) advocacy for an "evidential voice" for psychoanalysis. Still again, it seems to be Schafer (1983) who understands that Habermas has an "immediate position" (p. 234) relative to Spence (1990), who at least seems to regard Habermas to be a "strong," that is, ontological, hermeneutic philosopher.

2. For me this means that Polanyi is an objectivist philosopher, although others (Hanly 1990, Wallerstein 1985) do not agree.

3. But I do not think this phenomenon of pan-cultural recognition of facial, emotional displays is something from which mind–body reduc-tionists should take heart so easily. Let us say John Smith is observed to smile happily in circumstances in our culture where a smile is expected; another who observes this smile will "know" something about John Smith's experience, and this knowledge is asymbolic. Now, let us say John Smith is put into a hypnotic trance and is told a sexual joke involving a rainstorm. Let us also say that John Smith has been clinically studied and assessed to be the kind of person who hugely enjoys such jokes. Then John Smith is given a posthypnotic suggestion that when he awakens from the trance and hears the word "weather," he is to think of this joke and tell it to another. John Smith is awakened from the trance; a few minutes later he hears the word "weather," tells the joke, and smiles happily while telling the joke. Or, imagine John Smith has multiple personalities, each of which smiles on occasions to be expected in our culture. We cannot believe that the hypnotic trance or multiple-personality John Smith smiles have the same neurophys-iological array of events as the "ordinary" John Smith smile. How easily

can we imagine "serious" (Davidson 1980) psychophysiological laws that could explain such varied smiling?

4. I certainly include in my advocacy for research into psychoanalysis not only statistically controlled research into clinical process but also experimental methodologies outside the clinical situation. The "old chestnut" (e.g., Spence 1987) usually pulled out at this point is Freud's letter to Rosenzweig (see Gay 1988). Rosenzweig had written Freud describing how his research supported the psychoanalytic concept of repression. Freud wrote back that such experimentation could do "no harm" but was not needed, as the clinical process supplied sufficient evidence for the concept of repression. But Freud (again, see Gay 1988) was very interested in Potzl's research into preconscious stimulation effects on dream formation and, as well, Jung's research, which used a free-association type of test for purposes of diagnostic assessment. In other words, I believe Freud's interest in experimentation outside the clinical situation was aroused if the methodology seemed relevant to psychoanalysis. In any event, Freud (Gay 1988) was only trained in classical research procedures, was not aware of statistical sorts of control, and certainly could not even dream about our current technological (computer, video, etc.) capabilities.

Potzl's work was the "ancestor" of research into subliminal activation, experimental methodology to examine psychoanalytic propositions. L. Silverman (e.g., Silverman and Weinberger 1985) pioneered such research, including subliminal verbal stimulation. Silverman's research methodology has been subject to criticism (Balay and Shevrin 1988), and this criticism has been answered by D. Silverman (1989, and see Hardway 1986). The basic point is that this procedure produces real phenomena relevant to psychoanalytic propositions.

Shevrin (1992) has recently reviewed some of this research and advanced the methodology by using subliminal verbal material "tailored" to a particular subject-patient's conflicts as assessed by clinicians. Shevrin also has research findings that show "certain frequency features of brain responses" (p. 323) to be related to subliminal but not supraliminal stimulation of verbal material. However, we can question how such responses would differentiate, clinically, between repression and denial (Moore and Fine 1968), both of which involve dynamically unconscious procedures to maintain some experience out of consciousness. Once again, what is raised here is the possibility of "serious" (Davidson 1980) psychophysiological laws that would enable mind–body reductionism.

But imagine a full-fledged research program into "academic" areas of perception, thinking, and so forth, wherein all research subjects also were in a psychoanalysis. Even more, this research program could involve children in a psychoanalysis and then have a child development component built into it.

5. Murray (1961), now over 30 years ago, raised a powerful and eloquent voice for a societal need to continuously assess mental health values. These words, if anything, seem more cogent now than when Murray originally wrote them:

> that a natural, not a supernatural religion . . . [is] intended—one with only entities and forces *within* the order of nature, to be symbolized and commemorated; second, that the underlying propositions of this religion would be tested by their fruits and hence would be as susceptible as scientific theories to refutation and revision, and third, that the whole endeavor . . . [calls] for extensions rather than suppressions of . . . creativeness. [p. 16]

Is this utterly fantastic? Consider our present, extraordinary proliferation of therapeutic self-help groups for every sort of physical and emotional problem (cancer, obesity, addictions, etc.). Can this be taken to be an expression of the societal need insisted on by Murray? I think it accurate to say that the values that imbue these self-help groups, increasingly, are therapeutic and empirical: the usefulness of expressing one's feelings to another; the importance of acknowledging that one has a problem; the self-destructiveness of certain emotions, contrasted with self-affirmation of other affects (see, e.g., Bradshaw 1988). What seems clear is not only the fact of such an explosion in the frequency and diversity of self-help groups but an orientation away from the traditional, religious-centered Alcoholics Anonymous toward the kind of scientifically assessed but humanistic psychology Murray described. And what would be the effect on our society if, gradually, these proliferating self-help groups were to form some sort of loose federation? Would this not be a movement toward the kind of scientifically assessed humanistic religion envisioned by Murray? Erikson (1976) also had something important to say about the responsibility of psychoanalysis in this regard.

6. But Wilde knew there was something wrong, very wrong, with himself. Ellman (1988) notes in his biography how Wilde (1891b) in the novel describes Dorian Gray as follows:

> [Dorian] would often adopt certain modes of thought that he knew to be really alien to his nature, abandon himself to their subtle influences, and then, having as it were caught their colour and satisfied his intellectual curiosity, leave them with that curious indifference that is not incompatible with a real ardor of temperament, and that, indeed, according to certain modern psychologists, is often a condition of it. [pp. 319–320]

Ellman tells us that 4 years earlier Wilde in a letter described himself, not surprisingly, to have a "curious mixture of ardour and indifference" (p. 320).

But just who were these modern psychologists about whom Wilde (through the character of Dorian Gray) spoke? Certainly not Freud at this point in Freud's life (Gay 1988), and anyway, Wilde surely knew the difference between a physician and a psychologist. Wilde's father (Ellman 1988) probably was the preeminent ophthalmologist of his time. Dr. Joyce Steingart suggested to me that Wilde might have had William James in mind. This would be an irony because James, while a property mind–body dualist, could not accept anything like a concept of a dynamic unconscious. But James (1890) in his *Principles* was very much taken up with Janet's work (following Charcot) into phenomena related to multiple personalities, dissociated states, posthypnotic suggestion, and the like. James himself conceived of "*secondary personal selves*" (p. 227). I did learn that 250 copies of the original edition of James's *Principles* were sold to Macmillan and appeared in London in 1890. But then the chronology would be wrong in terms of the correspondence Ellman cites, wherein Wilde talks about modern psychologists. However, it is possible that Wilde, on his American tour (Ellman 1988), became familiar with James's concept of secondary personal selves. Also, of course, Wilde certainly could have been familiar with Janet's work from his visits to France. In any event, Wilde, I suggest, found this concept and research about unintegrated experiences relevant to his sense of estrangement from his feelings and/or his sense of his own incompatible emotional states.

7. We know (see esp. Bate 1963) the great importance Keats attached to the words "fellowship with essence"; in fact, they were part of a change of some five lines Keats implored the publisher to accept while the poem *Endymion* was in press.

REFERENCES

Abend, S., Porder, M. W., and Willick, M. S. (1983). *Borderline Patients: Psychoanalytic Perspectives*. New York: International Universities Press.

Adams, F. R. (1967). Stereotypy, social responsiveness, and arousal in a case of catatonia. *British Journal of Psychiatry* 118:1123–11.

Albee, E. (1962). *Who's Afraid of Virginia Woolf?* New York: Atheneum.

American Psychiatric Association. (1980). *Diagnostic and Statistical Manual of Mental Disorders*, 3d ed. Washington, DC: APA.

Arlow, J. A. (1985). The concept of psychic reality and related problems. *Journal of the American Psychoanalytic Association* 33:521–536.

Asimov, I. (1966). *The History of Physics*. New York: Walker.

Auden, W. H. (1939). In memory of Sigmund Freud. In *W. H. Auden: Collected Poems*, ed. E. Mendelson. New York: Random House, 1940.

Bach, S. (1977). On the narcissistic state of consciousness. *International Journal of Psycho-Analysis* 49:209–223.

———— (1980). Self-love and object love: some problems of self and object constancy, differentiation, and integration. In *Rapprochement: The Critical Sub-phase of Separation-Individuation*, ed. R. F. Lax, S. Bach, and J. A. Burland, pp. 171–198. New York: Jason Aronson.

———— (1985). *Narcissistic States and the Therapeutic Process*. New York: Jason Aronson.

Bacon, F. (1620). *Novum Organum: Great Books of the Western World*. Chicago: Encyclopedia Britannica, 1952.

Balay, J., and Shevrin, H. (1988). The subliminal activation method: a critical review. *American Psychologist* 43:161–178.

Balint, M. (1968). *The Basic Fault: Therapeutic Aspects of Regression*. London: Tavistock.

Bate, W. J. (1963). *John Keats*. Cambridge: Harvard University Press.

Bechtel, W. (1988a). *Philosophy of Mind: An Overview for Cognitive Science*. Hillsdale, NJ: Erlbaum.

———— (1988b). *Philosophy of Science: An Overview for a Cognitive Science*. Hillsdale, NJ: Erlbaum.

Beres, D., and Arlow, J. A. (1974). Fantasy and identification in empathy. *Psychoanalytic Quarterly* 43:26–50.

Bergmann, M. S., and Hartman, F. R. (1976). *The Evolution of Psychoanalytic Technique*. New York: Basic Books.

Bhaskar, R. (1975). Forms of realism. *Philosophica* 15:99–127.

Bion, W. R. (1962). *Learning from Experience*. London: Heinemann.

_____ (1967). *Second Thoughts: Selected Papers on Psychoanalysis*. New York: Jason Aronson.

Bird, B. (1957). A specific peculiarity of acting out. *Journal of the American Psychoanalytic Association* 5:630–647.

Blos, P. (1966). The concept of acting out in the transference. In *A Developmental Approach to Problems of Acting Out*, ed. E. N. Roxford, pp. 118–136. New York: International Universities Press.

Blum, H. P. (1973). The concept of the eroticized transference. *Journal of the American Psychoanalytic Association* 21:61–76.

Boesky, D. (1982). Acting out—a reconsideration of the concept. *International Journal of Psychoanalysis* 63:39–57.

Bradshaw, J. (1988). *Healing the Shame That Binds You*. Deerfield Beach, FL: Health Communication.

Brenner, C. (1955). *An Elementary Textbook of Psychoanalysis*. New York: International Universities Press, 1973.

_____ (1979). Working alliance, therapeutic alliance, and transference. *Journal of the American Psychoanalytic Association* 27:137–158.

_____ (1985). Countertransference as compromise formation. *Psychoanalytic Quarterly* 54:155–164.

Bretherton, I., and Boeghly, M. (1982). Talking about mental states: the acquisition of an explicit theory of mind. *Developmental Psychology* 18:906–921.

Breuer, J., and Freud, S. (1895). Studies in hysteria. *Standard Edition* 2:3–305.

Brown, D. E. (1991). *Human Universals*. Philadelphia: Temple University Press.

Brown, R. (1973). *A First Language*. Cambridge: Harvard University Press.

Bruner, J. S., Oliver, R., and Greenfield, P., et al. (1956). *Studies in Cognitive Growth*. New York: Wiley.

Bucci, W. (1985). Dual coding: a cognitive model for psychoanalytic research. *Journal of the American Psychoanalytic Association* 33:571–608.

_____ (1989). A reconstruction of Freud's tally argument: a program for psychoanalytic research. *Psychoanalytic Inquiry* 9:249–281.

_____ (1994). The multiple code theory and the psychoanalytic process: a framework for research. In *The Annual of Psychoanalysis*, vol. 22, pp. 243–263. Hillsdale, NJ: Analytic Press.

Buie, D. H. (1985). Borderline patients: psychoanalytic perspectives. *International Journal of Psycho-Analysis* 66:375–379.

Carpenter, H. (1981). *W. H. Auden: A Biography*. Boston: Houghton Mifflin.

Cassirer, E. (1923). *Substance and Function*. New York: Dover, 1953.

Caston, J. A. (1993). Can analysts agree? The problem of consensus and the psychoanalytic manikin. 1. A proposed solution. *Journal of the American Psychoanalytic Association* 41:395–422.

Caston, J. A., and Martin, E. (1993). The problem of consensus and the psychoanalytic manikin. 2. Empirical tests. *Journal of the American Psychoanalytic Association* 41:513–548.

Cavell, M. (1985). Self and some related issues: a philosophical perspective, part I and part II. *Psychoanalysis and Contemporary Thought* 8:3–44.

———— (1991). The subject of mind. *International Journal of Psycho-Analysis* 72:141–154.

Chrzanowski, G. (1980). Collaborative inquiry, affirmation, and neutrality in the psychoanalytic situation. *Contemporary Psychoanalysis* 16:348–386.

Compton, A. C. (1985). The concept of identification in the work of Freud, Ferenczi, and Abraham: a review and commentary. *Psychoanalytic Quarterly* 54:201–233.

Corbett, K. (1993). The mystery of homosexuality. *Psychoanalytic Psychology* 10:345–358.

Dahl, H., Teller, V., Moss, D., and Trujillo, M. (1978). Countertransference examples of the syntactic expression of warded-off contents. *Psychoanalytic Quarterly* 47:339–363.

Davidson, D. (1980). *Essays on Actions and Events*. New York: Oxford University Press.

Devitt, M. (1984). *Realism and Truth*. New Jersey: Princeton University Press.

Dickes, R. (1965). The defensive function of an altered state of consciousness: a hypnoid state. *Journal of the American Psychoanalytic Association* 13:356–403.

Downey, G. (1962). *Aristotle: Dean of Early Science*. New York: Franklin Watts.

Eagle, M. M., and Wolitsky, D. (1986). The process of psychoanalytic therapy: models and strategies by E. Peterfreund. *Psychoanalysis and Contemporary Thought* 9:79–102.

Edelheit, H. (1969). Speech and psychic structure: the vocal-auditory organization of the ego. *Journal of the American Psychological Association* 17:381–412.

Edelson, M. (1975). *Language, Interpretation, and Psychoanalysis*. New Haven, CT: Yale University Press.

Eissler, K. R. (1950). Ego-psychological implications of the psychological treatment of delinquents. *Psychoanalytic Study of the Child* 5:97–121. New York: International Universities Press.

———— (1953). The effect of the structure of the ego on psychoanalytic technique. *Journal of the American Psychoanalytic Association* 1:104–143.

Ekman, P. (1980). *The Face of Man: Expressions of Universal Emotions in a New Guinea Village*. New York: Garland STPM Press.

———— (1992). Facial expression of emotion: an old controversy and new findings. *Philosophical Transactions of the Royal Society London B* 335:65–69.

———— (1993). Voluntary smiling changes regional brain activity. *Psychological Science* 4:342–345.

Ekman, P., Sorenson, E. R., and Friesen, W. V. (1969). Pan-cultural elements in facial displays of emotions. *Science* 164:86–88.

Ekstein, R., and Friedman, S. W. (1957). Acting out, play action, and acting. *Journal of the American Psychoanalytic Association* 1:104–143.

Ellman, R. (1988). *Oscar Wilde*. New York: Vintage.

Epstein, L., and Feiner, A. (1979). *Countertransference*. New York: Jason Aronson.

Erikson, E. H. (1950). *Childhood and Society*. New York: Norton.

———— (1962). Reality and actuality. *Journal of the American Psychoanalytic Association* 11:452–474.

———— (1976). Psychoanalysis and ethics—avowed and unavowed. *International Review of Psycho-Analysis* 3:409–415.

Federn, P. (1926). Some variations in ego feeling. *International Journal of Psycho-Analysis* 7:433–444.

Fenichel, O. (1941). *Problems of Psychoanalytic Technique*. Albany, NY: Psychoanalytic Quarterly.

Ferenczi, S. (1929). The principle of relaxation and neocatharsis. In *Final Contributions to the Problems and Methods of Psychoanalysis*, pp. 108–125. New York: Basic Books, 1955.

———— (1931). Child analysis in the analysis of adults. In *Final Contributions to the Problems and Methods of Psychoanalysis*, pp. 126–142. New York: Basic Books, 1955.

Feyerabend, P. K. (1965). Problems of empiricism. In *Beyond the Edge of Certainty: Essays on Contemporary Science and Philosophy*, pp. 145–260. Englewood Cliffs: Prentice Hall.

———— (1981). *Realism, Rationalism, and Scientific Method*. Cambridge: Cambridge University Press.

Flavell, J. H. (1963). *The Developmental Psychology of Jean Piaget*. New York: Van Nostrand.

———— (1968). *The Development of Role-Taking and Communication Skills in Children*. New York: Wiley.

Fliess, R. (1942). The metapsychology of the analyst. *Psychoanalytic Quarterly* 11:211–227.

Fodor, J. A. (1987). *Psychosemantics*. Cambridge: MIT Press.

Fónagy, I. (1971). The function of vocal style. In *Literary Style: A Symposium*, ed. S. Chatman, pp. 149–174. London: Oxford University Press.

Forman, M. B. (1948). *The Letters of John Keats*. New York: Oxford University Press.

Freedman, N. (1994). More on transformation enactments in psychoanalytic space. In *The Spectrum of Psychoanalysis: Essays in Honor of Martin S. Bergmann*, ed. A. K. Richards and A. D. Richards, pp. 93–110. Madison, CT: International Universities Press.

Freeman, M. (1985). Psychoanalytic narration and the problem of historical knowledge. *Psychoanalysis and Contemporary Thought* 8:133–182.

Freud, A. (1936). The ego and the mechanisms of defence. In *The Writings of Anna Freud*, vol. 2. New York: International Universities Press, 1973.

Freud, S. (1887–1902). *The Origins of Psychoanalysis: Letters to Wilhelm Fliess, Drafts, and Notes*, ed. M. Bonaparte, A. Freud, and E. Kris. New York: Basic Books, 1954.

—— (1895). Project for a scientific psychology. *Standard Edition* 1:283–388.

—— (1896). Further remarks on the neuropsychoses of defense. *Standard Edition* 3:162–185.

—— (1899). Screen memories. *Standard Edition* 3:303–322.

—— (1900). The interpretation of dreams. *Standard Edition* 4/5.

—— (1905a). Three essays in the theory of sexuality. *Standard Edition* 7:125–243.

—— (1905b). Fragment of a case of hysteria. *Standard Edition* 7:3–124.

—— (1906). My views on the part played by sexuality in the etiology of the neuroses. *Standard Edition* 7:271–282.

—— (1908). Creative writers and day-dreaming. *Standard Edition* 9:143–153.

—— (1909). Analysis of a phobia in a five-year-old-boy. *Standard Edition* 10:3–152.

—— (1910a). Five lectures on psychoanalysis. *Standard Edition* 11:9–55.

—— (1910b) Leonardo da Vinci and a memory of his childhood. *Standard Edition* 11:59–139.

—— (1910c). The future prospects for psychoanalytic therapy. *Standard Edition* 11:139–152.

—— (1910d). Wild psychoanalysis. *Standard Edition* 11:219–230.

—— (1911a). Formulations on the two principles of mental functioning. *Standard Edition* 12:215–226.

—— (1911b). Psychoanalytic notes on an autobiographical account of a case of paranoia (*dementia paranoides*). *Standard Edition* 12:3–84.

—— (1912a). The dynamics of transference. *Standard Edition* 12:99–108.

—— (1912b). Recommendations to physicians practicing psychoanalysis. *Standard Edition* 12:109–120.

—— (1913). On beginning the treatment. *Standard Edition* 12:121–144.

—— (1914a). On narcissism: an introduction. *Standard Edition* 14:67–104.

—— (1914b). The Moses of Michelangelo. *Standard Edition* 13:209–240.

_____ (1914c). Remembering, repeating, and working through. *Standard Edition* 12:145–156.

_____ (1915a). Observations on transference-love. *Standard Edition* 12:157–174.

_____ (1915b). Thoughts for the times on war and death. *Standard Edition* 14:275–300.

_____ (1915c). Instincts and their vicissitudes. *Standard Edition* 14:111–140.

_____ (1915d). Repression. *Standard Edition* 14:146–158.

_____ (1915e). The unconscious. *Standard Edition* 14:159–216.

_____ (1916). Some character types met with in psychoanalytic work. *Standard Edition* 14:311–333.

_____ (1916–1917). Introductory lectures on psychoanalysis. *Standard Edition* 15:3–461.

_____ (1917). On transformation of instincts as exemplified in anal eroticism. *Standard Edition* 17:125–135.

_____ (1920a). The psychogenesis of a case of homosexuality in a woman. *Standard Edition* 18:145–172.

_____ (1920b). Beyond the pleasure principle. *Standard Edition* 18:3–66.

_____ (1921). Group psychology and the analysis of the ego. *Standard Edition* 18:67–145.

_____ (1923). The ego and the id. *Standard Edition* 19:12–63.

_____ (1925). An autobiographical study. *Standard Edition* 20:3–76.

_____ (1926a). Inhibitions, symptoms, and anxiety. *Standard Edition* 20:20–178.

_____ (1926b). The question of lay analysis. *Standard Edition* 20:179–260.

_____ (1927). The future of an illusion. *Standard Edition* 21:3–56.

_____ (1933). New introductory lectures on psychoanalysis (Lecture 31). *Standard Edition* 22:57–80.

_____ (1937a). Analysis terminable and interminable. *Standard Edition* 23:216–254.

_____ (1937b). Constructions in analysis. *Standard Edition* 23:257–269.

_____ (1939). Moses and monotheism. *Standard Edition* 23:7–140.

_____ (1940). An outline of psychoanalysis. *Standard Edition* 23:144–208.

Furth, H. G. (1987). *Knowledge as Desire: An Essay on Freud and Piaget.* New York: Columbia University Press.

Gadamer, H. (1977). *Philosophical Hermeneutics.* Berkeley and Los Angeles: University of California Press.

Galenson, E. (1971). A consideration of the nature of thought in childhood play. In *Separation-Individuation: Essays in Honor of Margaret S. Mahler,* ed. J. B. McDevitt and C. F. Settlage, pp. 41–59. New York: International Universities Press.

Gay, P. (1988). *Freud: A Life for Our Time.* New York: Norton.

Gediman, H. K., and Wolkenfeld, F. (1980). The parallelism phenomenon in psychoanalysis and supervision: its reconsideration as a triadic system. *Psychoanalytic Quarterly* 49:234–255.

Gedo, J. E. (1979). *Beyond Interpretation*. New York: International Universities Press.

────── (1981). Measure for measure: a response. Commentaries on John Gedo's *Beyond Interpretation*. *Psychoanalytic Inquiry* 1:289–316.

Geha, R. E. (1984). On psychoanalytic history and the "real" story of fictitious lives. *International Forum on Psychoanalysis* 1:221–292.

Gill, M. M. (1981). The boundaries of psychoanalytic data and technique: a critique of Gedo's *Beyond Interpretation*. Commentaries on John Gedo's *Beyond Interpretation*. *Psychoanalytic Inquiry* 1:205–232.

────── (1982). *Analysis of Transference*, vol. 1, *Theory and Technique*. Psychological Issues, no. 53. Madison, CT: International Universities Press.

────── (1983). The interpersonal paradigm and the degree of the therapist's involvement. *Contemporary Psychoanalysis* 19:200–237.

────── (1984a). Psychoanalysis and psychotherapy: a revision. *International Review of Psycho-Analysis* 11:161–179.

────── (1984b). Transference: a change in conception or only in emphasis? A response to commentaries on Merton Gill's *Analysis of Transference*. *Psychoanalytic Inquiry* 4:489–524.

────── (1985). The interactional aspect of transference: range of application and discussion. In *The Transference in Psychotherapy: Clinical Management*, ed. E. A. Schwaber, pp. 87–102, 121–139. New York: International Universities Press.

Gill, M. M., and Hoffman, I. Z. (1982). *Analysis of Transference*, vol. 2. Psychological Issues, no. 54. Madison, CT: International Universities Press.

Gleick, J. (1987). *Chaos: Making a New Science*. New York: Penguin.

Glover, E. (1952). Research methods in psychoanalysis. *International Journal of Psycho-Analysis* 33:403–409.

Goldberg, A. (1978). *The Psychology of the Self: A Casebook*. New York: International Universities Press.

Greenacre, P. (1950). General problems in acting out. In *Trauma, Growth, and Personality*, pp. 224–236. New York: International Universities Press, 1969.

────── (1957). The childhood of the artist: libidinal phase development and giftedness. *Psychoanalytic Study of the Child* 12:49–72. New York: International Universities Press.

────── (1966). Problems of acting out in the transference relationship. In *A Developmental Approach to Problems of Acting Out*, ed. E. N. Rexford, pp. 144–159. New York: International Universities Press.

────── (1971). Discussion of E. Galenson's paper, "A Consideration of the Nature of Thought in Childhood Play." In *Separation-Individuation,*

Essays in Honor of Margaret S. Mahler, ed. J. B. McDevitt and C. F. Settlage, pp. 60–69. New York: International Universities Press.

Greenson, R. R. (1965). The working alliance and the transference neurosis. *Psychoanalytic Quarterly* 34:155–181.

———— (1967). *Technique and Practice of Psychoanalysis.* New York: International Universities Press.

Grossman, W. (1992). The analyzing instrument and the clinical uses of theory. Paper presented at the Institute for Psychoanalytic Research and Development, New York, NY, October.

Grunes, M. (1984). The therapeutic object relationship. *Psychoanalytic Review* 71:123–143.

Guntrip, H. (1978). Psychoanalysis and some scientific and philosophical critics. *British Journal of Medical Psychology* 51:207–224.

Habermas, J. (1971). *Knowledge and Human Interests.* Boston: Beacon Press.

Haggard, E. A., Hiken, J. R., and Isaacs, R. S. (1965). Some effects of recording and filming on the psychotherapeutic process. *Psychiatry* 28:169–181.

Haggard, E. A., and Isaacs, R. S. (1966). Micromomentary facial expressions as indicators of ego mechanisms in psychotherapy. In *Methods of Research in Psychotherapy*, ed. L. A. Gottschalk and A. H. Auerbach, pp. 154–165. New York: Appleton-Century-Crofts.

Hamilton, V. (1993). Truth and reality in psychoanalytic discourse. *International Journal of Psycho-Analysis* 74:63–80.

Hanly, C. (1982). Narcissism, defense, and the positive transference. *International Journal of Psycho-Analysis* 63:427–444.

———— (1990). The concept of truth in psychoanalysis. *International Journal of Psycho-Analysis* 71:375–383.

———— (1994). Reflections on the place of the therapeutic alliance in psychoanalysis. *International Journal of Psycho-Analysis* 75:457–468.

Hardway, R. (1986). Facts and fantasies in subliminal psychodynamic activation: a quantitative analysis. Ph.D. diss., Ohio University.

Harré, R. (1970). *Principles of Scientific Thinking.* London: Macmillan.

Hartmann, H. (1939). *Ego Psychology and the Problem of Adaptation.* New York: International Universities Press.

Heidegger, M. (1927). *Being and Time.* New York: Harper & Row, 1962.

Heimann, P. (1950). On countertransference. *International Journal of Psycho-Analysis* 31:81–84.

Hobson, R. P. (1990). On acquiring knowledge about people and the capacity to pretend: response to Leslie (1987). *Psychological Review* 97:114–121.

Hoffman, I. Z. (1983). The patient as interpreter of the analyst's experience. *Contemporary Psychoanalysis* 19:389–442.

———— (1992a). Expressive participation and psychoanalytic discipline.

Contemporary Psychoanalysis 28:1–15.

——— (1992b). Some practical implications of a social constructivist view of the psychoanalytic situation. *Psychoanalytic Dialogues* 2:287–304.

——— (1993). The intimate authority of the psychoanalyst's presence. *Psychologist Psychoanalyst* 13:15–23.

Hoffman, I. Z., and Gill, M. (1988). Clinical reflections on a coding scheme. *International Journal of Psycho-Analysis* 69:55–64.

Holt, R. (1962). Individuality and generalization in the psychology of personality. *Journal of Personality* 30:377–404.

——— (1981). The death and transfiguration of metapsychology. *International Review of Psycho-Analysis* 8:129–143.

Holzman, P. S. (1983). Psychoanalysis: Is the therapy destroying the science? *Journal of the American Psychoanalytic Association* 33: 725–770.

Horowitz, M., ed. (1988). *Psychodynamics and Cognition*. Chicago: University of Chicago Press.

Isay, R. (1989). *Being Homosexual*. New York: Farrar, Straus, and Giroux.

Jacobs, T. J. (1991). *The Use of the Self: Countertransference and Communication in the Analytic Situation*. New York: International Universities Press.

Jacobson, E. (1957). Denial and repression. In *Depression: Comparative Studies of Normal, Neurotic, and Psychotic Conditions*, pp. 107–136. New York: International Universities Press.

James, W. (1890). *The Principles of Psychology*, vols. 1 and 2. New York: Dover, 1950.

Joseph, B. (1989). *Psychic Equilibrium and Psychic Change*. London: Routledge.

Kagan, J. (1981). *The Second Year*. Cambridge: Harvard University Press.

Kahn, M. M. R. (1968). Reparation of the self as an idolized internal object of perversion-formation. In *Alienation and Perversions*, pp. 11–17. New York: International Universities Press, 1979.

Kanzer, M. (1961). Verbal and non-verbal aspects of free association. *Psychoanalytic Quarterly* 14:327–350.

——— (1966). The motor sphere of transference. *Psychoanalytic Quarterly* 19:522–540.

Kaplan, A. (1964). *The Conduct of Inquiry: Methodology for Behavioral Science*. San Francisco: Chandler.

Keats, J. (1818). Endymion. In *Complete Poems and Selected Letters*, ed. C. D. Thorpe. New York: Odyssey, 1935.

Kendon, A. (1982). The organization of behavior in face-to-face interaction: observations on the development of a methodology. In *Handbook of Methods in Non-Verbal Behavior Research*, ed. P. Ekman and K. R. Scherer, pp. 440–491. Cambridge: Cambridge University Press.

Kernberg, O. F. (1975). *Borderline Conditions and Pathological Narcissism*. New York: Jason Aronson.

_____ (1984). *Severe Personality Disorders: Psychotherapeutic Strategies*. New Haven, CT: Yale University Press.

_____ (1987). Projection and projective identification: developmental and clinical aspects. *Journal of the American Psychoanalytic Association* 35:795–820.

Klein, G. S. (1966). The several grades of memory. In *Psychoanalysis—A General Psychology. Essays in Honor of Heinz Hartmann*, pp. 377–389. New York: International Universities Press.

Klein, M. (1957). *Envy and Gratitude*. London: Tavistock.

Kohut, H. (1973). Thoughts on narcissism and narcissistic rage. *Psychoanalytic Study of the Child* 27:360–400. New Haven, CT: Yale University Press.

_____ (1977). *The Restoration of the Self*. New York: International Universities Press.

Kosslyn, S. M., and Pomerantz, J. R. (1981). Imagery, propositions, and the form of internal representations. In *Readings in Philosophy of Psychology*, ed. N. Block, vol. 2, pp. 150–169. Cambridge: Harvard University Press.

Kris, E. (1952). *Psychoanalytic Explorations in Art*. New York: International Universities Press.

_____ (1956). The recovery of childhood memories in psychoanalysis. *Psychoanalytic Study of the Child* 2:54–88. New York: International Universities Press.

Kronenberger, L. (1976). *Oscar Wilde*. Boston: Little, Brown.

Kuhn, T. (1970). *The Structure of Scientific Revolutions*. Chicago: University of Chicago Press.

Lakoff, G. (1987). *Women, Fire, and Dangerous Things: What Categories Reveal about the Mind*. Chicago: University of Chicago Press.

Lauden, L. (1990). *Science and Relativism*. Chicago: University of Chicago Press.

Lear, J. (1990). *Love and Its Place in Nature*. New York: Farrar, Straus, and Giroux.

Leslie, A. M. (1987). Pretense and representation: the origins of "theory of mind." *Psychological Review* 94:412–426.

Leslie, A. M., and Frith, U. (1990). Prospects for a cognitive neuropsychology of autism: Hobson's choice. *Psychological Review* 97:122–131.

Levenson, E. A. (1972). *The Fallacy of Understanding*. New York: Basic Books.

Levy, R. I. (1973). *Tahitians: Mind and Experience in the Society Islands*. Chicago: University of Chicago Press.

Limentani, A. (1966). A re-evaluation of acting-out in relation to working through. *International Journal of Psycho-Analysis* 47:274–281.

Little, M. I. (1981). *Transference Neurosis and Transference Psychosis*. New York: Jason Aronson.

Loewald, H. W. (1960). On the therapeutic action of psychoanalysis. In *Papers on Psychoanalysis*, pp. 221–256. New Haven, CT: Yale University Press, 1980.

———— (1962). Internalization, separation, mourning, and the superego. In *Papers on Psychoanalysis*, pp. 257–276. New Haven, CT: Yale University Press, 1980.

———— (1970). Psychoanalytic theory and the psychoanalytic process. In *Papers on Psychoanalysis*, pp. 277–301. New Haven, CT: Yale University Press, 1980.

———— (1971a). On motivation and instinct theory. In *Papers on Psychology*, pp. 52–67. New Haven, CT: Yale University Press, 1982.

———— (1971b). The transference neurosis: comments on the concept and the phenomenon. In *Papers on Psychoanalysis*, pp. 302–314. New Haven, CT: Yale University Press, 1980.

———— (1975). Psychoanalysis as an art and the fantasy character of the psychoanalytic situation. In *Papers on Psychoanalysis*, pp. 352–371. New Haven, CT: Yale University Press, 1980.

———— (1976). Perspectives on memory. In *Papers on Psychoanalysis*, pp. 148–173. New Haven, CT: Yale University Press, 1980.

———— (1978). Primary process, secondary process, and language. In *Papers on Psychoanalysis*, pp. 178–206. New Haven, CT: Yale University Press.

———— (1980). Reflections on the psychoanalytic process and its therapeutic potential. In *Papers on Psychoanalysis*, pp. 372–383. New Haven, CT: Yale University Press.

Lothane, Z. (1992). *In Defense of Schreber: Soul Murder and Psychiatry.* Hillsdale, NJ: Analytic Press.

Luborsky, L. (1973). Forgetting and remembering (momentary forgetting) during psychotherapy. In *Psychoanalytic Research*, ed. M. Mayman. Psychological Issues, monograph 30. New York: International Universities Press.

Luria, A. R. (1981). *Language and Cognition.* New York: Wiley.

Mahl, G. F. (1977). Body movement, ideation, and verbalization during psychoanalysis. In *Communication Structures and Psychic Structures*, ed. N. Freedman and S. Grand, pp. 291–310. New York: Plenum.

Mahler, M., Pine, F., and Bergman, A. (1975). *The Psychological Birth of the Human Infant: Symbiosis and Individuation.* New York: Basic Books.

Mahoney, P. (1979). The place of psychoanalytic treatment in the history of discourse. In *Psychoanalysis and Discourse*, pp. 57–87. London: Tavistock, 1987.

Manicas, P. T., and Secord, P. F. (1983). Implications for psychology of the new philosophy of science. *American Psychologist* 38:399–413.

McDevitt, J. B. (1971). Discussion of E. Galenson's paper, "A consideration of the nature of thought in childhood play." In *Separation-*

Individuation: Essays in Honor of Margaret S. Mahler, ed. J. B. McDevitt and C. F. Settlage, pp. 70–74. New York: International Universities Press.

McDougall, J. (1980). *Plea for a Measure of Abnormality*. New York: International Universities Press.

—— (1985). *Theatres of the Mind*. New York: Basic Books.

McLaughlin, J. T. (1981). Transference, psychic reality, and countertransference. *Psychoanalytic Quarterly* 50:639–664.

Meehl, P. H. (1969). Subjectivity in psychoanalytic inference: the nagging persistence of Wilhelm Fliess's Achensee question. *Psychoanalysis and Contemporary Thought* 17:3–82, 1994.

Modell, A. H. (1976). "The holding" environment and the therapeutic action of psychoanalysis. *Journal of the American Psychoanalytic Association* 24:285–308.

Moore, B. E., and Fine, B. D. (1968). *A Glossary of Psychoanalytic Terms and Concepts*. New York: American Psychoanalytic Association.

Murray, H. A. (1961). Prospect for psychology. In *Proceedings of the Fourteenth International Congress of Applied Psychology* 1:11–32.

Nass, M. L. (1989). From transformed scream, through mourning, to the building of psychic structure: a critical review of the literature on music and psychoanalysis. *Annual of Psychoanalysis* 17:159–181.

Niederland, W. G. (1968). Schreber and Flechsig: a further contribution to the "kernel of truth" in Schreber's delusional system. *Journal of the American Psychoanalytic Association* 16:740–748.

Ogden, T. H. (1986). *The Matrix of the Mind*. Northvale, NJ: Jason Aronson.

Olineck, S. L., Poland, W. S., Grigg, K. A., and Graniter, W. L. (1973). The psychoanalytic work ego: process and interpretation. *International Journal of Psycho-Analysis* 54:143–151.

Paivio, A. (1986). *Mental Representation: A Dual Coding Approach*. New York: Oxford University Press.

Panel (1957). Acting out and its relation to impulse disorders, reported by M. Kanzer. *Journal of the American Psychoanalytic Association* 5:136–145.

—— (1985). Perspectives on the nature of psychic reality, reported by R. Roughton. *Journal of the American Psychoanalytic Association* 33:645–669.

—— (1986). Clinical aspects of language, reported by M. J. Weich. *Journal of the American Psychoanalytic Association* 34:687–698.

Piaget, J. (1924). Les traits principaux du logique de l'enfant. *J. Psych. Norm. Path.* 21:48–101.

—— (1937). *The Construction of Reality in the Child*. New York: Basic Books, 1954.

—— (1945). *Play, Dreams, and Imitation in Childhood*. New York: Norton, 1952.

_____ (1947). *The Psychology of Intelligence*. New York: Littlefield Adams, 1960.

_____ (1968). *On the Development of Memory and Identity*. Worcester, MA: Clark University Press.

Pine, F. (1982). The experience of self: aspects of its formation, expansion, and vulnerability. *Psychoanalytic Study of the Child* 37:143–168. New Haven, CT: Yale University Press.

_____ (1985). *Developmental Theory and Clinical Process*. New Haven, CT: Yale University Press.

_____ (1990). *Drive, Ego, Object, and Self: A Synthesis for Clinical Work*. New York: Basic Books.

Poland, W. S. (1986). The analyst's words. *Psychoanalytic Quarterly* 55:244–272.

Polanyi, M. (1958). *Personal Knowledge*. Chicago: University of Chicago Press.

Popper, K. R. (1959). *The Logic of Scientific Discovery*. London: Hutchinson.

Pribram, K. H. (1989). Psychoanalysis and the natural sciences: the brain-behavior connection from Freud to Sandler. In *Dimensions of Psychoanalysis*, ed. J. Sandler, pp. 139–164. Madison, CT: International Universities Press.

Putnam, H. (1981). *Reason, Truth, and History*. Cambridge: Cambridge University Press.

Pylyshyn, Z. W. (1978). When is attribution of beliefs justified? *Behavioral and Brain Sciences* 7:592–593.

Quine, W. V. (1969). *Ontological Relativity and Other Essays*. New York: Columbia University Press.

Racker, H. (1957). In *Transference and Countertransference*. New York: International Universities Press, 1968.

Rangell, L. (1981). A view of John Gedo's revision of psychoanalytic theory. Commentaries on John Gedo's *Beyond Interpretation*. *Psychoanalytic Inquiry* 1:249–266.

Rapaport, D. (1951). Consciousness. In *Problems of Consciousness*, pp. 18–57. New York: Josiah Macy Jr. Foundation.

_____ (1958). The theory of ego autonomy. In *The Collected Papers of David Rapaport*, ed. M. M. Gill, pp. 722–744. New York: Basic Books.

Rapaport, D., and Gill, M. M. (1959). The points of view and assumptions of metapsychology. In *The Collected Papers of David Rapaport*, ed. M. M. Gill, pp. 795–819. New York: Basic Books, 1967.

Reed, G. S. (1993). On the value of explicit reconstruction. *Psychoanalytic Quarterly* 62:52–73.

Reich, A. (1960). Further remarks on countertransference. In *Annie Reich: Psychoanalytic Contributions*, pp. 271–287. New York: International Universities Press, 1973.

Reik, J. (1944). *A Psychologist Looks at Love*. New York: Farrar and Rinehart.

Renik, O. (1993). *Countertransference Enactment and the Psychoanalytic Process*. In *Psychic Structure and Psychic Change*, pp. 135–158. Madison, CT: International Universities Press.

Reonhold, M. (1949). *Listening with the Third Ear: The Inner Experience of a Psychoanalyst*. New York: Farrar, Straus.

———— (1959). *Classical Drama: Greek and Roman*. Woodbury, NY: Barron's.

Rexford, E. N. (1966). A developmental approach to problems of acting out. In *A Developmental Approach to Acting Out*, ed. E. N. Rexford, p. 677. New York: International Universities Press.

Richards, A. D. (1984). Transference analysis: means or end. Commentaries on Merton Gill's *Analysis of Transference*. *Psychoanalytic Inquiry* 4:355–366.

———— (1991). The search for common ground: clinical aims and processes. *International Journal of Psycho-Analysis* 72:45–56.

Ricoeur, P. (1970). *Freud and Philosophy: An Essay on Interpretation*. New Haven, CT: Yale University Press.

Rieber, R. W. (1983). *Dialogues on the Psychology of Language and Thought Conversations with Noam Chomsky, Charles Osgood, Jean Piaget, Ulrich Neisser, and Marcel Kinsbourne*. New York: Plenum.

Rosenfeld, H. (1966). *Psychotic States: A Psychoanalytic Approach*. New York: International Universities Press.

———— (1982). Measurement of body motion and orientation. In *Handbook of Methods in Non-Verbal Behavior Research*, ed. P. Ekman and K. R. Scherer, pp. 199–274. Cambridge: Cambridge University Press.

Rubovitz-Seitz, P. (1991). Interpreting methodology, validation, and structuralist hermeneutics. *Psychoanalysis and Contemporary Thought* 14:563–594.

Russell, B. (1946). *History of Western Philosophy*. London: Allen and Unwin.

Sachs, H. (1942). *The Creative Unconscious: Studies in the Psychoanalysis of Art*. Cambridge: Sci-Art.

Salmon, W. C. (1984). *Scientific Explanation and the Causal Structure of the World*. Princeton: Princeton University Press.

Sandler, A. M. (1975). Comments on the significance of Piaget's work for psychoanalysis. *International Review of Psycho-Analysis* 2:363–367.

Sandler, J. (1976). Countertransference and role responsiveness. *International Review of Psycho-Analysis* 3:43–48.

Sass, L. A., and Woolfolk, R. C. (1988). Psychoanalysis and the hermeneutic turn: a critique of *Narrative Truth and Historical Truth*. *Journal of the American Psychoanalytic Association* 36:429–454.

Schafer, R. (1959). Generative empathy in the treatment situation. *Psychoanalytic Quarterly* 28:342–373.

_____ (1983). *The Analytic Attitude.* New York: Basic Books.

_____ (1984). Misconceiving historiography and psychoanalysis as art. Discussion of R. E. Geha's "On Psychoanalytic History and the 'Real' Story of Fictitious Lives." *International Forum for Psychoanalysis* 1:363–372.

_____ (1985a). Wild analysis. *Journal of the American Psychoanalytic Association* 33:275–300.

_____ (1985b). The interpretation of psychic reality, developmental influences, and unconscious communication. *Journal of the American Psychoanalytic Association* 33:555–570.

_____ (1991). A conversation with Roy Schafer. *The American Psychoanalyst.* Hillsdale, NJ: Analytic Press.

_____ (1992). *Retelling a Life: Narration and Dialogue in Psychoanalysis.* New York: Basic Books.

_____ (1994). The contemporary Kleinians of London. *Psychoanalytic Quarterly* 63:409–432.

Scherer, R. R. (1982). Methods of research on vocal communication: paradigms and parameters. In *Handbook of Methods in Non-Verbal Behavior Research,* ed. P. Ekman and K. R. Scherer, pp. 136–188. Cambridge: Cambridge University Press.

Schimek, J. (1975). A critical re-examination of Freud's concept of unconscious mental representation. *International Review of Psycho-Analysis* 2:171–187.

Schwaber, E. A. (1983). Psychoanalytic listening and psychic reality. *International Review of Psycho-Analysis* 10:379–392.

_____ (1985). The transference in psychotherapy. *Clinical Management.* New York: International Universities Press.

_____ (1992). Psychoanalytic theory and its relation to clinical work. *Journal of the American Psychoanalytic Association* 40:1039–1058.

Sedler, M. J. (1983). Freud's concept of working through. *Psychoanalytic Quarterly* 52:73–98.

Segal, H., and Britton, R. (1981). Interpretation and primitive psychic process: a Kleinian view. Commentaries on John Gedo's *Beyond Interpretation. Psychoanalytic Inquiry* 1:267–278.

Settlage, C. F. (1977). The psychoanalytic understanding of narcissistic and borderline personality disorders: advances in psychoanalytic theory. *Journal of the American Psychoanalytic Association* 25:805–834.

Shapiro, D. (1965). *Neurotic Styles.* New York: Basic Books.

Shapiro, J. (1993). On reminiscences. *Journal of the American Psychoanalytic Association* 41:395–422.

Shatz, M., Wellman, H., and Silber, S. (1983). The acquisition of mental verbs: a systematic investigation of the first reference to mental states. *Cognition* 14:301–321.

Shevrin, H. (1992). The Freudian unconscious and the cognitive unconscious: Identical or fraternal twins? In *Interface of Psychoanalysis and Psychology*, pp. 313–326. Washington, DC: American Psychological Association.

Silverman, D. C. (1989). Reply to Bayley and Shevrin critique of Silverman's subliminal psychodynamic activation research. *American Psychologist* 44:1422–1433.

Silverman, L. H., and Weinberger, J. (1985). Mommy and I are one: implications for psychotherapy. *American Psychologist* 40:1296–1308.

Singer, M. (1985). Borderline patients: psychoanalytic perspectives. *Psychoanalytic Quarterly* 54:270–278.

Smart, J. J. (1963). *Philosophy and Scientific Realism*. London: Routledge and Kegan Paul.

Socarides, C. (1978). *Homosexuality*. New York: Jason Aronson.

Spence, D. P. (1982). *Narrative Truth and Historical Truth*. New York: Norton.

_____ (1987). *The Freudian Metaphor: Toward a Paradigm Change in Psychoanalysis*. New York: Norton.

_____ (1990). The rhetorical voice of psychoanalysis. *Journal of the American Psychoanalytic Association* 38:579–604.

Spiegel, L. A. (1954). Acting out and defensive instinctual gratification. *Journal of the American Psychoanalytic Association* 2:107–119.

Stein, M. H. (1973). Acting out as a character trait: its relation to the transference. *Psychoanalytic Study of the Child* 23:347–364. New York: International Universities Press.

_____ (1981). The unobjectionable part of the transference. *Journal of the American Psychoanalytic Association* 29:869–892.

Steiner, G. (1990). *New Yorker*, January 22, pp. 133–136.

Steiner, R. (1987). Some thoughts on "La vive voix" by Ivan Fónagy. *International Review of Psycho-Analysis* 14:265–272.

_____ (1992). Some historical and critical notes on the relationship between hermeneutics and psychoanalysis. *British Psychoanalytical Society Bulletin* 28:7–38.

Steingart, I. (1969). On self, character, and the development of a psychic apparatus. *Psychoanalytic Study of the Child* 24:271–300. New York: International Universities Press.

_____ (1977). A comparative psychopathology approach to language behavior. In *Communicative Structures and Psychic Structures*, ed. N. Freedman and S. Grand, pp. 175–198. New York: Plenum Press.

_____ (1983). *Pathological Play in Borderline and Narcissistic Personalities*. New York: Spectrum.

_____ (1990). Discussant objective relations theory in perspective. *Psychoanalytic Inquiry* 10:270–282.

_____ (1992). Discussion of therapy transcript of Patient E from the Gill and Hoffman *Analysis of Transference*, vol. 2. Paper presented to the Candidate Society of the William Alanson White Institute.

Steingart, I., and Freedman, N. (1975). The organization of body-focused kinetic behavior and language construction in schizophrenia and depressed states. *Psychoanalysis and Contemporary Science* 4:423-450.

Steingart, I., Freedman, N., Grand, S., and Buchwald, C. (1975). The imprint of psychological differentiation in varying communication conditions. *Journal of Psycholinguistic Research* 4:241-255.

Stern, D. N. (1985). *The Interpersonal World of the Infant*. New York: Basic Books.

Stevenson, R. L. (1886). The strange case of Dr. Jekyll and Mr. Hyde. In *The Illustrated Robert Louis Stevenson*, pp. 1-63. London: Jupiter Books, 1957.

Stolorow, R. D., and Lachmann, F. M. (1980). *Psychoanalysis of Developmental Arrests: Theory and Treatment*. New York: International Universities Press.

Stone, L. (1961). *The Psychoanalytic Situation*. New York: International Universities Press.

_____ (1967). The psychoanalytic situation and transference: postscript to an earlier communication. *Journal of the American Psychoanalytic Association* 15:3-58.

_____ (1981). Some thoughts on the "here and now" in psychoanalytic technique and process. *Psychoanalytic Quarterly* 50:709-733.

Sullivan, H. S. (1954). *The Psychiatric Interview*. New York: Norton.

Terence. (163 B.C.). The self-tormentor. In *The Comedies of Terence*, ed. R. Graves. London: Cassell, 1963.

Thorpe, C. D. (1935). John Keats. *Collected Poems and Selected Letters*. New York: Oxford University Press.

Ungerer, J. A., Zelazo, P. R., Kearsley, R. B., and O'Leary, K. (1981). Developmental changes in the representation of objects in symbolic play from 18 to 31 months of age. *Child Development* 52:186-195.

Urbach, P. (1987). *Francis Bacon's Philosophy of Science: An Account and a Reappraisal*. LaSalle, IL: Open Court.

Vygotsky, L. S. (1934). *Thought and Language*. Cambridge: MIT Press, 1962.

Wallace, E. W. (1984). Psychoanalysis: history writing or story telling? Discussion of R. E. Geha's "On Psychoanalytic History and the 'Real' Story of Fictitious Lives." *International Forum for Psychoanalysis* 1:315-340.

Wallerstein, R. S. (1973). Psychoanalytic perspectives on the problem of reality. *Journal of the American Psychoanalytic Association* 21:5-33.

_____ (1984). The analysis of transference: a matter of emphasis or of theory reformation? In Commentaries on Merton Gill's *Analysis of*

Transference. Psychoanalytic Inquiry 4:325–354.

_____ (1985). The concept of psychic reality: its meaning and value. *Journal of the American Psychoanalytic Association* 33:555–570.

_____ (1990). Psychoanalysis: the common ground. *International Journal of Psycho-Analysis* 71:3–20.

Weinshel, E. (1988). Play and playing in adults and adult psychoanalysis: an addendum of the paper "On Inconsolability." *Bulletin of the Anna Freud Center* 2:108–127.

Weiss, E. (1942). Emotional memories and acting out. *Psychoanalytic Quarterly* 11:477–492.

Weiss, J., and Sampson, H. (1986). *The Psychoanalytic Process.* New York: Guilford.

Weitzenhofer, A. M. (1953). *Hypnotism.* New York: Wiley.

Werner, H., and Kaplan, B. (1963). *Symbol Formation.* New York: Wiley.

Wilde, O. (1891a). The decay of lying. In *Complete Works.* Garden City: Image/Doubleday, 1933.

_____ (1891b). *The Picture of Dorian Gray.* New York: Modern Library, 1968.

_____ (1896). The ballad of Reading Gaol. In *The Victorian Age. Prose, Poetry, and Drama,* ed. J. W. Bowyer and J. L. Brooks. New York: Appleton-Century-Crofts, 1938.

Will, D. (1980). Psychoanalysis as a human science. *British Journal of Medical Psychology* 53:201–211.

Winnicott, D. W. (1945). Primitive emotional development. In *Through Paediatrics to Psychoanalysis,* pp. 145–156. New York: Basic Books, 1975.

_____ (1949). Hate in the countertransference. In *Through Paediatrics to Psychoanalysis,* pp. 194–203. New York: Basic Books.

_____ (1951). Transitional objects and transitional phenomena. In *Through Paediatrics to Psychoanalysis,* pp. 229–242. New York: Basic Books.

_____ (1953). Psychosis and child care. In *Through Paediatrics to Psychoanalysis,* pp. 219–228. New York: Basic Books, 1975.

_____ (1955). The depressive position in normal development. In *Through Paediatrics to Psychoanalysis,* pp. 262–277. New York: Basic Books, 1975.

_____ (1956). Primary maternal preoccupation. In *Through Paediatrics to Psychoanalysis,* pp. 300–305. New York: Basic Books.

_____ (1960). The theory of the parent–infant relationship. In *The Motivational Processes and the Facilitating Environment.* New York: International Universities Press, 1965.

_____ (1967). Mirror-role of mother and family in child development. In *Playing and Reality,* pp. 111–118. New York: Basic Books, 1971.

_____ (1971a). Playing: a theoretical statement. In *Playing and Reality,* pp. 38–52. New York: Basic Books.

_____ (1971b). The place where we live. In *Playing and Reality*, pp. 104–410. New York: Basic Books.

Wisdom, J. O. (1967). Testing an interpretation within a session. *International Journal of Psycho-Analysis* 48:44–52.

CREDITS

INDEX

Abend, S., 175, 182, 183, 193n15, 194n20
Abuse. *See* Childhood sexual abuse
Acting out
  discharge and, 133
  ego feeling and, 145
  enacted symbol and, 134, 159–189
  Freudian concept of, 159–160
  language and, 32, 177
  psychic reality and, 133–134
  transference and, 16, 180–181
Adams, F. R., 11
Adaptation, working style and, 121–122
Albee, E., 101n9
Alexander, F., 66
Ambivalence
  transference resistance and, 81
  working style and, 123
Anal-rapprochement development
  mind emergence and, 96, 200, 202, 209–210, 211
  psychopathology and, 203, 204–205, 215
Analyst self-disclosure, countertransference and, 39–40, 61, 63–65
Anger
  clinical example, 224
  transference and, 106–107
Antiobjectivism, transference and, 57

Archeological metaphor, reconstruction and, 23–24
Aristotle, 244, 245
Arlow, J. A., 13, 37, 42, 73, 82, 86–89, 91–93, 100n7, 109
Asimov, I., 235, 244, 245
Attention, therapeutic relationship and, 122–123
Auden, W. H., 243, 244, 245, 246, 247

Bach, S., 193n15, 205
Bacon, F., 242, 244, 245
Balay, J., 256n4
Balint, M., 113, 188
Bate, W. J., 251, 258n7
Bechtel, W., 84, 231
Belief, reality and, 12
Beres, D., 13, 37, 82, 86–89, 91–93, 100n7, 109
Bergman, A., 193n17
Bergmann, M. S., 189
Berlin, B., 85
Bhaskar, R., 230, 236, 249, 251
Biology, empathy and, 86, 93
Bion, W. R., 83, 93, 96, 122
Bird, B., 178, 196n24
Blank screen, 99n2
Bleuler, E., 210
Blos, P., 160
Blum, H. P., 145
Boeghly, M., 210
Boesky, D., 16, 169

Borderline personality
  acting out and, 175–176,
    178–179
  countertransference and, 54
Bradshaw, J., 257n5
Brenner, C., 2, 39, 41, 51, 78–79,
  99n3, 107, 131n1
Bretherton, I., 210
Breuer, J., xvii, 19, 232
Britton, R., 190n1, 196n24
Brown, D. E., 85, 234, 235, 252
Brown, R., 203
Bruner, J. S., 170
Bucci, W., 21, 22, 23, 27, 32, 42,
  75, 76, 134, 138, 170
Buie, D. H., 176

Carpenter, H., 245, 246
Cassirer, E., 238
Caston, J. A., 237
Cathexis
  cognition and, 21–22
  primary process and, 20–21
  reconstruction and, 20
Cavell, M., 211, 214, 219n3, 222n8,
  222n9, 231
Charcot, J.-M., 258n6
Childhood, memory and, 18–19,
  20
Childhood sexual abuse, clinical
  example, 27–34
Chrzanowski, G., 63, 71, 74
Cognition
  acting out and, 164–165, 170
  cathexis and, 21–22
  pretense and, 208, 209
Color, culture, observation
  statement and, 84–86
Colvin, S., 254
Communication,
    countertransference and,
    137–138

Compton, A. C., 37
Concretization, of language, as
    enacted symbol, 150–159
Consciousness, free association
    and, 13
Contemplation, therapeutic
    relationship and, 40, 51–52
Convention
  reality and, 52–53
  reality testing and, 52
Corbett, K., 247
Countertransference
  analyst self-disclosure and,
    39–40, 61, 63–65
  anger and, 224–225
  borderline personality and, 54
  communication and, 137–138
  countertransference expression,
    69–70
  drama metaphor and, 109
  empathy and, 49–51
  fantasy as, 89–90
  fluctuations in, 107–108
  informative function of, 45
  interpretation and, 224
  language and, 47–48
  narrative and, 53–54
  norms and, 6, 120
  objectivity and, 54–55
  object relations and, 25, 36–37
  observability of, 6–7
  shaping and, 44
  transference and, 41
  unreality and, 55
  working style and, xviii, 35,
    37–76
Creative artist analogy, working
    style, 117–118
Creativity, 253–254
Culture
  emotion and, 234–235
  observation statement and,
    84–86

Dahl, H., 6, 48, 119, 157
Davidson, D., 7, 239, 240, 256n3, 256n4
Day residue, transference and, 42
Defense, narcissistic personality as, 95–96
Detachment, observation and, 109–110
Developmental factors, mother–child relationship, 199–203
Devitt, M., 12, 53, 84, 230, 236
Dickes, R., 145
Discharge, acting out and, 133
Discrepancy, reality and, 10–11
Distortion, truth and, 26–27
Dora case (Freud), 159, 161–162, 163, 168, 172
Downey, G., 245
Drama metaphor
    countertransference and, 109
    therapeutic relationship and, 55–56
Dream, day residue and, 42
Dream analysis, reconstruction and, 21
Drive theory
    acting out and, 133
    infant development and, 17
    love and, 104

Eagle, M. M., 111
Edelheit, H., 152
Edelson, M., 44, 155
Ego
    identification and, 38
    verbalization and, 38–39
Ego feeling, acting out and, 145
Ego relatedness, impingement and, 82
Eissler, K. R., 153, 154, 156, 157, 174, 193n19, 196n24, 199, 212
Ekman, P., 48, 85, 234

Ekstein, R., 191n9
Ellman, R., 246, 249, 257n6
Ellman, S., 193n17
Emotion, culture and, 234–235
Empathy
    biology and, 86, 93
    countertransference and, 49–51
    subjectivity and, 62–63
    transference and, 7, 37
    unconscious and, 38
Enacted symbol
    acting out and, 134, 159–189
    defined, 134–135
    as free associations, 138–142
    language and, 135
    transference as pathological play, 143–150
Epstein, L., 61, 63, 74, 124
Equivocality principle
    described, 4, 8
    interpretation and, 13
Erikson, E. H., xv, 93, 210, 220n5, 231, 243, 257n5
Expressive participation, countertransference and, 65–68

Fantasy
    free association and, 90–94
    shared/congruent, 89–90
    therapeutic relationship, mothering analogy, 122–123
Federn, P., 145
Feiner, A., 61, 63, 74, 124
Fenichel, O., 83
Ferenczi, S., 188, 189, 197n25
Feyeraband, P. K., 2
Fine, B. D., 12, 256n4
Flavell, J. H., 56
Fliess, R., 19, 37, 45, 55, 108, 115, 116, 121
Fodor, J. A., 84
Fónagy, I., 48, 165

Free association
  consciousness and, 13
  countertransference expression,
    69–70
  enacted symbol as, 138–142
  fantasy and, 90–94
  interpretation of, 162
  language and, 151, 157
  psychoanalysis and, xvi–xvii
  transference and, 61
Freedman, N., 7, 22, 48
Freeman, M., 57, 75
Freud, A., 170, 173, 174, 191n9,
  192n13
Freud, S., xvi, xvii, xxii, 2, 8,
  11–12, 13, 14, 16, 17, 18, 19,
  20, 21, 22, 23, 24, 25, 26, 27,
  29, 32, 35, 36, 37, 38, 39, 40,
  41, 42, 43, 45, 49, 54, 58, 60,
  67, 68, 69, 73, 75, 78, 79, 80,
  81, 84, 89, 95, 96, 98, 99n2,
  103, 104, 105, 106, 107, 108,
  112, 113, 114, 115, 121, 122,
  123, 126, 129, 130, 133, 135,
  142, 143, 144, 145, 146, 150,
  155, 156, 159, 160, 161, 162,
  163, 164, 165, 169, 172, 177,
  183, 189, 192n13, 192n15, 203,
  210, 211, 214, 215, 217, 219n4,
  227, 229, 231, 232, 233, 236,
  237, 238, 239, 240, 242, 243,
  245, 246, 247, 248, 250, 251,
  252, 253, 254
Friedman, S. W., 191n9
Frith, U., 221n8
Frosch, J., 160
Furth, H. G., 208, 209, 210

Gadamer, H., 229, 232, 252,
  255n1
Galenson, E., 193n18
Galileo, 245
Gay, P., xvii, 233, 256n4, 258n6

Gediman, H. K., 44
Gedo, J. E., 37, 94, 185, 186, 187,
  193n15, 195n23, 195n24
Gill, M. M., 1, 4, 5, 6, 13, 36, 38,
  40, 41, 44, 45, 53, 54, 57, 58,
  59, 60, 61, 63, 64, 65, 69, 70,
  71, 72, 73, 74, 75, 94, 96,
  101n10, 107, 109, 119, 124,
  125, 186, 225, 231
Gleick, J., 240
Glover, E., 238
Goldberg, A., 37, 152, 153,
  193n15
Greenacre, P., 160, 161, 168,
  190n6, 252
Greenson, R. R., 14, 78, 79, 150,
  158, 159
Grossman, W., 93
Grunes, M., 114
Guntrip, H., 238, 240

Habermas, J., 255n1
Haggard, E. A., 6, 48, 238
Hamilton, V., 237
Hanly, C., 14, 17, 95, 128, 202,
  214, 255n2
Hardway, R., 256n4
Harré, R., 230, 236
Hartman, F. R., 189
Hartmann, H., 17, 45, 51, 58, 69,
  73, 121, 134, 138, 156, 210, 231
Hatred, countertransference and,
  54
Heidegger, M., 229, 232, 252,
  255n1
Heimann, P., 51, 107
Here-and-now therapeutic
  relationship, 72–73, 74
Heterosexuality, 247–248
Historical truth
  material truth and, 24, 26
  narrative truth and, 8
Hobson, R. P., 221n8

Hoffman, I. Z., 63, 64, 65, 66, 67, 68, 69, 70, 71, 72, 75, 76, 94, 96, 101n10, 107, 109, 118, 124, 125, 126, 127, 128
Holt, R., 7, 48, 49, 238
Holzman, P. S., 7
Homosexuality, 246–247
Horowitz, M., 48
Human nature, theory of, 108–109
Hypothesis construction, science and, 239–241
Hysteria, memory and, 19

Identification, defined, 37–38
Imagistic schema, meaning and, 76
Impingement
  ego relatedness and, 82
  love and, 113–114
Infant development, drive theory/perception, 17
Infectious concept, of interpretation, 96–97
Innocence, reality and, 12
Insight
  interpretation and, 98–99
  language and, 23
  love and, 113
  as self-contemplation, xvi
  transference and, 110–111
Interpretation
  countertransference and, 224
  defined, 82
  equivocality principle and, 13
  of free association, 162
  infectious concept of, 96–97
  insight and, 98–99
  language and, 76
  love and, 118–119
  narrative and, 94–95, 98
  neutrality and, 58–59, 60–61
  object relations and, 78, 124

  orientation in, 96–97
  reality and, 70–71
  resistance and, 223–224
  scholarship analogy, 111–112
  shaping and, 97–98
  therapeutic alliance and, 14
  transference neurosis and, 76–77
  truthfulness of, as object relations experience, 76–101
Isaacs, R. S., 6, 48

Jacobs, T. J., 5, 44, 71, 128, 134, 135, 136, 137, 138–142, 144, 238
James, W., 230, 258n6
Joseph, B., 37

Kagan, J., 210, 214
Kahn, M. M. R., 204
Kanzer, M., 160, 161, 192n12
Kaplan, A., 99n2, 134, 138, 155, 163, 165
Kaplan, B., 22
Kay, P., 85
Keats, J., 250, 251, 253, 254, 258n7
Kendon, A., 157
Kernberg, O. F., 213, 215, 216, 217, 218, 222n10, 225, 226
Klein, G. S., 161, 193n16
Kohut, H., 94, 96, 97, 104, 120, 189, 204, 213, 214, 216
Kosslyn, S. M., 21
Kris, E., 239, 252, 253
Kronenberger, L., 249
Kuhn, T., 2

Lachmann, F. M., 189
Lakoff, G., 85, 234
Language
  acting out and, 32, 177
  cognition and, 21–22
  concretization of, as enacted symbol, 150–159

Language (*continued*)
countertransference and, 6–7,
47–48
enacted symbol and, 135
expressiveness, 16
free association and, 13, 157
insight and, 23
interpretation and, 76, 223–224,
226–227
litigious, 15
mind development and, 210
narcissistic personality disorder
and, 213–214
psychic reality and, 152
symbol and, 163–164
transference and, 43–44, 147
verbalization, ego and, 38–39
Laudan, L., 35, 84, 98
Lear, J., 118
Leslie, A. M., 208, 209, 219n3,
220n7, 221n8
Levenson, E. A., 36, 39, 55, 61, 62,
63, 69, 71, 74, 75, 76, 93, 94, 97,
101n10, 107, 109, 124, 127
Levy, R. I., 235
Libido, as life instinct, 133
Limentani, A., 160
Litigious language, 15
Little, M. I., 195n24
Loewald, H. W., 43, 60, 76–77, 78,
79, 80, 96, 97, 98, 110, 115,
118, 124, 128, 129, 130, 131,
133, 142, 207, 219n4, 250
Lothane, Z., 12
Love
as educator, 126
experience of, 103–104
impingement and, 113–114
insight and, 113
interpretation and, 118–119
psychic reality and, 119–121,
126–127
scholarship analogy, 111–112

termination and, 129–131
therapeutic relationship and,
105–106, 111, 113
transference and, 80–81, 99, 103
truth and, 114–115
Luborsky, L., 68, 241
Luria, A. R., 203

Mahl, G. F., 191n12
Mahler, M., 199, 200, 214, 215
Mahoney, P., 15, 190n5
Manicas, P. T., 231, 239, 240, 241
Martin, E., 237
Masochism, countertransference
and, 51
Material truth, historical truth
and, 24, 26
McDevitt, J. B., 193n18
McDougall, J., 196n24, 204
McLaughlin, J. T., 39, 71, 99n2,
107, 128, 134
Meaning
acting out and, 170
imagistic schema and, 76
realization of, 151
Meehl, P. H., 94, 237
Memory
childhood and, 18–19, 20
narrative/historical truth, 8
truth and, 25–26
Mind
emergence of, 208–212
self and, 211
Mind control, sadomasochistic
fantasy and, 96, 210
Mind emergence, anal-
rapprochement development
and, 96
Modell, A. H., 97, 113, 185
Moore, B. E., 12, 256n4
Mother–child relationship,
developmental factors,
199–203

Multiple encoding, cognition and, 22
Murray, H. A., 257n5

Narcissism
anal-rapprochement development, 205
love and, 104
Narcissistic personality
as defense, 95–96
therapy with, 213–214
Narrative
countertransference and, 53–54
interpretation and, 94–95, 98
report by, 238
Narrative truth, historical truth and, 8
Nass, M. L., 253
Neurotic reality testing, 15
Neutrality
interpretation and, 58–59, 60–61
scholarship and, 101n12
Niederland, W. G., 12
Nonverbal communication
countertransference and, 6–7
symbol and, 155
Norms, countertransference and, 6, 120

Objectivity
countertransference and, 54–55
psychic reality and, 16–17
Object relations
countertransference and, 36–37
interpretation and, 78, 124
primary maternal preoccupation, 122
therapeutic relationship and, 35
transference and, 25
truth of interpretation, 76–101
Observation
detachment and, 109–110

participant observation, working style and, 71
reality and, 15
science and, 18
Observation statement, culture and, 84–86
Ogden, T. H., 220n5
Olineck, S. L., 49, 50
Osgood, C., 86

Paivio, A., 21
Panel, 44, 100n8, 160, 161
Participant observation, working style and, 71
Pathological play
etiology of, as transference, 199–222
projective identification and, 216–218
transference as, enacted symbol, 143–150
Perception, infant development and, 17
Philosophy of science, science and, 241–242
Piaget, J., 12, 56, 163, 165, 170, 171, 173, 174, 190n2, 193n16, 202, 210
Pine, F., 95, 96, 199, 202, 225
Play
enacted symbol, transference as pathological play, 143–150, 166–167
pathological play, etiology of, as transference, 199–222
pretense and, 208
symbol and, 208–209
Poland, W. S., 35, 44
Polanyi, M., 232, 233, 236, 251
Pomeranz, J. R., 21
Popper, K. R., 14, 239
Pretense, play and, 208
Pribram, K. H., 133

Primary maternal preoccupation,
    object relations, 122
Primary process
    acting out and, 163–164
    cathexis and, 20–21
Projective identification,
    pathological play and, 216–218
Psychic reality
    acting out and, 133–134
    adaptation and, 121–122
    comprehension of, 229–258
    historical/material truth, 24
    language and, 152
    love and, 119–121, 126–127
    reality and, 16–17
    terror and, 27
Psychoanalysis
    free association and, xvi–xvii
    reconstruction in, 18–34
    science and, 2
    therapeutic relationship and,
        xvii–xix
Psychopathology
    anal-rapprochement
        development and, 203,
        204–205, 215
    comparative, 212–216
Putnam, H., 52, 84, 230, 236, 237
Pylyshyn, Z. W., 209

Quine, W. V., 84, 220n7

Racker, H., 44, 48, 51, 71, 72
Rage, narcissistic personality
    disorder and, 213–214
Rangell, L., 187
Rapaport, D., 73, 193n16, 231
Reality
    convention and, 52–53
    interpretation and, 70–71
    relativity and, 125
    science and, 229–231

transference and, 2, 3–18
truth and, 1, 126
Reality testing
    convention and, 52
    schizophrenic/neurotic, 15
Reconstruction, in psychoanalysis,
    18–34
Regression
    subjectivity and, 63
    transference and, 36
Reich, A., 51
Reik, J., 14, 104
Relativity, reality and, 125
Renik, O., 71, 128, 134
Reonhold, M., 56, 109
Repetition compulsion
    object relations and, 77–78
    resistance and, 113
Repression, reconstruction and, 19
Resistance
    interpretation and, 223–224
    repetition compulsion and, 113
    transference and, 46
Rexford, E. N., 160
Richards, A. D., 59, 61, 96
Ricoeur, P., 2, 229
Rieber, R. W., 86
Rosch, E., 85
Rosenfeld, H., 155, 196n24
Rubovitz-Seitz, P., 229
Russell, B., 244

Sachs, H., 86
Sadomasochism, anal-
    rapprochement development,
    205
Sadomasochistic fantasy, mind
    control and, 96, 210
Salmon, W. C., 2
Sampson, H., 14, 238
Sandler, A. M., 170
Sandler, J., 5, 6, 184, 185
Sass, L. A., 236

Schafer, R., 1, 2, 5, 12, 14, 37, 38,
    40, 45, 47, 51, 52, 55, 56, 57,
    70, 72, 94, 97, 100n8, 107, 108,
    109, 114, 115, 116, 117, 118,
    121, 124, 127, 128, 134, 230,
    237, 240, 255n1
Scherer, R. R., 155
Schimek, J., 20
Schizophrenic reality testing, 15
Scholarship
    interpretation and, 111–112
    neutrality and, 101n12
Schwaber, E. A., 4, 8, 9–11, 12,
    18, 39, 42, 45, 46, 47, 75, 82,
    98, 99n2, 108, 115, 169
Science
    hypothesis construction and,
        239–241
    narrative report and, 238
    observation and, 18
    philosophy of science and,
        241–242
    psychoanalysis and, 2
    reality and, 229–231
    theory formation and, 233
Second self, working style and,
    116–117
Secord, P. F., 231, 239, 240, 241
Sedler, M. J., 146
Segal, H., 190n1, 196n24
Self
    crystallization of, 199, 202
    mind and, 211
Self-contemplation, insight as, xvi
Settlage, C. F., 207
Sexual abuse. See Childhood
    sexual abuse
Sexuality
    expressive participation, 65–68
    transference and, xvii
Shaping
    countertransference and, 44
    interpretation and, 97–98

    transference and, 43–44, 57
Shapiro, D., 34n2
Shapiro, J., 97, 239
Shatz, M., 210
Shevrin, H., 256n4
Silverman, D., 256n4
Silverman, L. H., 256n4
Singer, M., 194n20
Smart, J. J., 2
Socarides, C., 247
Spence, D. P., 2, 24, 26, 94,
    255n1, 256n4
Spiegel, L. A., 204
Statistical procedure, 240–241
Stein, M. H., 78, 192n12
Steiner, G., 118, 231, 252, 255n1
Steingart, I., 7, 48, 69, 97, 103,
    112, 127, 157, 160, 174, 190n4,
    191n9, 195n24, 202, 203, 205,
    217, 219n1, 219n5, 222n10
Steingart, J., 258n6
Stern, D. N., 210, 219n3, 221n8
Stevenson, R. L., 217
Stolorow, R. D., 189
Stone, L., 59, 60, 61, 78, 99, 116,
    123, 150
Subjectivity
    empathy and, 62–63
    psychoanalysis and, 1–2
    regression and, 63
Sullivan, H. S., 71, 104
Surprise, analytic attitude and, 14
Symbol. See also Enacted symbol
    acting out and, 163–164, 165
    cognition and, 21–22
    language and, 154–155
    play and, 208–209

Telepathy, 86
Terence, 251
Termination, transference and,
    129–131
Terror, psychic reality and, 27

Theory formation, science and,
    233
Therapeutic alliance, interpretation
    and, 14
Therapeutic relationship
    attention and, 122–123
    contemplation and, 40, 51–52
    drama metaphor and, 55–56
    here-and-now, 72–73, 74
    love and, 105–106, 111, 113
    mothering analogy, 122–123
    psychoanalysis and, xvii–xix
    unconscious and, 36
Thorpe, C. D., 250, 253, 254
Transference
    acting out and, 160, 161,
        180–181
    anger and, 106–107
    countertransference and, 41
    determinants for, 40
    empathy and, 37
    insight and, 110–111
    as joint product, 40–41
    language and, 43–44, 147
    love and, 80–81, 99, 103
    object relations and, 25
    as pathological play, enacted
        symbol, 143–150
    pathological play, etiology of,
        199–222
    reality and, 2
    real/unreal in, 3–18
    regression and, 36
    resistance and, 46
    sexuality and, xvii
    shaping and, 57
    termination and, 129–131
    types of, 79
    unreality and, 55
    working style and, 35, 37–76
Transference neurosis, 60
    interpretation and, 76–77
    regression and, 36

Transference resistance,
    ambivalence and, 81
Truth
    distortion and, 26–27
    historical/material truth, 24, 26
    of interpretation, as object
        relations experience,
        76–101
    interpretation and, 97–98
    love and, 114–115
    memory and, 25–26
    narrative/historical, 8
    reality and, 1, 126

Unconscious
    empathy and, 38
    reconstruction and, 20
    therapeutic relationship and, 36
Unconscious experience, database
    of, 84–85
Understanding, insight and,
    110–111
Ungerer, J. A., 201
Unreality, transference and, 3–18
Urbach, P., 242, 244, 245

Verbalization, ego and, 38–39
Vygotsky, L. S., 203

Wallace, E. W., 34n1
Wallerstein, R. S., 1, 35, 58, 70,
    100n8, 255n2
Weinberger, J., 256n4
Weinshel, E., 194n21
Weiss, E., 145, 152, 163, 171
Weiss, J., 14, 238
Werner, H., 22, 134, 138, 155, 163,
    165
Wilde, O., 246, 247, 249, 250,
    257n6
Will, D., 231, 239, 240

Winnicott, D. W., 41, 44, 54, 77,
    82, 96, 100n9, 113, 120, 122,
    123, 131, 183, 189, 190n7,
    194n20, 201, 207, 208, 215,
    220n5, 250
Wisdom, J. O., 14
Wolitsky, D., 111
Wolkenfeld, F., 44
Woodruff, G., 209
Woolfolk, R. C., 236
Work ego, 115–117

Working style
    adaptation and, 121–122
    ambivalence and, 123
    countertransference and, xviii
    creative artist analogy, 117–118
    participant observation and,
        71
    second self and, 116–117
    transference/
        countertransference, 35,
        37–76